CATABASIS: VERGIL AND THE WISDOM-TRADITION

CATABASIS
VERGIL AND THE WISDOM-TRADITION

BY

RAYMOND J. CLARK

1979

B. R. GRÜNER — AMSTERDAM

ISBN 90 6032 104 9

Printed in the Netherlands

FOR

VIVIEN,

SANDRA, SUZANNAH, AND SALLY

AND

TO MR. H. W. STUBBS

cum gratiis

PREFACE

There exists no book in English, so far as I know, which brings together into a continuous examination the widely scattered fragments of the *"Descent into the Underworld"* theme, for which the Greeks used the term *"Catabasis"*, and none in any language which attempts to do this from a Vergilian viewpoint. This book is principally designed to trace the development of the theme from the Near East through its long career in Greek and Roman literature and cult as a background to Vergil's cumulative and innovative version of the "Descent of Aeneas" in the Sixth Book of the *Aeneid* and to pinpoint more fully than hitherto Vergil's originality in his use of the theme. It covers therefore a literary tradition of about 2000 years in the pre-Christian era.

The theme itself is rich in folklore and inextricably connected with the mythological deeds of the heroes Gilgamesh, Heracles, Odysseus, Orpheus, Peirithous, Theseus, Aeneas, and many others who descended alive and returned from the Land of the Dead. The study of these descent and return myths along with an exploration of their locales, underworld geography, and ritualistic implications, has an intrinsic fascination. With my main purpose in mind I have, however, endeavoured more than anything else to emphasise the "contemporary twist" which expresses the object of the mythographer in each case and, for reasons which will become apparent, to develop the wisdom-tradition as distinct from the vegetation-tradition of underworld myths.

The book also offers by its very nature a close analysis of several major works — the *Epic of Gilgamesh,* Homer's *Odyssey* XI, and Vergil's *Aeneid* VI — which, it is hoped, may serve as a good introduction to early epic poetry and to the traditions of culture. To assist non-Classical readers who have an interest in the Classical heritage I have paraphrased or added translations to most Greek and Latin passages. Translations of the *Aeneid* are taken from W. F. Jackson Knight, *Virgil: The Aeneid* (Penguin Classics 1956) and are reprinted by kind permission of Penguin Books Ltd. I have also included fairly full notes to the extensive background literature, so as to make it possible for readers to pursue any topic of special interest to them. Since Vergil, like Homer before him, is both the culmination of a mythological tradition and the source of a new one, I had originally planned an epilogue sketching the apocalyptic use of the theme in modern descent literature from Dante onwards. But the book is already long enough, so that I can do no better than recommend to the interested reader the brief summary entitled "Underworld Themes in Modern Fiction" by H. W. Stubbs in *The Journey to the Other World* ed. H. R. E. Davidson (London 1975), 130—149.

My own curiosity in Underworlds owes a great deal to the lectures of the late Vergilian scholar W. F. Jackson Knight and to a reading of his *Cumaean Gates*. Subsequently Mr. H. W. Stubbs of the University of Exeter put his unrivalled learning at my disposal in supervising a doctoral thesis completed in 1969, of which this book is a substantial revision. The dedication to him expressed in my thesis remains as my tribute for his teaching, friendship, and encouragement. In addition I wish to record special thanks both to Colin G. Hardie of Magdalen College, Oxford, for carefully reading an earlier draft and for providing me with the kindest of constructive advice which I have incorporated, and to Professor G. Wilson Knight for inviting me to make use of his late brother Jackson Knight's library, before it was dispersed, and for many other kindnesses. To others, too, I express sincere gratitude: to Dr. Charles T. Murphy for his assistance and hospitality during my stay at the Villa Vergiliana at Cuma in the summers of 1965 and 1971; to Professor F. W. Clayton, Mr. John D. Christie, and Professor R. B. Onians for helpful suggestions; and to my colleagues in Memorial University of Newfoundland for their encouragement. The book has been published with the help of a grant from the Humanities Research Council of Canada, using funds provided by the Canada Council, and to this body I express sincere thanks. It should hardly be necessary to add that for the views presented in this book the responsibility is mine. Finally to Vivien *dilectissimae uxori*, to whom with my children I offer now this book, I express profound gratitude for her constant support.

MEMORIAL UNIVERSITY OF NEWFOUNDLAND 1976

CONTENTS

Acknowledgement

The photographs for Plates 1 and 2 are by courtesy of the Biblioteca Apostolica Vaticana.

Plate 1. *Vergilius, Vaticanus Lat. 3225*, Fol. 48^{v}: The Sibyl throwing the honeyed offering to Cerberus as she and Aeneas enter the Underworld; see pp. 87 and 213f.

Plate 2. *Vergilius, Vaticanus Lat. 3225*, Fol. 53^{v}: Musaeus leads Aeneas and the Sibyl to Anchises and the Souls who are drinking from the stream of Lethe; see pp. 166f. and 177ff.

ABBREVIATIONS

A.B.V.	J. D. Beazley, *Attic Black-Figure Vase-Painters* (Oxford 1956).
A.J.A.	*American Journal of Archaeology*
A.J.P.	*American Journal of Philology*
A.N.E.T.$^{1-3}$	*Ancient Near Eastern Texts* ed. J. B. Pritchard (1st.-3rd. editions, Princeton 1950, 1955, and 1969)
A.R.V.^{2}	J. D. Beazley, *Attic Red-Figure Vase-Painters* (2nd. ed. Oxford 1963)
A.R.W.	*Archiv für Religionswissenschaft*
B.A.S.O.R.	*Bulletin of the American Schools of Oriental Research*
B.S.A.	*Annual of the British School at Athens*
C. & M.	*Classica et Mediaevalia*
C.F.	*Classical Folia*
C.I.L.	*Corpus Inscriptionum Latinarum* (Berlin 1862—)
C.J.	*Classical Journal*
C.P.	*Classical Philology*
C.Q.	*The Classical Quarterly*
C.R.	*The Classical Review*
F.Gr.H.	F. Jacoby, *Fragmente der griechischen Historiker* (Berlin 1923—)
F.H.G.	C. Müller, *Fragmenta Historicorum Graecorum* (Paris 1841—1870)
F.L.	*Folklore*
G. & R.	*Greece and Rome*
H.S.C.P.	*Harvard Studies in Classical Philology*
J.A.O.S.	*Journal of the American Oriental Society*
J.B.L.	*Journal of Biblical Literature and Exegesis*
J.C.S.	*Journal of Cuneiform Studies*
J.H.S.	*The Journal of Hellenic Studies*

J.N.E.S.	*Journal of Near Eastern Studies*
J.R.S.	*The Journal of Roman Studies*
J.S.S.	*Journal of Semitic Studies*
M.D.A.I.(A.)	*Mitteilungen des deutschen archäologischen Instituts, Athenische Abteilung*
M.E.F.R.	*Mélanges d'archéologie et d'histoire de l'École Française de Rome*
Mus. Helv.	*Museum Helveticum*
P.A.P.S.	*Proceedings of the American Philosophical Society*
P.B.S.R.	*Papers of the British School at Rome*
P.Oxy.	*The Oxyrhynchus Papyri* (London 1898—)
P.P.	*La Parola del Passato*
P.V.S.	*Proceedings of the Virgil Society*
R.E.	Pauly-Wissowa, *Real-Encyclopädie der classischen Altertumswissenschaft* (Stuttgart 1894—)
R.H.R.	*Revue de l'Histoire des Religions*
Roscher	*Ausführliches Lexikon der griechischen und römischen Mythologie*, hrsg. von W. H. Roscher (Leipzig—Berlin 1884—1937)
T.A.P.A.	*Transactions and Proceedings of the American Philological Association*
W.S.	*Wiener Studien*

CHAPTER I

INTRODUCTION: NEAR EASTERN DESCENTS

1. *Introduction*

In the Sixth Book of Vergil's *Aeneid*, Aeneas, the hero of the poem, makes a journey down into the Underworld, where he meets several of the illustrious dead before being reunited with his father, whom he consults about what lies in store for him and his companions now that they have at last arrived in Italy. The consultation over, he returns to the world of the living. It is one of the most famous parts of Vergil's poem, notable in its own right and as a direct source of Dante's inspiration in the *Inferno, Purgatorio*, and *Paradiso*. Vergil, as is well known, draws for his account partly upon certain aspects of Stoic and philosophical doctrine, but more upon Greek legends of Hades, in particular Homer's account in *Odyssey* Book Eleven (known as the *Nekyia*) of the journey made by Odysseus in order to consult the spirits of the dead, and such traditional myths (surviving in a variety of literary formulations) as those which relate the expeditions of Heracles and Orpheus to the Underworld, the former to bring back Cerberus, the latter to bring back Eurydice. Such expeditions are known to scholars as "*Catabaseis*", from the Greek word for "Descent", *Κατάβασις*. We may say, then, that Vergil's description of Aeneas' Descent is a magnificent composite literary integration of Odysseus' Visit to Hades and numerous other Greek "catabatic" myths.

In an impassioned appeal to the Sibyl of Cumae to assist him visit his dead father Anchises through the Entrance to the Lower World at Avernus in Italy, Aeneas gives us the clue as to who were at least some of his prototypes by naming a few — but not all — of those persons who on rare occasions in the past had dared to venture on a Journey of the Dead. Who these exceptional persons were, and why and where and how they made the Journey to the World of Shades and what they saw and learnt in the infernal regions are intriguing questions. It is partly as answers to them that I have attempted here a connected account of this recurring theme in the two thousand years up to and including Vergil. And in endeavouring to indicate the remarkable versatility of the theme during its considerable career I have placed especial emphasis upon answering the question: what did these various Visitants to the Land of the Dead find in the infernal regions and with what did they return? It is, moreover, a reasonable assumption that Vergil, who is known to have devoted a great deal of research to the writing of his poem, and as we have just noted makes Aeneas appeal to several catabatic heroes as his prototypes, read much of this tradition, though a detailed comparison reveals that Vergil never merely borrows, he always transforms: the elements are traditional but their impact is new. It is my purpose to illustrate this point at length by showing the development of the Journey into the Underworld theme from its origins, and by emphasising those aspects of the tradition in particular which Vergil was to take up and reforge.

In broad terms Vergil was the first to make of the theme an instrument of national aspiration and social criticism. It would, however, be a mistake to think that only Vergil adapted the theme to his own day and that the descents before Vergil were completely devoid of contemporary overtones of their own. It is a commonplace of literary criticism that no fictional pattern has much chance of survival unless it corresponds with human experience or aspiration. And in looking carefully at what the various visitants to the Land of the Dead obtained in the World Below, we shall see that Vergil's predecessors likewise exploited and transmuted the traditional myths and legends to suit their needs and those for whom they wrote. This explains why there is no "fixed" version of the numerous pre-Vergilian catabatic myths about Odysseus or Heracles or Theseus or Orpheus or any other visitant to the Land of the Dead. Consequently in the next four chapters of this book I look in detail at the locales, underworld geography, ritualistic and other implications, and above all at the "contemporary twists" of earlier catabatic myths which express the object of the mythographer in each case. To show how Vergil utilized this material — how, in short, he adapted the theme as never before when he gave it an obvious contemporary twist and made Aeneas return from the Underworld with a message relevant to the glorious Golden Age of

Rome under Augustus — will be the object of the final two chapters. In this chapter, which is introductory, we shall look behind the Greek at the Near Eastern origins of the catabatic theme, which in turn requires that we attempt to define further the kind of tradition we are tracing.

Let us begin by drawing a distinction between those myths in which a god or goddess makes the descent and those in which a human being descends into the World Below. The distinction is maintained in Greek and Roman myth as, for example, between the goddess Persephone and the mortal Aeneas. These therefore are obviously two separate branches of the catabatic tradition. But since the esssential *differentia specifica* between them are not so obvious and hold important implications for the scope of our study, we shall enquire into them with reference to Near Eastern myths a little more closely than has hitherto been customary.

II. *The fertility-tradition*

The fertility-tradition of underworld myths can be adequately illustrated from the descents of the Sumerian goddess Inanna and the Akkadian goddess Ishtar — these two descents also exemplify the rapid change that has taken place in recent years with the discovery of new texts and fragments — and a few others.

In the Sumerian myth of Inanna's Descent into the Underworld,[1] which goes back to the first half of the second millennium B.C., Inanna, the tutelary deity of Erech, "queen of heaven" and goddess of love and war whom the shepherd Dumuzi had "married", descends into the Land of No Return ruled over by her sister Ereshkigal, the goddess of death and gloom, on the pretext of attending the funeral of Ereshkigal's husband. With a terror that is practically unknown to

[1] See S. N. Kramer, "*Inanna's Descent to the Nether World* Continued and Revised", *J. C. S.* 5(1951), 1—17, which incorporates the Yale tablet (to be mentioned presently) but not the new finds mentioned in nn. 6, 7, and 10 below. Quotations are from this version, whose line references correspond to the rendering in *A.N.E.T.* 52—57. Note that the second edition of *A.N.E.T.* (1955) still does not include the Yale tablet, while the third edition of 1969 merely mentions it in a note.

Greek underworld myths, Inanna is stripped of her apparel at each of the seven gates of the Underworld until she appears naked upon her knees before the pitiless Queen of the Dead and the seven Judges of the Underworld, who by fastening upon her their "eye of death" turn her into a corpse. For three days she hangs there impaled upon a stake, until the god Enki sends two creatures below to revive her with the food and water of life.

Inanna's fertility-role is in fact less conspicuous in the extant description of this descent than in a hymn of the Dumuzi-Inanna cult describing her "sacred marriage" enacted at the New Year.[2] But in the Semitic counterpart to this descent found on tablets dating from the end of the second millennium B.C. and telling of the Akkadian goddess' descent through the seven gates of the Underworld, it is clear that reproduction among beasts and men ceases while she is detained in the Underworld (obv. 77—79).[3] And we shall see shortly below that, as in the Akkadian version, the descents made by divine personages will generally be found to have fertility implications.

Why the descending goddesses Inanna and Ishtar undertook the descents — the stories are so structurally alike that they may be taken together — and how they escaped from the Underworld has been pieced together from new tablets only in recent years. Twenty years ago and before, it was almost universally believed that Inanna and Ishtar had ventured on the journey below in order to bring back from the Underworld their husband-lover Dumuzi and Tammuz respectively, who were detained there against their will.[4] Testimony to the Akkadian Tammuz's resurrection was alleged to have been found in

[2] The hymns describing the *ἱερὸς γάμος* of the Dumuzi-Inanna cult are edited and translated by S. N. Kramer, "Cuneiform Studies and the History of Literature: The Sumerian Sacred Marriage Texts", *P.A.P.S.* 107(1963), 485ff. See esp. 489f. for the ritual-practice (these pages also provide good answers for those interested in the question: how do rituals of this kind arise?), and 506f. for Inanna's fertility significance.

[3] Line references by obverse and reverse of the tablets are to E. A. Speiser's translation in *A.N.E.T.*[3] 107—109.

[4] See e.g. A. Falkenstein, "Zu 'Inannas Gang zur Unterwelt,", *Archiv. für Orientforschung* 14(1942), 113—138 and P. Maurus Witzel, "Zur sumerischen Rezension der Höllenfahrt Ischtars", *Orientalia* 14(1945), 24—69. Cf. also *id.* "Ischtar gegen Tammuz?" *Orientalia* 21(1952), 435—455.

the words of Belili, Tammuz's sister, the Akkadian Geshtinanna, who refers to "the day when Tammuz comes up to me" (rev. 56). At the same time Ereshkigal's instruction to her vizier Namtar was then without explanation: "If she [Ishtar] does not give thee her ransom price, bring her back" (rev. 46). This line evidently did not fit in with the above reconstruction of the myth.

Ereshkigal's remark in the Akkadian descent indeed continued unexplained until the publication of a tablet from Yale, which includes Ereshkigal's parting instruction in the Sumerian version: "If Inanna would ascend from the nether world let her give one substitute as her substitute" (276f.).[5] The tablet goes on to describe how Inanna is then released from the Underworld and is accompanied on her release by *gallas*, or underworld demons, who seek to obtain a suitable substitute for her. Twice they attempt to seize a victim and twice Inanna intervenes. But when she sees how her husband Dumuzi, instead of mourning for her death, "had dressed himself in a noble garment, seated himself nobly on (his) seat", she says, "*As for him*, carry him off" (341). Dumuzi forthwith begs the Sumerian sun-god Utu to turn him into a snake so that he might escape the demons; and here the text of the Yale tablet breaks off.

A new tablet from Ur, first published by Kramer in 1963, adds another thirty lines and shows that Utu heeded Dumuzi's plea after all. In the form of a snake Dumuzi fled first to the home of his sister Geshtinanna and then to his "holy sheep fold", where eventually the *gallas* caught up with him and lacerated his body.[6] The end was still left inconclusive. But another new myth called *The Death of Dumuzi* supplements the finale and shows that after being changed three times into a gazelle, rather than a snake, Dumuzi was finally caught and dragged down into Hell.[7]

[5] For the Yale tablet see n.1 above.

[6] The Ur tablet was first published by S. N. Kramer, *P.A.P.S.* 107(1963), 492f. and 515f.

[7] This myth, found on tablets dating from about 1750 B.C., was presented in its restored state first by S. N. Kramer in 1960 at the International Congress of Orientalists in Moscow, and then translated by him in his *Mythologies of the Ancient World* (New York 1961), 109—115. Compare the very different account of Dumuzi's death in T. Jacobsen and S. N. Kramer, "The Myth of Inanna and Bilulu", *J.N.E.S.* 12(1953), 160ff.

The main outlines of the story have been so far pieced together. But one vital ingredient was still left vague. Kramer at first thought that Dumuzi not only "dies" as Inanna's substitute but "stays dead" forever if Inanna is to live.[8] By a curious coincidence the evidence for the resurrection of Attis and Adonis has been found somewhat wanting in recent years.[9] However, a reading by Falkenstein of another Ur tablet inscribed with the very end of Inanna's Descent — "You (Dumuzi), half the year! Your sister (Geshtinanna), half the year!" — shows with reasonable certainty that Dumuzi remained in the Underworld for only half the year and his sister Geshtinanna replaced him for the other half.[10]

These new developments challenge old ideas. The view once put forward by Oppenheim that Ishtar, like Christ, descended into the Netherworld in order to "'redeem'... 'lost' souls even at the cost of her life"[11] is now rendered obsolete. The myth suggests the very opposite, that Dumuzi is actually deprived of eternal life by his wife's jealousy; and as such Inanna-Ishtar's descent can no longer be considered the prototype of Christ's. It is now clear, too, that she did not descend in order to fetch up Dumuzi-Tammuz. Her descent was rather an act of territorial expansion, in which she attempts to seat herself

[8] See e.g. his *Mythologies of the Ancient World*, 10. The consequences this would hold for Biblical studies are examined by E. M. Yamauchi, "Tammuz and the Bible", *J.B.L.* 84(1965), 283—290.

[9] Attis is not revived except in one, late source (Firmicus Maternus, *De errore* 3), which M. P. Nilsson, *Geschichte der griechischen Religion* 2(Munich 1950), 623, dismisses as speculative. The sources for Adonis' resurrection (Lucian, Origen, Jerome, Cyril of Alexandria) are also late; see P. Lambrechts, "La 'résurrection' d'Adonis" in *Mélanges Isidore Levy* (Bruxelles 1955), 207—240. In his *Attis: van Herdersknaap tot God* (Brussel 1962) Lambrechts endeavours to show further that Attis was a minor mortal follower of Cybele and does not appear as a god either in iconography or in texts before A.D. 150.

[10] See A. Falkenstein, review of C. J. Gadd and S. N. Kramer, *Ur Excavations Texts VI* (London 1963) in *Bibliotheca Orientalis* 22(1965), esp. 280—282 on no. 10 line 10. Kramer subsequently accepted Falkenstein's interpretation in "Dumuzi's Annual Resurrection", *B.A.S.O.R.* 183(1966), 31. For discussion of the relationship of Sumerian and Akkadian versions of this myth see also Falkenstein, "Die Sumerische und der Akkadische Mythos von Inannas Gang zur Unterwelt" in *Festschrift Werner Caskel* ed. E. Gräf (Leiden 1968), 87—110.

[11] A. Leo Oppenheim, "Mesopotamian Mythology III", *Orientalia* 19(1950), 139.

on Ereshkigal's throne so as to make herself mistress not only of Heaven but of the Underworld as well.[12]

Such a drastic modification of old ideas should make us wary also of overstressing the general features of other catabatic myths in which all too often similarities are countered by fundamental differences. Already Frankfort has given us good reason to believe that Osiris, the Egyptian giver of fruit and lord of the Underworld, whose resurrection signified his life in the beyond and whose power was recognized when life breaks forth periodically from the earth, was not a "dying god", as Sir James G. Frazer in his monumental work *The Golden Bough* calls him along with Tammuz, Attis, Adonis and others, but a "dead god" who altogether belonged to the world of the dead and was often depicted as a mummy.[13] Hazardous it is, then, even from this consideration alone — the different kind of Afterlives they reflect is another[14] — to regard the Egyptian god Osiris and the Mesopotamian Tammuz as expressions of the same type of "rising and dying fertility-god".

To return to Inanna's descent, it is further surmised by Falkenstein[15] — he adduces corroborating evidence from a passage in "Dumuzi's dream" — that Geshtinanna took her brother's place in the Underworld by offering herself out of love as a substitute for him. If this is true, and I think it is quite likely, then Geshtinanna was a substitute for Dumuzi as Dumuzi was, though not willingly, for Inanna. It is evidently a widespread motif in the Near East. For the principle that no one may leave the Underworld unless an acceptable substitute is available is to be found also in the Sumerian descent-myth *Enlil and Ninlil*.[16] Enlil, the chief god of the Sumerian pantheon, is banished to the Underworld by the other gods for sexual impropriety with the

[12] The motive for the descent is clarified in the two articles by Falkenstein in n.10 above.

[13] H. Frankfort, *Kingship and the Gods* (Chicago 1948), esp. 184f. and 298.

[14] While in Egypt the reality of death "was hidden under the elaborate rituals proclaiming belief in survival" (Frankfort, *op. cit.* 281), man's inescapable fate in the Mesopotamian "House of Death" was at best a wraith-like lingering in limbo. The latter is called by G. S. Kirk, "Greek Mythology: Some New Perspectives", *J.H.S.* 92(1972), 82, the "model from which [the Greek Hades] is surely derived."

[15] See the review article cited in n.10 above.

[16] For this myth see further at n.41 below.

goddess Ninlil who follows him below. The goddess' last act causes great concern to Enlil, who knows that she will soon give birth to the moon-god Nanna-Sin. Since he does not want this god to dwell for ever in the world below, he must devise a means for the new god's release. Accordingly he disguises himself first as the gate-keeper of Nippur, then as the gate-keeper of the World of the Dead, and thirdly as the ferryman of the River of Death. Thus unrecognized he makes love again to Ninlil in the Underworld and so impregnates her with three further offspring. These three underworld deities are then given as substitutes for the release of their older brother Sin, who thereby ascends to his proper place in heaven.

Alongside this underworld myth explaining the organization of the world and the birth of the gods may be placed another Sumerian myth which is also concerned with creation. In *Enki and Ninhursag*[17] the cause of trouble is again sexual excess: Ninhursag is furious with Enki for having tasted some "forbidden fruit" in the form of plants that have been grown from his seed. In anger the goddess withdraws from him, apparently into the Underworld, and by so depriving Enki of her "eye of life" brings him close to death until she returns.

The withdraw-motif is common in the fertility pattern of descent myths. In the Hittite *Myth of Telipinu,* the god of vegetation, according to one version, is regarded as having taken some offence and departed from the world in a huff; in another version he is sent on the orders of his father, the Weather-god, into the depths of Ocean, whence in due course he retrieves the captive sun from the Netherworld.[18]

Finally in the Canaanite descent-myth of Baal the withdraw-motif is humanized in a different guise again. The god is lured this time into the Underworld by Mot's invitation to a feast which cannot be decently refused. And while Baal is detained in the world below his place in the Upperworld is taken by an inferior god called Ashtar, who like

[17] Trans. S. N. Kramer, *A.N.E.T.*[3] 37—41. For a structural analysis of this and the former myth in comparison with others (not underworld), see G. S. Kirk's excellent book *Myth: its Meaning and Functions* (Cambridge 1970), 91ff., 101—107.

[18] The two versions are analysed by Th. H. Gaster respectively in *Thespis*[2] (New York 1966), 295—315 and "A Hittite Seasonal Myth", *F.L.* 84(1973), 339—343.

Dumuzi assumes sovereignty until he is ousted on Baal's return.[19] Perhaps no other Near Eastern myth so closely resembles Inanna-Ishtar's descent as does this one of Baal, though in one important respect the Mesopotamian and Canaanite myths are at variance. In the former a goddess descends to the lower world: in the latter the descent is made by a male. The difference, I believe, represents a climatic rather than a patriarchal twist.[20] For whereas seasonal vegetation is uppermost in the myth of Inanna-Ishtar (the latter's stay below ground marks a period of infertility on earth which lasts until after the goddess has been sprinkled with the water of life and returns), Baal, whose opponent Mot represents the devastations of drought, himself symbolises primarily the return of the fertilising rain. Thus the Canaanite, like the Mesopotamian, is an aetiological myth which explains seasonal or climatic changes.

Enough has been said of underworld myths of this kind, it is hoped, to clarify the essential specific differences between them and Aeneas' descent. The myths in which a god or goddess descends into the lower world are closely associated with fertility patterns or creation myths and the Underworld is primarily thought of not as an Afterworld where the dead may be consulted, as it is in the secular tradition of Aeneas, but as a place of retreat or home of hostile forces, whither the deity for some reason withdraws or is allured or is sent in punishment or exile or disappears in an act of aggrandizement.[21] It is not, then, primarily to the fertility-tradition of underworld myths that we

[19] See e.g. Th. H. Gaster, *Thespis*², 123ff. and 153—244. Precise details of the seasonal significance are disputed, but on Gaster's interpretation Ashtar and Tammuz may be presumed to be active from the time when the rains fail in May until the winnowing of the crops in June/July (the month to which Tammuz gave his name); for the ritual lamentation of Tammuz's death in this month see S. Langdon, *Babylonian Menologies and the Semitic Calendars* (London 1935), 119—123.

[20] For the tendency to regard such differences as due to sociological change see e.g. Jane Harrison, *Themis* (Cambridge 1927), 420f. However, the close knowledge of e.g. the reverence paid to the Virgin Mother by Catholics in our own day should make us wary of interpreting "matrist" religious attitudes in terms of a "matriarchal" society.

[21] For a full-scale study of violent entrances into hostile Underworlds, see J. Kroll's excellent monograph *Gott und Hölle: der Mythos vom Descensuskampfe* (Leipzig und Berlin 1932).

must look for the nearest antecedents to Aeneas' Descent into the Underworld, which is inspired rather by Aeneas' desire to visit and consult with his dead father Anchises. More akin by far to this is the secular tradition of underworld myths represented in the Near East by Gilgamesh's journey to his ancestor Utnapishtim, in which the mortal Gilgamesh, rather than a deity, makes a Journey of the Dead in quest of information. The Greek myth of Persephone-Kore's abduction into the underworld Kingdom of Hades, which causes the death of the crops, is evidently part of the fertility-tradition. But since Persephone retains the characteristics of the pre-Greek Goddess of Death[22], the two traditions are intertwined. Hence the goddess' descent is fused with her role as Queen of the Netherworld and lies behind several myths in which a mortal visits the World of the Dead either in the attempt to retrieve the goddess herself from the world below or to receive from her an initiate's welcome. In the following pages, however, it will be my especial aim with Aeneas in mind to develop what may be termed the wisdom-tradition of underworld myths as distinct from the fertility- or vegetation-tradition.

III. *The wisdom-tradition*

The Babylonian *Epic of Gilgamesh* tells of the catabatic journey of the man Gilgamesh.[23] He is two-thirds divine, but for all that he is a man subject to human aspirations and suffering. We begin our study of Classical *catabaseis* with this Epic because it is the oldest secular catabatic myth in Near Eastern literature, possibly the oldest in the world, and because a certain affinity exists between it and the Vergilian descent.

The Epic was almost certainly current as early as the third millennium B.C. and has been pieced together from tablets inscribed in Old Babylonian dating from the first half of the second millennium and from a later Assyrian recension and from Hittite and Hurrian translations discovered on tablets at Boghaz-Köy in central Anatolia.

[22] See esp. on p. 92 below.

[23] Details of the Journey are given shortly below.

Many of the episodes in the Epic go back to Sumerian forerunners, but as we shall see shortly below only the unified Epic seems to have told of the catabatic journey of the man Gilgamesh, and this was originally, as we have said, an Akkadian, that is Semitic, tale. That it had an extraordinarily wide circulation can be inferred from its dispersal in several translations throughout the Near East, and since most of the Akkadian tablets were found in Ashurbanipal's library at Nineveh, it must have survived down to as late as the seventh century B.C.

The probability that Vergil's research into the catabatic tradition extended directly to the Near East I would take to be very unlikely. His intimate acquaintance with Greek traditional mythology, and in particular with Homer's *Nekyia* which describes the earliest Visit to Hades in the Western world, on the other hand, can be taken for granted. The Homeric epic, of course, is itself the culmination of a long tradition, some of it going back, as archaeology confirms, to the Mycenaean Age, in which the events were set. There is no need here to rehearse the mistrust[24] that was once felt on the subject of the spread of ideas into Greece from the Near East. Greek myth, as is now recognized by many Classicists and Orientalists alike, is known to have derived much of its form and content from the myth and ritual of the Near East. The intimate relation between the two has recently been expressed succinctly thus: "the great civilizations lay in the East, and from the first, Greece's face was turned towards the Sun. Greece is part of Asia; Greek literature is a Near Eastern literature."[25] The Sumerian scholar Samuel Noah Kramer from an Oriental

[24] Suffice to mention that Ganschinietz in his monumental article "Katabasis" (published 1919) in *R.E.* 10.2359—2449 esp. 2391 was struck by the amazing likeness of Babylonian poetry and thought to the Greek, but nevertheless denied a genetic link.

[25] M. L. West, *Hesiod: Theogony* (Oxford 1966), 30f. Cf. also the detailed arguments in e.g. T. J. Dunbabin, *The Greeks and their Eastern Neighbours* (London 1957), T.B.L. Webster, "Homer and Eastern Poetry", *Minos* 4(1956), 104—116, Albin Lesky, "Griechischer Mythos und Vorderer Orient", *Saeculum* 6(1955), 35—52, M. C. Astour, *Hellenosemitica*[2] (Leiden 1967) with its vast bibliography, and the many works dealing with this matter which are cited below. G. S. Kirk, *Myth: its Meaning and Functions*, 132, accordingly writes: "the study of Mesopotamian myths is rewarding not only for their unusual richness in complexity and

viewpoint is somewhat more expansive: "Sumerian influence penetrated the Greek and Hebrew world through the Canaanite, Hittite, and Akkadian literature. Particularly through the latter, since it is well known, that in the second millennium B.C. the Akkadian language was the *lingua franca* of practically the entire literary world."[26] Against a background of cultural intercourse such as this it would not be surprising if Homer were somehow influenced by the Epic.

The question of the date of transmission for the spread of ideas from the Near East into Greece, on the other hand, is very much *sub judice*. In the case of Hesiod's cosmological and theogonical myths, which are very closely related indeed to Near Eastern myths like the Babylonian theogony of Dunnu and the Babylonian *Enuma Elish* and the Hurrian myth of Kumarbi, it has been argued that the orientalising period in the late ninth or eighth century B.C., when contacts were renewed after the dark ages, was as crucial in this process as the Minoan-Mycenaean period itself.[27] However for the purposes of this study, which recognizes in the catabatic myths a more remote affinity, I am content to state that except for some sheerly Oriental derivations like the Chimaera Homer is working generally (with particular exceptions mentioned at various places in the text below) on assimilated tradition which has been thoroughly hellenized and humanized, rather than on new (like Hesiod's preaching of the Asiatic goddess Hecate). It is not unlikely, after all, that some knowledge of the Gilgamesh Epic or its prototypes was introduced to Greece in the second millennium B.C. and was hellenized to provide a kind of background that might be drawn upon by anyone wishing to publicise a Heracles or Odysseus. Any resemblances between Aeneas' descent and Gilgamesh's are, therefore, more probably due to what Vergil inherited

fantasy... but also for their influence as a model for Greek myths... The lively discussion... of these myths... should be of deep concern to Hellenists."

[26] S. N. Kramer, "Cuneiform Studies and the History of Literature", *P.A.P.S.* 107(1963), 487.

[27] P. Walcot, *Hesiod and the Near East* (Cardiff 1966), *passim;* and for the theogonic text of Dunnu see W. G. Lambert and P. Walcot, "A New Babylonian Theogony and Hesiod", *Kadmos* 4(1965), 64—72. Cf. however M. L. West, *Hesiod: Theogony*, 14 and 28f.

through Homer and other early Greek tradition than to his direct acquaintance of the Near Eastern catabatic tradition itself.

Even a brief sketch of the contents of the Epic[28] reveals its humanity and appeal. After a short introductory passage praising the city Uruk (Biblical Erech, modern Warka), we are told how the king Gilgamesh gains a friend in Enkidu; how both set out to reach a cedar forest, whose fierce guardian Huwawa (Humbaba in the Assyrian version) they kill; and how Gilgamesh, after refusing an offer of marriage from the goddess Ishtar herself, must needs overcome the Bull of Heaven, for which Enkidu suffers and dies. Beside himself with grief at the loss of his friend, Gilgamesh sets out alone in search of his ancestor Utnapishtim, the Babylonian hero of the flood, that he might learn from him the secret of immortality. Having reached the mountain called Mashu, whose peaks reach up to heaven and down to the netherworld beneath, Gilgamesh finds its gate guarded by a Scorpion-man and his wife, who warn that no mortal has passed through this gate before. Gilgamesh, however, being two-thirds divine, is permitted to pass and after journeying through the mountain-tunnel for twelve double-hours he emerges into a bright garden of jewels. Here he meets the Semitic sun-god Shamash, who likewise tries to discourage him from going further. But Gilgamesh is persistent and continues his journey until he meets a Circe-like figure called Siduri dwelling by the sea. She too seeks to dissuade him from the quest. Only Shamash, she tells him, has ever journeyed across the Ocean and, beyond that, lie the Waters of Death. But he prevails upon her and she directs him to Urshanabi, the ferryman of Utnapishtim, who also tries to make Gilgamesh change his mind. In a fit of rage Gilgamesh now smashes what seems to be a vital part of the boat. As a consequence Urshanabi cannot take Gilgamesh across the waters until three hundred (or in the Assyrian version one hundred and twenty) punting-poles are cut down from a forest. This task is soon accomplished by Gilgamesh, who is at last ferried across. But

[28] N. K. Sandars, *The Epic of Gilgamesh* (Harmondsworth revd. 1964) offers a readable account in which different versions are conflated without line references. The most complete translation is that of A. E. Speiser in *A.N.E.T.*³ 72—99, with additions by A.K. Grayson, *op. cit.* 503—507. References by Tablet, column and line, are to this work unless otherwise specified.

Utnapishtim appears far from encouraging. His own immortality, he says, was a gift bestowed by the gods themselves: but where is the god who wills Gilgamesh's immortality? He agrees even so to help Gilgamesh obtain immortality provided the latter can but keep awake for seven days. But Gilgamesh fails the test. Utnapishtim sends him therefore to a "washing place", which may have denoted a fountain of youth.[29] By not thinking to drink from its magical waters Gilgamesh apparently misses a second opportunity to win immortality. Finally he is directed to a prickly herb of youth that grows beneath the waters. This he obtains. But on the journey back to Uruk, Gilgamesh puts it down in order to bathe and loses it to a snake, who snatched and ate it and thereby won for itself the immortality that might have been man's.[30] Urshanabi, for having ferried Gilgamesh to Utnapishtim's shore, is banned by Utnapishtim from ever making the crossing again, and therefore accompanies Gilgamesh back to Uruk. The Epic ends with an "inorganic appendage" to be described shortly below.

The female who guards the approaches to Ocean, the boat of which a part is missing, the boatman, the quest for ancestral wisdom, and other motifs in the *Epic of Gilgamesh* which bear some affinity to the Greek catabatic tradition will be reserved for discussion in later chapters.

Instead for the rest of this chapter we shall confine the argument, in connection with Gilgamesh's long and arduous journey through the mountain and across Ocean and the Waters of Death in order to

[29] A. Leo Oppenheim, "Mesopotamian Mythology II", *Orientalia* 17(1948), 56. It is a widely held idea that man lost the opportunity of gaining immortality through some trivial accident or mistake. Oppenheim compares the well-known episode of the unlucky cook in the romance of Alexander the Great, who failed to draw the correct conclusions when rinsing a certain fish. A nearer parallel is to be found in the Akkadian myth of Adapa, who after a submarine descent failed to eat the bread and water of life that was proffered to him (*A.N.E.T.* 101—103).

[30] M. P. Nilsson, *The Minoan-Mycenaean Religion and its survival in Greek Religion*² (Lund 1950), 629 n. 29 thinks that the herb was "a magical means to restore the dead to life" and was, therefore, of another order than the fruits in the Hebrew, Persian, Egyptian and Greek-Minoan Gardens. This is hardly decisive. In the Epic immortality or second youth was won by a living snake, not a dead one—the snake itself being not dissimilar from the serpent in *Genesis*, on which see J. G. Frazer, *Folk-lore in the Old Testament* (London 1918), vol. 1.76f. and H. W. Stubbs, "Satan, Loki, and Prometheus", *Orpheus* 3(1956), 152—156.

obtain ancestral wisdom, to some of the implications of Professor Webster's claim that the seer Teiresias, who gave Odysseus information in the Homeric *Nekyia*, took over the role that belonged to Utnapishtim.[31] In that case the ancestral part of Utnapishtim will presumably have been made over to Odysseus' mother Anticleia; as we shall see, communing with the family-ancestor in the Underworld remains a persistent element in the catabatic tradition. Of particular interest for us here is Webster's further observation, added without comment, that Utnapishtim was located "in the upper world" and that Teiresias when assigned Utnapishtim's role was "placed in Hades".[32] The point that Utnapishtim's "upper world" is, within the structure of the Epic, in effect an Otherworld and to all intents an Underworld will be argued here for three reasons. Firstly, it prepares us for the view, hardly conclusive on the evidence assembled at this point but to my mind probable if considered within the whole context of the two journeys, that Homer is somehow indebted to the *Epic of Gilgamesh*. Secondly, while endeavouring for ourselves to reach a point from which to view the significance of Utnapishtim's "upper world", we can hardly overlook the composite nature of Gilgamesh's journey; and this will lead us directly to touch on what may be called the Babylonian Epic's "Homeric problem" and to the very beginnings of the catabatic tradition. Thirdly, it raises several issues which help us to understand more clearly what a *catabasis* is.

Once Gilgamesh passes the gate of the Mashu guarded by the Scorpion-people, "Wardens of Shamash,/Both at his rising and setting" (Tablet IX. ii. 9—10),[33] and begins to travel "along the road of the sun" (Tablet IX. iv. 45) through the heart of the mountain, it seems that he has already gone where no mortal has ventured before. As he nears the end of the tunnel, "the dawn breaks" (Tablet IX. v. 45) and he finds himself in a jewelled garden where Shamash the sun-god walks in early morning. Gilgamesh has evidently passed through the confines of the world of mortals into the beyond, the country of dawn "Eastward in Eden". The "Mashu", meaning "Twins", can be

[31] T. B. L. Webster, *From Mycenae to Homer*² (London 1964), 82f. and 247f.
[32] *Ibid.* 248, cf. 83.
[33] R. Campbell Thompson, *The Epic of Gilgamish* (Oxford 1930), 42.

none other than the mythical twin-peaked mountain of the sun, the place of both sunset and sunrise frequently depicted on early Babylonian cylinder seals. They are not, then, to be thought of in strictly geographical terms and their common identification with the mountains of Lebanon and Anti-Lebanon probably does not belong to the earlier strata of material and would only have real meaning for anyone in Syria or Palestine, where of course the Epic was known.

Having journeyed through the mountain to the Garden of the Sun, Gilgamesh must yet cross Ocean in a boat to another land beyond. Insofar as Siduri tells Gilgamesh that only the sun-god Shamash has ever made the Ocean-crossing before him, and insofar as the boat of Urshanabi might be regarded as a doublet of the boat of the sun, this part of Gilgamesh's journey, too, seems to resemble a "Journey of the Sun". The reduplication within the Epic points to the episodic nature of Gilgamesh's journey and to the composite nature of the Epic itself. There is no need to go through once again all of the arguments adduced by Kramer and others to show that of five extant poems in the Sumerian Gilgamesh cycle — namely *Gilgamesh and Huwawa* (known also as *Gilgamesh and the Land of the Living*), the *Death of Gilgamesh*, *Gilgamesh and the Bull of Heaven*, *Gilgamesh, Enkidu, and the Nether World*, and *Gilgamesh and Agga* — only the last seems not to have been utilized in the Epic, while motifs taken from poems which are not Gilgamesh poems are incorporated too.[34] Suffice it to say that Kramer has indicated that he knows of no Sumerian prototype for Gilgamesh's journey through the mountain.[35] And I can find no precise counterpart to Gilgamesh's Ocean-crossing either.

Both observations suggest that whoever the epic-maker was — and I doubt that he was many[36] — he has skilfully reworked traditional material to create a catabatic tale not actually found in his sources.

A number of poems may, however, have suggested the idea for

[34] S. N. Kramer, "The Epic of Gilgamesh and its Sumerian Sources", *J. A. O. S.* 64(1944), 7—23 and 83.

[35] *Ibid.* 18. n. 82.

[36] Kramer, *op. cit.* 13, speaks of the "creators" of the Babylonian Epic: but the creation of such a well-conceived poetic unity may be chiefly the work of a single bard.

such a tale to the epic-maker. Foremost among these is the Sumerian poem *Gilgamesh, Enkidu, and the Nether World*, told in the Epic's "inorganic appendage", to which reference has been made above.[37] Here Enkidu descends into the Underworld to fetch up the mysterious *pukku* and *mikku* which Gilgamesh somehow had dropped thither; but he fails to observe Gilgamesh's warning not to break the underworld tabus and is accordingly "caught" in the Underworld. This is not a proper *catabasis* because Enkidu does not come back. Only his spirit is allowed to return, through a hole in the ground, and Enkidu converses briefly with Gilgamesh about what he has seen in the Land of the Dead. This earlier poem of Enkidu's descent may then have provided the idea for Gilgamesh's Journey of the Dead in the Epic. And the brilliant conception of the Babylonian redactor lay in making Enkidu's death the motivation for Gilgamesh's journey in quest of immortality from the one man who had succeeded in obtaining it, Utnapishtim. This man is none other than Gilgamesh's own ancestor who was preserved from the flood and now lives not in this world but in a land "far away, at the mouth of the rivers" (Tablet XI. 195). He is the hero of the Akkadian flood-story and the counterpart of the Sumerian flood-hero Ziusudra, who according to *The Deluge* was immortalized in a faraway land called Dilmun, "where the sun rises" (line 261).[38] The Babylonian bard has very evidently utilized the story of the Flood even though this tale originally had nothing to do with Gilgamesh. And he has not only changed the third person of the Flood-story to the first person so as to make Utnapishtim the narrator of his own experiences, but has also innovated the theme by making Gilgamesh the first man ever to cross Ocean and visit him. Thus Gilgamesh's Journey through the mountain and Gilgamesh's Ocean-

[37] P. 26. Gilgamesh's questioning of Enkidu is oddly joined to the main story of the Epic (see Kramer, *op. cit.* 23), but his desire to learn the nature of the Land of Shades is a natural sequel to his own failure to obtain immortality. The poem is now properly edited by A. Shaffer, *Sumerian Sources of Tablet XII of the Epic of Gilgamesh* (Pennsylvania PhD., 1963).

[38] *The Deluge,* trans. S. N. Kramer, *A.N.E.T.* 42—44, is now fully edited by M. Civil in *Atra-Hasis: The Babylonian Story of the Flood* ed. W. G. Lambert and A. R. Millard (Oxford 1969), 138—143. This work shows also that the Akkadian flood-story has a much closer relationship with Gilgamesh XI than does the Sumerian version.

crossing, for which no prototypes can be found, appear to be innovations called into being by Gilgamesh's search for his "translated" ancestor in a world that in the Epic has become a Land of the Departed.

Furthermore, the Ocean-crossing in the Epic is merged with the idea of a crossing over the Waters of Death, which are said by Siduri in the Assyrian version to lie between the sea and Utnapishtim's shore (Tablet X. ii. 25). When after three days Urshanabi's boat reaches these waters the ferryman bids Gilgamesh take each of the poles he had earlier cut down in turn for a single thrust, presumably so that his hand should not touch a single drop of the now fatal water.[39] The conflation between the Ocean and the Waters of Death conveys a very obvious mortuary significance, borrowed perhaps from the Sumerian river of death. Although Urshanabi, as has been rightly observed,[40] is not a ferryman of the dead, he may be modelled on one.[41] We can add to this that the above mentioned Descents into the Underworld by the goddesses Inanna and Ishtar seem also to have been drawn upon. Ishtar threatens to smash the doors of the Underworld and bring up the dead in both the Epic at Tablet VI. 96—100 and her Descent at lines 17—20 (obv.).[42] And the same myths as newly interpreted now make intelligible the reason why Gilgamesh in declining Ishtar's offer of marriage at Tablet VI. 46ff. refers to the terrible treatment which the goddess had meted out to her former lover Tammuz and others.[43] These descents, then, in all probability

[39] As R. Campbell Thompson, *The Epic of Gilgamish*, 85, supposes.

[40] See Th. H. Gaster, *The Oldest Stories in the World* (Boston 1958), 50.

[41] For the Sumerian belief that the dead were ferried by a boatman (the prototype of Charon?) across a river, see the myth *Enlil and Ninlil* described on p. 19 above and further in S. N. Kramer, *The Sumerians* (Chicago 1964), 133, 145ff. Cf. also the tantalising reference to the Magan-boat, which might be a boat of the dead, in the obscure lines 112—114 of the Huwawa poem (*A.N.E.T.* 49). The Sumerian hero Lugalbanda, who was known to the Babylonian bard, also appears to have crossed an underworld river, see S. N. Kramer, *History Begins at Sumer*² (London 1961), 283f.

[42] Peter Jensen, *Das Gilgamesch-Epos in der Weltliteratur,* vol. 2 (Marburg 1929), 177, compares this episode to Helios' threat to descend to Hades and shine among the dead below (at Hom. *Od.* 12. 382f.).

[43] "For Tammuz, the lover of thy youth,
Thou hast ordained wailing year after year.
Having loved the dappled shepherd-bird,

formed part of the tradition from which the Babylonian redactor conceived the idea of Gilgamesh's "descent" through the subterranean tunnel of the mountain, and over the waters of Ocean and Death, to the Afterworld of his departed ancestor Utnapishtim.

In this context it is not altogether inappropriate that Gilgamesh's journey seems to have followed a journey of the Sun. The dead are often thought of as dwelling either beneath the surface of the earth where they have been interred, or in a land across Ocean or River beyond the horizon where the sun goes.[44] There seem accordingly to be two widespread classes of mortuary myth, "the ocean type, in which the dead are supposed to cross the ocean, and the cave type, in which the dead are supposed to enter a cave, on the way to their rest."[45] Both types appear to have been fused in the Epic and to have acquired mortuary significance. Indeed the Ocean-crossing to Utnapishtim's shore and the subterranean journey to the jewelled Garden of the Sun are in many ways doubtlets. And to judge from the constituent parts of Gilgamesh's journey, the hero seems to travel to both west and east; the eastern setting being curiously paralleled by the Homeric passage that locates Odysseus in the east among the

> Thou smotest him, breaking his wing.
> In the grooves he sits, crying 'My wing!'
> Then thou lovedst a lion, perfect in strength;
> Seven pits and seven thou didst dig for him.
> Then a stallion thou lovedst, famed in battle;
> The whip, the spur, and the lash thou ordainedst for him. ...
> Then thou lovedst the keeper of the herd...
> Yet thou smotest him, turning him into a wolf. ...
> Then thou lovedst Ishullanu, thy father's gardener...
> Thou smotest him, and turn[edst] him into a *mole*. ...
> If thou shouldst love me, thou wouldst [treat me] like them."

The goddess Ishtar here seems to have behaved as a sorceress with the power to turn her lovers into animals.

[44] The belief is attested with impressive documentation in E. B. Tylor, *Primitive Culture* (repr. New York 1958), ch. 13, and M. C. Stokes, "Hesiodic and Milesian Cosmogonies", *Phronesis* 7(1962), 19—21. Other references are given in an exploratory article by H. Wagenvoort, "The Journey of the Souls of the Dead to the Isles of the Blessed," *Mnemosyne* 24(1971), 113ff.

[45] W. F. Jackson Knight, *Cumaean Gates* republished with revisions in *Vergil: Epic and Anthropology* ed. J. D. Christie (London 1967), 144.

"dance-floors of early Dawn" (*Od.* 12.3f.). Precisely how the journey is to be envisaged is therefore something of a mystery. But it is sufficient for our purpose to emphasise that Gilgamesh sets out from Uruk towards the Sunset Mountains and travels in quest of an ancestor to and beyond the edge of the Unknown. His journey to the "upper world" of Utnapishtim can therefore, within the context of the Epic, be regarded as a Journey of the Dead made by a living man in the flesh; and as such it has no known Sumerian counterpart though it incorporates several Sumerian tales strung together as ordeals to be overcome within the framework of the mortuary nature of the myth.

A more detailed comparison between the *Epic of Gilgamesh* and Homer's *Nekyia* indicates a further variation between them which requires explanation. Odysseus' Visit to Hades is to a veritable Land of the Dead, whereas Utnapishtim and his wife are visited by Gilgamesh in a Blessed Abode that is more akin to Homer's "Elysian Plain", whither a few highly favoured mortals, instead of dying in the ordinary way, were "translated" and continue body and soul to live for ever (*Od.* 4.561—569). Utnapishtim's is not, then, an abode for the Ordinary Dead like the Kingdom of Hades visited by Odysseus. But since both catabatic heroes commune with an ancestor in an Otherworld, which is also an Afterworld, the difference is only one of emphasis. If the emphasis is on the ancestor, especially if only recently dead, the fact of death may be stressed; and if the hero meets his dead ancestor, why not also his dead companions on the same journey? Thus Odysseus meets not only his mother Anticleia, and the prophet Teiresias, but also his comrades Achilles, Agamemnon, Ajax and others. Aeneas likewise meets a host of the dead, and Dante too. Different aspirations are, of course, represented by each.

Thus allowing for the difference of emphases between the two types of Afterworld — and both are conflated side by side in the Vergilian Underworld — a *catabasis* can be defined as a Journey of the Dead made by a living person in the flesh who returns to our world to tell the tale. Such Journeys in the flesh are to be distinguished from mere Visions of the Otherworld. Shortly before his death Enkidu himself has such a vision in the Seventh Tablet of the *Epic of Gilgamesh*, which could hardly have given the Mesopotamian Underworld worse publicity. St. Paul, too, had a vision of his own conducted tour through the torments in Hell according to the apocryphal *Apocalypse of Paul* (chapters 31—44), to which Dante, doubting his own fitness for the journey, indirectly alludes[46] at *Inferno* 2.32 —

"Io non Enea, io non Paolo sono"
"I am not Aeneas, I am not Paul" —

thereby in effect acknowledging the "descents" of both Aeneas and Paul as his prototypes. The visionary genre, of which I have cited St. Paul's infernal journey as an instance, becomes exceedingly popular especially in the Christian literature of the Middle Ages.[47]

Catabatic Journeys are also distinguishable — though the distinction is not always observed[48] — from the phenomenon known as *ecstasis* (ἔκστασις), which denotes rather a kind of astral travel or wandering among the celestial spheres by a person's projected soul which is temporarily released from the body.[49] Nor are Journeys of

[46] See T. Silverstein, "Did Dante know the Vision of Saint Paul?" *Harvard Studies and Notes in Philology and Literature* 19(1937), 231—247, arguing for Dante's debt to the Vision, specifically at *Inferno* 3.34—42 and 11.3—13 to the Long Latin Text of the Vision. For the Latin texts see *id. Visio Sancti Pauli* (London 1935) and M. R. James, *Apocrypha Anecdota* in *Texts and Studies: Contributions to Biblical and Patristic Literature* II.3 (Cambridge 1893), 1—42. An earlier Greek text (for which see C. Tischendorf, *Evangelia Apocrypha* II. 34ff.) was written probably in the third century.

[47] For other instances see e.g. E. Norden, *Aeneis Buch* VI^3, 9f.; H. R. Patch, *The Other World According to Descriptions in Medieval Literature*, esp. chap. 4; and D. D. R. Owen, *The Vision of Hell: Infernal Journeys in Medieval French Literature* (Edinburgh 1970), all with extensive bibliographies. See also G. Dagron, "La Vie Ancienne de Saint Marcel L'Acémète", *Analecta Bollandiana* 86 (1968), 310 (for a knowledge of which I am grateful to Dr. John Whittaker), telling of the resurrection by the fifth century St. Marcellus of the monk Paul, who then narrates his Journey after Death. This Byzantine episode modelled upon the Resurrection of the Centurion's daughter in the New Testament presupposes already a veritable tradition of descent literature.

[48] It is not observed even by Ganschinietz (see n. 24 above), who includes within the catabatic tradition such psychic excursions as that of Cleonymus the Athenian *ap.* Clearchus of Soli's dialogue *On Sleep* in Proclus *In Rem.* 2. 113. 19ff. Kroll (=Clearchus fr. 8 Wehrli). Jack Lindsay in *The Clashing Rocks* (London 1965), *passim* errs further in grouping both kinds of journeys with Shamanism.

[49] The literary genre of such soul-journeys in Greece was apparently inaugurated by Plato's Er the Armenian in *Rep.* 10. 614ff., though it is worth comparing Parmenides' earlier experience described in his Proem and the soul-journeys attributed

the Dead to be confused with the consultations of ghosts at Entrances to Hades or at Oracles of the Dead by means of "necromancy" (νεκυομαντεία), which is a ritual Calling up of the Dead to the Land of the Living. To illustrate this distinction we need only turn again to the *Epic of Gilgamesh* and point to the journey made by Gilgamesh to his ancestor on the one hand, and to the séance of Enkidu at the end of the Epic on the other.

It is worth adding, perhaps, in view of the fact mentioned earlier that the dead are sometimes believed to dwell at the edge of the world as well as below the surface, that these two death-beliefs and myth-types are frequently found fused in classical *catabaseis*. Moreover many stories of Journeys into the Unknown seem to have been cast into a kind of catabatic framework — especially since in pre-scientific antiquity a journey into unchartered waters was regarded as a Journey into the Otherworld. A case could perhaps be made for regarding Jason's Argonautic voyage past the Clashing Rocks in quest of the Golden Fleece as such an otherworldly story in origin. The Rocks apparently mark the frontiers between this world and the beyond.

to later philosophers, on which see Norman W. DeWitt, "Epicurus, *Περὶ Φαντασίας*", *T.A.P.A.* 70 (1939), 414—427. For how Plutarch uniquely integrates the "ecstatic" and "catabatic" traditions in the apocalyptic myth *De genio Socratis* 589F—592E describing Timarchus' descent into the underground cave of Trophonios at Lebadeia in Boeotia, where he then experiences a "Himmelsreise der Seele", see my "Trophonios: The Manner of his Revelation", *T.A.P.A.* 99 (1968), 63—75, where references may be found to several other soul-wandering figures such as Epimenides, Hermodorus, Hermotimus of Clazomenae, Thespesios of Soli, and, if Plutarch is to be believed in the myth just mentioned, Socrates too. Er, Aristeas of Proconnesus, Abaris, Empedotimos (though his revelation was "in the body") and Pythagoras are all admirably discussed by J. D. P. Bolton, *Aristeas of Proconnesus* (Oxford 1962), disputing E. Rohde's suggestion in *Psyche*[8], 328 that Maximus of Tyre (*Dissert.* 16. 2f., 38.3) preserves the primitive version supposedly underlying the antishamanistic account in Herodotus 4.13-16 — a view which had led K. Meuli, *Hermes* 70(1935), 121—176 to suggest that Aristeas was a Greek shaman of the Scythian type. Also to be included in the genre is the story of the boy in the experiment at which Aristotle assisted (=Clearchus, fr.7 Wehrli), fully discussed with relation to a Jewish Sage in H. Lewy, "Aristotle and the Jewish Sage according to Clearchus of Soli", *Harv. Theol. Rev.* 31 (1938), 205—235. For the persistence of the experience in religious belief up to the present see W. F. Jackson Knight, *Elysion* (London 1970).

The Golden Fleece, which by a trick of language may once have been a Golden Apple,[50] seems to be an ancient talisman of immortality; waters of immortality and ambrosia lie beyond the Rocks in many folktales and in Homer. And in view of the date of Greek exploration in the Black Sea, the destination is more likely to be a late localization of the Otherworld than an original ingredient of the story.[51] If so, history has been expressed through mythology and mythology rationalized into history. Furthermore, given the widespread conception of Death's Entrance as a voracious mouth in the Near East,[52] the portrayal of Jason in art as being actually swallowed alive and again as emerging from the mouth of a dragon-like seamonster[53] (here it is apparent that the clashing rocks are envisaged as jaws) is remarkable. In addition to similar experiences attributed

[50] See R. Roux, *Le Problème des Argonautes* (Paris 1949), 35—38 on the ambiguity of the word *μῆλον* meaning both "apple" and "sheep".

[51] For an eighth century dating of Greek exploration in the Black Sea, see now R. Drews, "The Earliest Greek Settlements on the Black Sea", *J. H. S.* 96 (1976), 18—31. If, as I believe, the Argonautic story was originally not based on a historical voyage to Colchis — for an opposed view that Jason's voyage was based on a historical journey into the Euxine by the Greeks in search of gold in the late fourteenth or early thirteenth century B. C., see J. R. Bacon, *The Voyage of the Argonauts* (London 1925) — then in all probability the river Phasis, along which the Argonauts reached their destination, was originally a Pylos- or Avalon- or Brazil-type name denoting an otherworldly river. Geographically it marked the bounds of the world in the east (cf. Ap. Rhod. *Argon.* 2. 1261, Hes. *Cat. Women* fr. 45—45a ed. Evelyn White, Mimn. fr. 11. 5ff. ed. Bergk, Hecat. *ap.* schol. Ap. Rhod. *Argon.* 4. 259, Pind. *Pyth.* 4. 211) as e.g. Plato at *Phaedo* 109 says the Pillars of Heracles marked its western limits. According to J. D. P. Bolton, *Aristeas of Proconnesus*, 55ff. the river Phasis, which Herodotus identifies with the modern Rion, was once no other than the Tanais (=modern Don) and was believed originally to be straits leading from Palus Maeotis (=modern Sea of Azov) to Ocean; Ocean did not exist and the legendary "straits" turned out to be a river, the Tanais-Don. Thus the myth precedes the discovery.

[52] The Jewish conception is evident from *Isaiah* 5.14, *Habakkuk* 2.5, *Proverbs* 1.12, and *Psalms* 141.7. In the Canaanite myth already discussed, Baal's descent into the maw of a monster and Anat's descent into the earth presumably led to the same place (see Th. H. Gaster, *Thespis*², 206, 214). For comparable Greek references, see W. F. J. Knight, *Vergil: Epic and Anthropology*, 182f.

[53] Both scenes are reproduced in S. Reinach, *Répertoire des Vases Peints*² (Paris 1922), 1. 101f. and 137.

to Heracles, Perseus, perhaps Menestratus,[54] and the parody of the theme in the pure comic fiction of Lucian's *Verae Historiae*, the Jewish culture-hero Jonah was also swallowed and ejected after three days from the "belly of hell".[55] In apocryphal literature[56] and art[57] Our Lord's Descent into Hell, too, came to be depicted in like imagery — perhaps prompted by the close association of Jonah's experience with Christ's at *Matthew* 12.40f. Nevertheless in the Greek journeys of this kind, which are influenced by quests of treasure and exploration, death is largely forgotten, except for heroic encounters with dragons and other monsters.[58] And since they are neither actual descents into the world of the dead nor central to the wisdom-tradition, which it is my purpose with Aeneas in mind to develop, they, along with the underworld myths of the vegetation-tradition already excluded, are placed outside the scope of this book.

[54] For the swallowing of Heracles, see Lycophr. *Alex.* 34 with Tzetzes *ad loc.* and Sext. Empir. *Adv. Math.* 1. 255; and for Perseus, see Lycophr. *Alex.* 837—841 with Tzetzes *ad loc.* and Achil. Tat. 3.7.7. Menestratus is said by Pausanias at 9. 26.7f. to have armed himself with fishhooks before offering himself to the dragon, which, despite the forty parallels to combats with dragons adduced by J. G. Frazer in his *Pausanias's Description of Greece* (London 1898) *ad loc.*, would be a more suitable protection against being actually swallowed, a somewhat different theme.

[55] *Jonah* 1.17 and 2.2, on which see e.g. L. Radermacher, "Walfishmythen *A.R.W.* 9(1906), 248—252.

[56] Hades in the second part of the apocryphal *Gospel of Nicodemus* (Greek recension ch. 20) known as the "*Descensus Christi ad Inferos*" ed. C. Tischendorf, *Evangelia Apocrypha*[2] (Lipsiae 1876), 327 complains of a pain "in his belly" (!) as the Saints await release by Christ.

[57] For Our Lord's Descent through Hell's mouth, often represented as a fish's, perhaps Leviathan's, see R. Hughes, *Heaven and Hell in Western Art* (London 1968), 175—213, to whose collection may be added the notable print by Hearne of Christ releasing the Saints from the jaws of a huge monster in W. Hone, *Ancient Mysteries* (London 1832), 140 and cf. A. Jameson, *History of our Lord as exemplified in works of art*[3] (London 1872), 2.259 for a remarkable thirteenth century print. Christ also, of course, harrows hell through a pit.

[58] We shall of course meet with dragon and monster elements at the end of Odysseus' Visit to Hades, and also at the beginning of the Underworld Journeys of Heracles, Dionysus, and Aeneas. By contrast, the snake at the end of Gilgamesh's Journey is not the kind of evil dragon that one fights, but the ordinary snake that renews its skin. The two can be amalgamated, as in the Christian interpretation of *Genesis* (H. W. Stubbs, *Orpheus* 3 [1965], 155), but they are originally separate.

CHAPTER II

THE HOMERIC NEKYIA

1. *Prophetic wisdom and prophetic roles*

The *Nekyia*, as we have already indicated, is the word given by the ancients to the Eleventh Book of the *Odyssey* in which Odysseus narrates to his hosts, the King and Queen of the Phaeacians, the story of his Visit to the Land of the Dead after he had left the goddess Circe on the island of Aeaea and of the magical rites by which the ghosts of the dead were called up.[1] To discover the purpose of the *Nekyia* the main question to be asked is this: why did Odysseus undertake the Visit to Hades and what did he obtain? If we can find the answer to this we shall also have gone a fair way towards answering a second question which has long occupied the attention of Homeric scholars, namely: is the *Nekyia* an integral part of the *Odyssey* or a later addition to it? In seeking answers to these questions we shall need to consider the nature and assignment of the underworld prophecies themselves, their relationship to the instructions and "prophecies" offered by Circe, and the fulfillment of various pieces of ghostly information in the subsequent events of the *Odyssey*. The discussion of these matters throws into relief the extant beginnings of the wisdom-tradition of the Descent-theme in Greece. We shall reserve the wider concerns of Odyssean underworld tradition and topography on the one hand, and the catabatic, as distinct from

[1] It is so used by Strabo 5.4.5, p. 244 to designate the whole underworld visit of Odysseus at the Avernian *νεκυομαντεῖον* near Cumae. See further Eust. *Od.* 1667. 37; Max. Tyr. 14.2; Diod. Sic. 4.39; Plut. 740E; and cf. the schol. MV on *Od.* 24.1, where *νέκυια* is used to mean "descent" (see p. 53 below). Cicero thrice (IX. 10, 11, and 18) in letters to Atticus dated March 49 B.C. employs the word contemptuously of Caesar's entourage meaning "Hell let loose". For the alleged Avernian setting and for the question how far Odysseus' *Nekyia* seems to have represented a *catabasis* as distinct from a *nekyomanteia*, see Parts Two and Three of this chapter.

the necromantic, significance of Odysseus' Journey on the other, for the Second and Third Parts of this chapter respectively.

The Journey to Hades is prescribed for Odysseus by Circe who explains that before he can leave her island for his native Ithaca he must first journey "to the homes of Hades and dread Persephone to consult the soul of Theban Teiresias, the blind seer whose mind abides steadfast":

> *ἀλλ' ἄλλην χρὴ πρῶτον ὁδὸν τελέσαι καὶ ἱκέσθαι*
> *εἰς 'Αΐδαο δόμους καὶ ἐπαινῆς Περσεφονείης,*
> *ψυχῇ χρησομένους Θηβαίου Τειρεσίαο.*
>
> (10.490—492)

Circe presently provides Odysseus with instructions on how to reach the World of Shades. Odysseus must sail across Ocean in a ship that needs no pilot[2] until he comes to the groves of Persephone.[3] On the far shores of Ocean live the Cimmerians in a land of perpetual night through which the sun's rays never penetrate.[4] A short walk will take him to the dark home of Hades. There into Acheron flows Pyriphlegethon and Cocytus, which is an offspring of Styx; a rock marks the meeting-place of the two roaring rivers[5]. Here as he is bidden Odysseus digs a pit (*βόθρος*) and makes appropriate sacrifices to the dead.[6] No sooner is blood spilt than ghostly phantoms of brides, unwedded youths, old men, tender maidens, and slain warriors come flocking about the pit: but these ineffectual phantoms are powerless to think or speak unless they are first given a drink of blood and by drawing his sword Odysseus permitted none of these to taste the blood and speak.[7] What follows falls into five sections. At first three spirits (*ψυχαί*) *came up* in succession and conversed with Odysseus in turn: Elpenor, a comrade not long dead; the seer Teiresias; and Odysseus' mother Anticleia. Odysseus then *saw* a long line of famous women who came forward to relate their ancestries. Homer does not say of

[2] *Od.* 10.505.
[3] *Od.* 10.510.
[4] *Od.* 11.11—19.
[5] *Od.* 10.512—515.
[6] *Od.* 10.516—540; 11.23—50.
[7] *Od.* 11.36ff.

these women that Odysseus saw their ghosts but them — though we can assume that it was their ghosts that appeared. Odysseus then breaks off his narrative to say that it is time for bed, but his listeners press to hear more. So Odysseus continues with a description of his ghostly meeting with three more spirits, those of Agamemnon, Achilles, and Ajax, great heroes of the Trojan War. Finally as he *looked around* the Underworld he saw King Minos giving judgement to the dead, while in another quarter Orion and Heracles hunted game and the three great sinners Tityus, Tantalus, and Sisyphus bore their everlasting punishment; and he has time only to speak to Heracles. The five scenes balance one another but not quite as symmetrically as Webster would have us believe.[8]

The precise purpose of the Visit to Hades is explicitly given by Circe. It is to consult with Teiresias "who will tell you of the way and the measures of your path home, how you may go over the teeming deep":

ὅς κέν τοι εἴπῃσιν ὁδὸν καὶ μέτρα κελεύθου
νόστον θ', ὡς ἐπὶ πόντον ἐλεύσεαι ἰχθυόεντα.

(10.539—540)

Indeed the ghost of the seer in the *Nekyia* immediately knows for what purpose Odysseus has come to him: "*νόστον δίζηαι,*" he begins by saying, "you are enquiring of your return home" (11.100). Anticleia's ghost nevertheless is unaware of the purpose of her son's visit and she therefore asks him how he came to be in the Land of the Dead. Odysseus' reply shows well enough that he understands the reason for his coming: "My mother, necessity has brought me down to the house of Hades, to consult the soul of Theban Teiresias":

μῆτερ ἐμή, χρειώ με κατήγαγεν εἰς 'Αΐδαο
ψυχῇ χρησόμενον Θηβαίου Τειρεσίαο.

(11.164—165)

[8] *Pace* T. B. L. Webster, *From Mycenae to Homer*², 246 the numbers in the second and fifth parts do not balance, though admittedly more ghosts are promised in the Minos list. Three ghosts are mentioned in both the first and fourth scenes though Ajax does not come up to the trench or speak. In the fifth scene only Heracles speaks.

The purpose of the consultation is more fully explained to the ghost of Achilles. "I came", says Odysseus, "in the hope that Teiresias might speak some plan whereby I might reach rugged Ithaca":

ἦλθον Τειρεσίαο κατὰ χρέος, εἴ τινα βουλὴν
εἴποι, ὅπως Ἰθάκην ἐς παιπαλόεσσαν ἱκοίμην.

(11.479—480)

Finally he recalls the purpose of his underworld consultation to a similar end while narrating in a flashback his adventures to Penelope:

ὣς γάρ μοι ψυχὴ μαντεύσατο Τειρεσίαο
ἤματι τῷ ὅτε δὴ κατέβην δόμον Ἄϊδος εἴσω,
νόστον ἑταίροισιν διζήμενος ἠδ' ἐμοὶ αὐτῷ.

(23.251—253)

There can be no doubt, then, about the ostensible reason for Odysseus' journey. It was to consult Teiresias' ghost about his Homecoming.

Yet very little — all too little say both Separatists and Unitarians alike — seems to have been said about it in the event. Consider what information Odysseus actually obtains. He learns from Teiresias that the wrath of Poseidon has already been incurred for his having blinded the Cyclops Polyphemus. Poseidon will therefore make the return difficult. The prophet then predicts the disasters which will befall the crew if the cattle of Helios on the island of Thrinakie are harmed:

ἀλλ' ἔτι μέν κε καὶ ὣς κακά περ πάσχοντες ἵκοισθε,
αἴ κ' ἐθέλῃς σὸν θυμὸν ἐρυκακέειν καὶ ἑταίρων,
ὁππότε κε πρῶτον πελάσῃς εὐεργέα νῆα
Θρινακίῃ νήσῳ, προφυγὼν ἰοειδέα πόντον,
βοσκομένας δ' εὕρητε βόας καὶ ἴφια μῆλα
Ἠελίου, ὃς πάντ' ἐφορᾷ καὶ πάντ' ἐπακούει.
τὰς εἰ μέν κ' ἀσινέας ἐάᾳς νόστου τε μέδηαι,
καί κεν ἔτ' εἰς Ἰθάκην κακά περ πάσχοντες ἵκοισθε·
εἰ δέ κε σίνηαι, τότε τοι τεκμαίρομ' ὄλεθρον
νηΐ τε καὶ ἑτάροις· αὐτὸς δ' εἴ πέρ κεν ἀλύξῃς,
ὀψὲ κακῶς νεῖαι, ὀλέσας ἄπο πάντας ἑταίρους,
νηὸς ἐπ' ἀλλοτρίης.

(11.104—115)

Ominous indeed are the last four lines: "But if you hurt them, then for you I foretell destruction, for ship and comrades. And you yourself, if you escape, will come home late, in evil plight, with all your comrades lost, upon a foreign ship". Odysseus is told moreover that upon reaching Ithaca he will find suitors in his house, wooing his wife with gifts:

δήεις δ' ἐν πήματα οἴκῳ,
ἄνδρας ὑπερφιάλους, οἵ τοι βίοτον κατέδουσι
μνώμενοι ἀντιθέην ἄλοχον καὶ ἕδνα διδόντες.

(11.115—117)

With vengeance he will overcome the suitors, "whether by guile or openly with a sharp sword":

ἀλλ' ἦ τοι κείνων γε βίας ἀποτίσεαι ἐλθών·
αὐτὰρ ἐπὴν μνηστῆρας ἐνὶ μεγάροισι τεοῖσι
κτείνῃς ἠὲ δόλῳ ἢ ἀμφαδὸν ὀξέϊ χαλκῷ,...

(11.118—120)

There follows enigmatic advice about Odysseus' last journey to a people knowing nothing of the sea until Odysseus meets a wayfarer, who mistakes an oar which Odysseus shall carry for a winnowing-fan, and then a final prediction about the manner in which Odysseus will meet his death. But the events of the *Odyssey* stop short of the realization of this part of Teiresias' prophecy.

The information which was promised by Circe is felt by modern readers to have got short shrift from Teiresias. This impression is intensified when Odysseus returns to Circe and she herself not only repeats much of the information but adds substantially to it. She adds information concerning Odysseus' future journey past the Sirens and the choice that lies ahead between the Planctae and Scylla and Charybdis.[9] She speaks in greater detail than Teiresias about the island of Thrinakie; she knows exactly the number of herds Helios

[9] At *Od.* 12.55—59, 73, 101 Circe speaks first of two and then of three ways, as the Planctae, Scylla, and Charybdis are approached. Circe's directions to Odysseus may be the model of the three paths described by the goddess in the revelation to Parmenides; see E. A. Havelock, "Parmenides and Odysseus", *H.S.C.P.* 63 (1959), 138.

has on the island, how many heads are in each herd, and with what immortal nature these animals are endowed.[10] She then repeats verbatim from Teiresias' speech (pp. 40f. above) the fatal consequences which will follow if the cattle of Helios are harmed: "But if you hurt them, then for you I foretell destruction, for ship and comrades. And you yourself, if you escape, will come home late, in evil plight, with all your comrades lost".[11] That Circe should seem to know so much more than Teiresias about Odysseus' way home has led to the widely favoured view that she renders Teiresias' prophecy superfluous and as well the motive which she herself supplied for Odysseus' consultation with the seer. "The inference is surely irresistible", remarks Woodhouse, "that Odysseus had been sent on a fool's errand to Hades, when, after all, Kirke could have told him as much as, or even more than, he had learnt in Hades from the far-famed seer".[12] Page goes even further and infers that "the Visit to the Underworld was originally independent of the *Odyssey*, and that it has been artificially inserted into its present surroundings".[13]

The prophecies of Teiresias and Circe are not however mere doublets. Circe's function is clearly distinguishable from Teiresias'. I shall attempt to delineate their respective roles and those of the various ghosts whom Odysseus meets in the *Nekyia* in a way that elucidates, it is hoped, the nature and scope of the wisdom which Odysseus re-

[10] *Od.* 12.127—136. On the origins in fact and folklore of the Homeric Cattle of the Sun see D. L. Page, *Folktales in Homer's Odyssey* (Camb. Mass. 1973), 79—83.

[11] *Od.* 12.139—141 = *Od.* 11.112—114.

[12] W. J. Woodhouse, *The Composition of Homer's Odyssey* (Oxford 1930), 145. Similarly E. Rohde, *Psyche*[8] (London 1925), 33 n. 61 thinks that Teiresias fulfils Circe's requirement "only very partially and superficially". And J. A. K. Thomson, *Studies in the Odyssey* (Oxford 1914), 94f. believes the *Nekyia* to be "badly motivated". But whereas Rohde infers that Odysseus' descent did not form part of the original plan of the *Odyssey*, Thomson is led from a consideration of Odysseus' chthonic nature (see p. 55 below) to the opposite conclusion. U. von Wilamowitz-Moellendorff, *Homerische Untersuchungen* (Berlin, 1884), 145 considers the information given by Teiresias about Odysseus' voyage and the suitors superfluous and useless. This view is shared by G. S. Kirk, *The Songs of Homer* (Cambridge 1962), 238 who thinks that Teiresias' prophecy about the oar was the original prophecy.

[13] D. L. Page, *The Homeric Odyssey* (Oxford 1955), 32. (Professor Page's analyses of the *Nekyia*, though I do not accept several of his conclusions, are a brilliant and invaluable collection of the problems from the analytical viewpoint.)

ceives from each. It is as well to begin by observing the point where Circe's verbatim repetition of Teiresias' prophecy concerning Thrinakie ends. For at that point Teiresias continues (see p. 40f.) with the words *νηὸς ἐπ' ἀλλοτρίης*, "upon a foreign ship". And this is then followed by the prophet's prediction of the suitors, whom Circe does not mention. The divergences between the speeches of Circe and Teiresias and the repetition to which we have already called notice prompt three questions. First, why does not Teiresias, as does Circe, mention the dangers of the Sirens, Planctae, Scylla, and Charybdis? Second, why do Circe and Teiresias both mention the cattle of Helios at Thrinakie (to which Circe adds some details about the cattle and Teiresias adds the reference to a foreign ship)? Third, why does not Circe, as does Teiresias, mention the suitors at all? The answers to these three questions will in fact provide the clues essential to the distinctive roles of each.

The charge laid against Teiresias is that the information he gives in the *Nekyia* is superfluous and useless. But has the seer performed so badly? He warns Odysseus of the dangers which await him on the island of Thrinakie because he prophesies the future and Helios' cattle can affect Odysseus' destiny. Odysseus clearly has a destiny if he reaches Ithaca: but if Odysseus falls into the trap on the island of Thrinakie he may not reach his home and may not have a destiny. It is clear furthermore that the issue with the suitors is dependent both upon the protasis in line 112 *εἰ δέ κε σίνηαι*, "if you harm the cattle", and the further protasis in 113 *εἴ πέρ κεν ἀλύξῃς*, "and if you escape". These conditions are seized upon by Page who writes: "the peculiar uncertainty of the prophet in this passage has often been remarked: 105 *αἴ κε*, 110 *εἰ μέν κε*, 112 *εἰ δέ κε*, 113 *εἴ πέρ κεν*: Teiresias ought to be able to do better than this".[14] But should we expect Teiresias' prediction to be more precise than this? For Odysseus' destiny is still in the balance;[15] he has incurred Poseidon's wrath already by

[14] *Ibid.* 49 n. 10.

[15] The protasis in line 112 is the vital condition of the eight lines which follow. We have just seen that Page disapproves whenever Teiresias says 'if' (previous n.), but when he quotes *op. cit.* 41 from Teiresias' speech without the protasis (lines 115ff.) he imparts to the apodosis a false ring of certainty. Odysseus does have options ahead, though Athene may say afterwards that her personal conviction

blinding the Cyclops Polyphemus but he still has the chance of returning home (with comrades too) provided he avoids the wrath of Helios.[16] The logic of the prophecy therefore is: 'if all goes well at Thrinakie, you will be home sooner: if not, your return will be delayed — for more than seven years in fact — and the suitors will have time to get active and Penelope will not know what to do'. Apart from the trap on the island of Thrinakie which might affect his destiny Teiresias is not interested in other details of the journey home. Consequently he offers no advice about Scylla and the rest.

No sooner has Odysseus returned from the Land of Shades than Circe offers at once to point out the way and make each thing plain.[17] But this in fact she does only after she has first welcomed Odysseus and enquired into each thing, and in turn Odysseus has duly told her all that he has learnt from the ghosts: " *αὐτὰρ ἐγὼ τῇ πάντα κατὰ μοῖραν κατέλεξα,*" he says, "I told her everything in order" (12.35). She begins only then to point out the way and make each thing plain. And she relates, as it were, the Mariner's Mirror but not the future. To her the cattle are only one risk along with the other dangers and she appears not to know Odysseus' destiny. She does not mention Odysseus' returning home "upon a foreign ship" because presumably she does not know how Odysseus will get home; nor does she know about the Phaeacians; nor does she know about the menace from the Suitors in Ithaca. She could in fact have told Odysseus nothing without the clue furnished by Teiresias that his route to Ithaca was to be by way of Thrinakie.[18]

(*ἀλλ' ἐνὶ θυμῷ/ᾔδε', Od.* 13.339f.) always was that Odysseus would come home after losing all his comrades. The seer's function was to predict these vital options since they affect Odysseus' Homecoming.

[16] On the wraths of the gods Helios, Poseidon, and Zeus, as they affect Odysseus' *Nostos*, see the excellent discussion by W. J. Woodhouse, *The Composition of Homer's Odyssey*, 29—40. (I differ only in one particular from Woodhouse *op. cit.* 32 regarding the force of the wrath of Helios. Surely the protasis at *Od.* 11.113 makes clear that the wrath of this god would have embraced Odysseus too had he personally taken part in the violation?) On Helios' threat to shine in the Underworld cf. chap. 1 n. 42.

[17] *Od.* 12.25ff.

[18] The Homeric episode thus seems to have a similar framework to Vergil's Aristaeus epyllion at the end of the fourth *Georgic*, which has been subjected to the

Yet from the poet's viewpoint neither Circe nor Teiresias can fail to warn Odysseus of the fatal consequences of violating Helios' cattle. For although Circe may not know about the threat from Suitors in Ithaca, she can be assumed to know all about her father Helios' cattle[19] and the especial dangers involved in harming them. Both therefore mention the incident, but they are offering two kinds of prophecy. Circe's prophecy is a kind of spacial projection into the future which can foresee and advise on how to pass from Aeaea through the dangers which lie within fairly local seas — hence the Sirens, the Wandering Rocks, Scylla and Charybdis, and Thrinakie. Teiresias' prophecy *e contra* is real prediction in the sense of foretelling how destiny may be shaped. Hence the importance of Thrinakie and the reference to the foreign ship. Hence, too, the Suitors who will be busy in Ithaca. Hence also the distant prophecies about a future journey and death at the end, with which should be compared the prophetic assurance given Menelaus in similar circumstances.[20] But since Scylla and the rest were not in Odysseus' horoscope, Teiresias does not mention them. Had Teiresias been consulted by one of the six victims of Scylla, it might have been a different matter! In the light of the foregoing interpretation might not *ὁδὸν καὶ μέτρα κελεύθου* mean not just the geography of the way home but the rest of Odysseus' earthly pilgrimage?

An abrupt transition from Teiresias to Anticleia shows how eager is Odysseus to talk also with his mother's ghost. If Webster was right to suggest that Teiresias took over the role that originally belonged to Utnapishtim, one suspects also that the ancestral part of Utnapishtim's role was made over to Odysseus' mother Anticleia.[21] At any

same criticism, namely that Cyrene could have told her son what to do without Proteus. But, like Circe, Cyrene is helpless until Proteus supplies the clue that the wrath of Orpheus was the cause of her son's troubles. Once she knows of Orpheus' wrath she knows how to appease it. For further discussion of the Aristaeus epyllion see pp. 96—98.

[19] Circe is the daughter of Helios; for her genealogy see *Od.* 10. 137—139.

[20] In the proto-*Nekyia* at *Od.* 4.351ff. esp. 561—69. See further p. 97 below.

[21] T. B. L. Webster, *From Mycenae to Homer*, 247f. supposes further that Anticleia, since she gives Odysseus eschatological information concerning the fate of

rate communing with the family ancestor in the Underworld remains a persistent element of the catabatic tradition from Homer onwards. Rohde goes so far as to think that the purpose of Teiresias in the *Nekyia* was really to introduce Odysseus to his mother and former companions, and that this meeting was Odysseus' prime motive.[22] If Rohde is right, Teiresias might be a Hermes figure. Certainly he does give directions at *Od.* 11.145ff. This is hardly his job. But Teiresias in the *Nekyia* in effect has two functions: he is both prophet and guide.

The confrontation of Odysseus with his mother, whose recent death is now revealed to him, develops into a fine domestic scene. How fares his father and his son? Does Penelope still rule in Ithaca? Or has some usurper taken over? The ghost of Anticleia dispels her son's fears thus:

σὸν δ' οὔ πώ τις ἔχει καλὸν γέρας, ἀλλὰ ἕκηλος
Τηλέμαχος τεμένεα νέμεται καὶ δαῖτας ἐΐσας
δαίνυται, ἃς ἐπέοικε δικασπόλον ἄνδρ' ἀλεγύνειν·
πάντες γὰρ καλέουσι.

(11.184—187)

"Your princely right", she affirms, "has not yet passed into other hands but Telemachus is in peaceful possession of the royal lands and attends all public banquets such as the dispenser of justice should enjoy: for all men invite him". Page takes this speech as "alone enough to show how little this poet knew or cared about the central theme of the *Odyssey* — the courting of Penelope by disorderly suitors in Ithaca.[23] And he raises further objection to Anticleia's admonition at *Od.* 11.223—224: "Bear all these things in mind, that you may tell them hereafter to your wife". This last utterance is, he says, "a conclusion of almost comical vapidity — *unless Odysseus is in fact telling the story to his wife*".[24] Page's arguments, in sum, invite

the dead in the Underworld (*Od.* 11.216—222), took the part of Enkidu who enlightens Gilgamesh about the Underworld. See pp. 27 and 29 above.

[22] E. Rohde, *Psyche*[8], 35, argues that the questioning of Teiresias is a mere device borrowed from Menelaus' enquiry of the Old Man of the Sea, Proteus, in the proto-*Nekyia* (*Od.* 4.351ff).

[23] D. L. Page, *The Homeric Odyssey*, 40.

[24] *Ibid.* 47.

us to believe that the Journey to Hades, which in our *Odyssey* is narrated to the King and Queen of the Phaeacians, was originally unconnected with the present *Odyssey* in which the suitors are the central theme. This further assumes the existence of two *Odysseys* preceding the extant version, namely an *Odyssey* with suitors and originally without the *Nekyia*, and an *Odyssey* with a *Nekyia*, which was narrated to Penelope, but perhaps without suitors.[25]

But Anticleia has not, to be sure, ruled out the suitors' existence for all time. She takes exceeding care not to mislead Odysseus and her words are carefully chosen: "*σὸν δ' οὔ πώ τις ἔχει καλὸν γέρας*", she says at *Od.* 11.184. The affirmation that Odysseus' princely right has "not yet" (*οὔ πώ*) passed into other hands by no means rules out the possibility of trouble in the future: but it settles present fears. Nor does Odysseus' questioning of his mother's ghost about suitors prove ignorance by this poet of Teiresias' recent allusion to them. Teiresias has not said that the suitors had yet begun their wicked machinations. We have already seen that the affairs in Ithaca are in some measure dependent upon how Odysseus handles the situation at Thrinakie. If Odysseus had thought enough about Teiresias' prophecy, he would probably have deduced that Penelope had not yet remarried. But since the menace from suitors is one hypothesis dependent upon the mishandling of a situation which has not yet arisen, he does seek confirmation and he wants to know the situation in Ithaca now. This Teiresias would not, or could not, tell, but Anticleia, within a year or so, can. She, unlike the seer, cannot ascertain the future but she can describe the recent past: the *πώ* means, in effect, "when I saw them last". There exists no clearer indication than this that the two ghosts are offering Odysseus different kinds of information. Teiresias

[25] According to D. L. Page, *op. cit.* 42 the original Odyssean Visit to Hades included Anticleia (whose speech is taken as proof that this poet was unaware of suitors), Teiresias, and the heroes of the Trojan War. Teiresias' allusion to suitors is then suspected of having been added to the *Nekyia* after it had been attached to the *Odyssey*-with-suitors (*op. cit.* 41f.). Presumably the veiled references to suitors by Agamemnon's ghost (see pp. 48f. below) must be taken as further additions to the *Nekyia*. How many stories are purported to have been in the *Odyssey*-with-the *Nekyia* narrated to Penelope, Page does not however make clear: did Odysseus return straight home after his underworld journey and find his wife awaiting him peacefully?

predicts: whereas the ghost of Anticleia can only provide her son with information that she took with her to the grave.[26] Had she described Penelope as being pestered already by disorderly suitors, as Page would presumably have her tell, her information would have been plainly inaccurate and she would have ruined her son's life with worry for the next seven years with Calypso. It is perfectly reasonable to assume that the suitors had not yet begun their evil work for the suitor Antinoos expressly says that up to the time Telemachus went to Pylos, in the year that Odysseus returned, the suitors had been active for three years and were starting a fourth.[27] The chronology is confirmed by Athene in a remark to Odysseus which can hardly be overlooked.[28]

So far answers have been suggested to three questions. Why did Circe add to and repeat much, but not all, of the information given by Teiresias? Why did not Anticleia tell Odysseus about the presence of suitors? And why did not Odysseus obtain all the information about Ithaca from Teiresias himself? Little evidence has emerged so far to support Page's thesis that Odysseus' Journey to Hades originally existed independently of our *Odyssey*. We will consider finally the one instance where Odysseus does in the *Nekyia* receive constructive advice.

This comes from the lips of the murdered King Agamemnon's ghost. He warns Odysseus to take appropriate measures to avoid the kind of fate he himself had met with because of his wife's scheming

[26] D. L. Page, *The Homeric Odyssey*, 41, objects that if Anticleia is describing Ithaca at the time of her death, Telemachus being then only about thirteen years old is too young to be acting as Anticleia describes. But this objection is hardly decisive. Neoptolemus cannot have been much older when he fought at Troy, or Ascanius when he moved in royal circles. Even in history Cyrus, the younger son of Darius II, was given the command of Asia Minor in his early teens; and in the year 1400 A. D. Henry V was made his father's deputy in Wales at the age of thirteen and spent the next seven years in almost continuous warfare.

[27] *Od.* 2.89—90.

[28] *Od.* 13.375—378:

> *διογενὲς Λαερτιάδη, πολυμήχαν' Ὀδυσσεῦ,*
> *φράζευ ὅπως μνηστῆρσιν ἀναιδέσι χεῖρας ἐφήσεις,*
> *οἳ δή τοι τρίετες μέγαρον κάτα κοιρανέουσι,*
> *μνώμενοι ἀντιθέην ἄλοχον καὶ ἕδνα διδόντες.*

when he returned from Troy: "Do not", he says, "yourself ever be soft even with your wife. Do not declare unto her every tale you know, but tell a part and keep a part concealed... And I will tell you another thing you should lay to heart: bring your ship to your beloved land in secrecy and not openly, for women are no longer to be trusted" (11.441—443 and 454—456). How often must Odysseus have pondered upon the striking similarity between his own circumstances and those that led up to Agamemnon's death. Both Returning Husbands had left at home a Waiting Wife exposed overlong to the intrigues of a Suitor or Suitors. Both had left an Only Son too young to claim the inheritance, and a Kingdom which in the absence of the legitimate ruler might fall to alien rule or misgovernment. Not without point, then, was the hint that Odysseus should work under a cloak of secrecy. Yet the Alexandrine critics athetized both passages.[29] The rejection of these lines, however, is weakened if they can be shown to be organic to the structure of the *Odyssey*; if, that is, Agamemnon's advice was subsequently heeded by Odysseus when he returned home.

On five separate occasions is the issue raised in the *Odyssey* whether Odysseus should return home openly or under cover. First Teiresias predicts that Odysseus will slay the suitors "whether by guile or openly with a sharp sword" (11.120), but he offers Odysseus no specific advice. The advice to return "in secret", *κρύβδην*, and "not openly", *μηδ' ἀναφανδά*, comes from Agamemnon's ghost. When Odysseus later lands in Ithaca the goddess Athene, too, tells him to keep his identity concealed.[30] On the fourth and fifth occasions Odysseus, in disguise as a disreputable vagabond, tells first Eumaeus and then Penelope a false tale: how he, a Cretan, sailed to Egypt and then to Phoenicia and finally came to Thesprotia, whose king, Pheidon, informed him that Odysseus had just left to consult the oracle of Zeus at Dodona as to whether he should return to Ithaca "openly or

[29] For criticism of the Alexandrian atheteses (lines 454—456 are moreover missing in most ancient texts) on mainly stylistic grounds see M. van der Valk, *Textual Criticism of the Odyssey* (Leiden 1949), 192 and 225.

[30] *Od.* 13.308—310:

μηδέ τῳ ἐκφάσθαι μήτ' ἀνδρῶν μήτε γυναικῶν,
πάντων, οὕνεκ' ἄρ' ἦλθες ἀλώμενος, ἀλλὰ σιωπῇ
πάσχειν ἄλγεα πολλά, βίας ὑποδέγμενος ἀνδρῶν.

secretly", ἢ ἀμφαδὸν ἦε κρυφηδόν.[31] This is Odysseus' cover story, the relation of which to the *Nekyia* will be considered further in the following section of this chapter.

Of the greatest importance for the argument here is Odysseus' meeting with Athene. For when Odysseus awakes after his boat journey from Scherie, his heart leaps with joy to learn from the goddess herself that he is, at last, in Ithaca itself. She recognizes Odysseus despite the pack of lies that he at first tells[32] and after revealing herself to him she informs him of the situation in Ithaca. It is then that she emphasises upon Odysseus the necessity to remain concealed and congratulates him upon the cunning he has already shown: "Another wanderer would have hastened eagerly to see in his hall his children and his wife: but you are not yet minded to know or learn anything until you have further tested your wife" (13.333—336). She then urges him to consider how best to devise an end to the suitors who are busily courting Penelope, at which Odysseus exclaims, "Heavens! I would surely have perished in my palace *by the evil doom of Atreus' son Agamemnon* had not you, O Goddess, duly told me each thing! But come, weave a plan how I may wreck vengeance upon them":

> ὢ πόποι, ἦ μάλα δὴ 'Αγαμέμνονος 'Ατρεΐδαο
> φθίσεσθαι κακὸν οἶτον ἐνὶ μεγάροισιν ἔμελλον,
> εἰ μή μοι σὺ ἕκαστα, θεά, κατὰ μοῖραν ἔειπες.
> ἀλλ' ἄγε μῆτιν ὕφηνον, ὅπως ἀποτίσομαι αὐτούς.
>
> (13.383—386)

According to Page who quotes this passage but omits the words italicised (thus tacitly ignoring Odysseus' allusion to Agamemnon), Odysseus first heard about the troubles at home *after his return to Ithaca.*[33] Yet how was Odysseus to know that he would suffer Agamemnon's fate had he not met Agamemnon's ghost in the *Nekyia*? Athene has not told him. The alternatives are that Calypso has told him about it and Odysseus simply has not mentioned it, or the poet absentmindedly assumes that it was common knowledge all over the

[31] *Od.* 14.330 and 19.299.
[32] *Od.* 13.228—286.
[33] D. L. Page, *The Homeric Odyssey*, 42.

Mediterranean. But both of these assumptions are unsatisfactory alike, for it is the habit of the poet to tell whence his characters derive their information. Odysseus' gasp of surprise at Athene's mention of suitors — her description of them at *Odyssey* 13.378 recalls Teiresias' description at *Odyssey* 11.117 — does not therefore prove the contention that this poet was unaware of Teiresias' earlier prophecy about the suitors in Ithaca. On the contrary Athene has just confirmed what Odysseus feared most: Teiresias had been right about Thrinakie, and now he is right about the suitors. Odysseus' reference to Agamemnon was in fact prompted by Athene's confirmation of his own worst fears. He had already intended not to reveal himself in the first place; and this policy he is the more able to adopt since he reached Ithaca, as Teiresias had warned he might, with all his comrades lost. Odysseus' outburst is also therefore an expression of relief, because the goddess offered to help him along lines he was already following. In short, Odysseus' allusion to Agamemnon shows that he knows all about Agamemnon already. The allusion is important both in showing the relevance of Agamemnon's remarks in the *Nekyia* and in demonstrating that there has already been a *Nekyia* in the suitors-story.

By way of summary we can now formulate some answers to the main question posed at the beginning of this chapter. Odysseus, like Gilgamesh, crosses Ocean in a boat of which a part seems to be missing.[34] And in each case a Journey is made to a World of the Departed by a hero in quest of information. But it is a different kind of information that each seeks. In this regard it is worth observing that what Gilgamesh seeks is given to Menelaus because he married Helen, and that immortality has already been offered to Odysseus by the nymph Calypso and refused by him[35] (in an episode which exhibits in its own right several characteristics of a descent-story),[36]

[34] See also pp. 73 and 160—162 below.

[35] *Od.* 5.136f., 209, and 7.257.

[36] The story-roots based on a comparison of *Weltmärchen* are as follows: (1) an otherworldly nymph or fairy entices a mortal into her home; (2) the mortal is the object of union with his fairy bride and stays for one or seven years; (3) feeling the sensual pleasures grow pale or sensing appalling dangers to himself the mortal hero desires to revisit the world of mortals and, often with divine help, manages to

since he prefers to return home and enjoy the happy old age of a Nestor. Odysseus' *Nekyia* is thus undertaken not to obtain immortality, but to learn the way home; and it is an integral part of his Homecoming, or *Nostos*, from Troy. Accordingly he consulted Teiresias to this end, and he obtained some extremely relevant information from him regarding his kingdom and future destiny. He obtained also from Agamemnon's ghost natural information based on the experience that sent that Returning Hero to the grave, in the form of the practical hint to return home secretly; and from his mother Anticleia, who possessed knowledge of the recent past, he learnt how his family and kingdom in Ithaca were disposed at the time of her death. The information, which is in part ancestral, pertains then ultimately to the restoration of his family and kingdom and serves to emphasise both the unity of the theme underlying the *Nostos* and the final Vengeance of Odysseus upon the Suitors. Thus Odysseus' Visit to Hades is the climax to his Wanderings. It inspires him to return home, liberate his kingdom, and restore order. We shall find that the Trojan hero Aeneas will be similarly inspired after his Journey into the Underworld to go on to Latium and restore or impose order in Italy.

escape; (4) the hero returns again to the otherworld. All four elements are found in the folksong of Tannhäuser; the fourth is missing in the extant versions of the tale of True Thomas or Thomas the Rhymer (but is supplied by Sir Walter Scott); while the first and fourth components are necessarily absent in the *Odyssey*, since there the folktale is adapted to the Return. Odysseus is brought to Calypso through shipwreck and is afterwards happily re-united with Penelope. Thomas in the Scottish tale escapes from an underworld fairyland, apparently like Tam Lin just in time to avoid being slain as a surrogate victim. The terror of Tannhäuser, who escapes from the Underworld of the Venusberg through fear of damnation, seems to be a rationalization by Christian medieval tradition, just as his subsequent return to the fairy bride, upon his failing to obtain absolution for his earlier sensual living with her, is an anti-clerical twist. For the danger in which Odysseus finds himself, see the article by W. S. Anderson, "Calypso and Elysium", *C. J.* 54(1958), 2—11. Anderson follows an earlier suggestion by H. Güntert connecting Calypso's isle of Ogygia with the Elysian Afterworld. The best short treatment of the folktale is by S. Baring-Gould, *Curious Myths of the Middle Ages*, 209—229. That the folktale was drawn upon by Homer seems not to be widely recognized, to judge from recent Homeric folklore studies.

2. *Origins: tradition and topography*

The foregoing analysis, of course, neither rules out the possibility of interpolations elsewhere nor implies that all the elements of the *Nekyia* belonged originally to the story of Odysseus. It is in fact a reasonable assumption that the Catalogue of Fair Women in the *Nekyia*, like the Iliadic Catalogue of Ships, was once an independent poem of the Hesiodic Boeotian type which the Homeric poet incorporated.[37] Moreover, it is to the credit of the Alexandrian scholar Aristarchus that he noticed that lines 568—627 of Book Eleven (describing Odysseus' visit to the region of the Underworld which includes Heracles) do not belong to the main thread of the story. But even so, it is very much a debatable point whether this passage is to be regarded as spurious — as is thought by the scholiast H on *Odyssey* 11.568, *νοθεύεται μέχρι τοῦ "ὣς εἰπὼν ὁ μὲν αὖθις ἔδυ δόμον ''Αϊδος εἴσω"* — rather than as having been modelled by Homer upon another independent poem, perhaps an epic *Catabasis* of Heracles,[38] which is merely the product of a later stage of composition than the main body of the text. The decision we take on this matter is even crucial to the interpretation of Book Eleven as a whole. For only by treating these lines as a post-Homeric fabrication could the scholiasts MV on *Odyssey* 24.1 have said that Book Eleven is not really a *Nekyia* (Descent) but a *Nekyomanteia* (Calling up of the Dead). Page refers to the

[37] I say "Hesiodic Boeotian type" because T. B. L. Webster, *From Mycenae to Homer*², 178f. postulates a "common ancestor in pre-migration poetry" to account for the variations between Hesiod's Catalogues of Women and the Homeric version. Their close connection was extensively noted by R. Pfeiffer, "Hesiodisches und Homerisches, zu neuen und altern Papyri", *Philologus* 92(1937), 1ff., and D. L. Page, *The Homeric Odyssey*, 36—39 argues that the Hesiodic Catalogues are the actual source and model of the Homeric "interpolation". Similarly Page in *History and the Homeric Iliad* (Berkeley 1951), 152 argues that the Catalogue of Ships was originally a Boeotian composition, though as R. Hope Simpson and J. F. Lazenby, *The Catalogue of the Ships in Homer's Iliad* (Oxford 1970), 186f. point out, this assumption is not actually proved by the internal evidence of the Catalogue itself.

[38] See P. Von der Mühll, "Zur Erfindung in der Nekyia der Odyssee", *Philologus* 93(1938), 8—11 and R. Merkelbach, *Untersuchungen zur Odyssee* (Munich 1951), 191. Cf. also my pp. 211ff. and 220ff. below.

scholiasts' verdict with approval.[39] And certainly the ritual preliminaries do suggest that the scene is a tombside set-up where anyone can rouse the ghost of the buried hero with animal-sacrifice and chthonic ritual. But the care which has been taken over the blending of these lines into their surrounding passage so as to effect a transition from a *Nekyomanteia* to a *Catabasis* — the internal evidence showing this will be detailed more closely in the following section — suggests that Homer may have deliberately conflated necromantic practice with the concept of a Journey of the Dead. It seems worthwhile, therefore, to reconsider the traditions and topography that might shed some light upon the origins of the *Nekyia* in Greece. In doing so we shall have to take account of several conflicting theories which seek to represent Homer's Ithacan Odysseus as also a Boeotian, Corinthian, and Thesprotian hero. But my intention here is not so much to enumerate once more all the evidence pertaining to these hypotheses, as to offer a fresh evaluation of them in the light of recent discoveries.

The trench-ritual, as we have just said, resembles a necromantic séance and implies even a ghost-cult. The notion that Odysseus' consultation with Teiresias is the *nekyomanteia* proper and the central part of the *Nekyia* is developed most remarkably by J. A. K. Thomson, though I hope to show why the theory ultimately lacks conviction. Thomson argues that Homer's Catalogue of Women provides a *prima facie* case for assuming a Boeotian origin for this part of the *Nekyia.* And from the prophet's recurring epithet in the phrase "Theban Teiresias" he concludes that the very core of the *Nekyia* must be based on an actual very ancient Boeotian tradition of a visit by Odysseus to consult the seer, not at the edge of the world, but in the prophet's own native Boeotian home.[40] Indeed it has often been pointed out that Boeotia is a province richer than most in subterranean prophets; witness especially Amphiaraos' underground cave in Cnopia near Thebes and Trophonios' underground cave near Lebadeia. The argument appears convincing, therefore, that the Boeotian consultation was originally told in a Boeotian *Odyssey* before Odys-

[39] *The Homeric Odyssey*, 48 n.3.

[40] J. A. K. Thomson, *Studies in the Odyssey*, esp. 24—28 (and for Teiresias' home see n. 44 below).

seus was thought of as an Ithacan, that is before his tribe went to Ithaca.[41] And to support his conjecture further Thomson makes two lines of reasoning converge upon Boeotia. In the first place he claims to have traced Odysseus' ancestry through the tomb of his paternal grandfather Arkeisios-Arkesilaos to Boeotia, actually to Lebadeia where Trophonios' cult was situated; the chain of reasoning being that Arkeisios at *Odyssey* 14.182 is a "hypocoristic" form of Arkesilaos, a Boeotian hero in the Homeric Catalogue of Ships (*Iliad* 2.495) and that a hero of that name is buried at Lebadeia according to Pausanias 9.39.3.[42] Secondly, he finds a remarkable number of etymological coincidences from which he infers that Odysseus is ultimately identical in both name and nature with his maternal grandfather Autolykos of Parnassus, whose name means Very Wolf.[43] So Odysseus' Visit to the Shades was required by his chthonic nature, but was actually attached to him by virtue of his connection with Trophonios; which was in fact the basis for Thomson's belief that the *Nekyia* formed part of the original plan of the *Odyssey* (see n. 12 above).

It is a consequence of Thomson's reasoning, which he does not state but surely implies, that for the purposes of the *Nekyia* Teiresias was taken from the cult at Telphousa or Orchomenos[44] and was superimposed on Trophonios' cult as the person consulted. And Tro-

[41] *Op. cit.* 91—93. (But see my p. 72 below.)

[42] *Op. cit.* 20f.

[43] To find in "Odysseus" the stem *λυκ-*, "Wolf", which appears in "Auto*lyk*os", Thomson *op. cit.* 16ff. appeals to the forms *'Ολυσ(σ)εύς*, sometimes *'Ολυττεύς*, *'Ολισσεύς* from which the Latin forms *Ulysses*, *Ulixes*, or *Olixes* are derived. The wolf in Odysseus is allegedly supported, if it is recognized that the Indo-germanic words for Bear and Wolf are frequently contaminated, by his paternal grandfather Arkeisios, *ἄρκτος (ἄρκος)*, "Bear", while his other name Arkesilaos (see above) is said by various mythographers to have been the son of *'Αρχίλυκος* or *'Αρηίλυκος* or simply *Λύκος*, the Wolf (Diod. 4.67; schol. on Hom. *Il.* 2.494; Hygin. *Fab.* 97). Even so we can scarcely accept that Odysseus' grandfather was reincarnated in the grandson during the grandfather's own lifetime (Thomson p. 90 n.2)!

[44] For Teiresias' death and grave near the spring of Telphousa and for his cult at Orchomenos see A. Schachter, "A Boeotian Cult Type", *B.I.C.S.* 14(1967), 15 n. 32 and E. Rohde, *Psyche*[8], 104 n.8 respectively. Telphousa is now identified with the spring of Hagios Nikolaos by J. Fontenrose, "The Spring Telphusa", *T.A.P.A.* 100(1969), 119—131.

phonios' Oracle has one striking feature in common with Homer's *Nekyia* which marks it off from other oracles of which we have knowledge, namely the absence of a professional intermediary. At least none is mentioned by Homer, and the consultant at Lebadeia had to descend by himself into the underground cave known in some sources as the *καταβάσιον*, which itself implies a kind of catabatic ritual.[45] But this consideration apart, most of the other pillars on which Thomson builds his superstructure quickly collapse. The Catalogue of Fair Women, as we have noted already on p. 53 above, is almost certain to have been incorporated into the *Nekyia* from an independent poem which was not necessarily Boeotian. Furthermore, even if we accept the etymological arguments and the equation of Odysseus' grandfather Arkeisios with Arkesilaos, which is itself dubious,[46] there is good reason to be suspicious about the Boeotians in the Catalogue[47] — even Homer perhaps regarded them as expendable (cf. *Iliad* 17.597ff.). Finally the presence of the Boeotian seer need not imply a Boeotian *Odyssey* at all.

[45] On the *καταβάσιον* see schol. on Aristoph. *Clouds* 508 and the *Suda* s.v. *Τροφωνίου κατὰ γῆς παίγνια*. For the descent by the consultant himself cf. Strabo 9.2.38 (*καταβαίνει δ'αὐτὸς ὁ χρηστηριαζόμενος*), Maximus of Tyre, *Dissert.* 14.2 (the consultant is *ὑποφήτης αὐτάγγελος*), Philostratus, *Vit. Apoll.* 8.19. (pointing out the uniqueness of the Oracle, *μόνον γὰρ ἐκεῖνο* [sc. *μαντεῖον*] *δι' αὐτοῦ χρᾷ τοῦ χρωμένου*), and Pausanias 9.39. That a "descent" is involved is suggested also by the title of a work, unfortunately now lost, called *ἡ εἰς Τροφονίου Κατάβασις* by Dicaearchus, a pupil of Aristotle and contemporary of Theophrastus (see Athenaeus 13.594EF and 14.641EF), and by the Delian historian Semos, who mentions the descent made at the Oracle by Parmeniscus of Metapontum in the fifth book of his *Δηλίας* (*F. Gr. Hist.* 396F10 *ap.* Athenaeus 14.614A). The custom of descending into the Trophonion with honey-cakes was already familiar enough in the fifth century to invite Aristophanes' scorn in the *Clouds* 506—508; and the theme of the descent was doubtless parodied too in Cratinus' *Τροφώνιος*, on which see J. M. Edmonds, *The Fragments of Attic Comedy* (Leiden 1957), I. 101—105. For further references to the ritual and the oracle see my article "Trophonios: the Manner of his Revelation", *T.A.P.A.* 99(1968), 63ff.

[46] It is hardly proved by Rhys Carpenter, *Folk Tale, Fiction and Saga in the Homeric Epics* (Berkeley 1946), who develops the etymological suggestions into a fullscale Bearson interpretation of the *Odyssey* in which Odysseus is the sacred hibernating bear of cult and folktale. This ingenious interpretation unfortunately lacks conviction from many aspects.

[47] See on this D. L. Page, *History and the Homeric Iliad*, 152.

This last statement perhaps requires amplifying. Teiresias of course plays a very ancient role indeed if, as was suggested in chapter 1 above, he took over the role that originally belonged to Utnapishtim in the *Epic of Gilgamesh*. But the seer need not himself have appeared in this role at a very early date. Webster holding that behind the *Odyssey* lies a distinct Mycenaean borrowing of the *Epic of Gilgamesh* supposes an ancient invocation of Teiresias, whom he takes to be a very old figure to be identified with the Qerasija of the Knossos tablets.[48] Kirk similarly supposes that Teiresias was a Boeotian figure well established in North Mycenaean tradition.[49] But quite apart from the difficult question of whether or not Teiresias was established in Mycenaean saga, one excellent reason for Odysseus' consultation of the Shade of Teiresias is that the seer was well known from Theban Epic, and he could as well have been borrowed from this source as from an agelong Mycenaean tradition.[50] Even if Homer was unaware of Teiresias' virtual suicide from drinking the cold water from the spring of Tilphousa,[51] he presumably knew that Teiresias had died, and this made him readily available for consultation without having Odysseus journey to Thebes. Hence Teiresias' presence in the *Nekyia* may indicate Homer's debt to a recent Theban Epic rather than to Mycenaean tradition and it does not imply that Homer took over Odysseus' Visit to the Dead from a Boeotian original. Even if Homer's description of the ritual is indebted to Boeotia — and *nekyomanteia* are by no means restricted to this district of Greece — the *Nekyia* is, as I hope to show more fully below, much more than a Witch of En-

[48] *From Mycenae to Homer*², 109 and 248. Webster also suggests here that Teiresias' death in Colophon (*Nostoi*, ed. Allen, 5.108) might indicate that the immigrants in Asia Minor brought with them an Oracle of Teiresias. This argument would help supply a post-migration reason for Teiresias' part in the *Nekyia* but still does not take us very far.

[49] G. S. Kirk, *The Songs of Homer*, 237, cf. 107ff.

[50] As kindly pointed out to me by H. W. Stubbs, for whose view on Homer's readiness to borrow from Theban epic (whether or not Homer himself had composed a Theban epic, as E. V. Rieu suspected) see his "Homer, Thebes and Argos", *P.C.A.* 50(1953), 19.

[51] Aristoph. fr. 701 (Hall and Geldart); Pind. fr. 188 (Bowra); Paus. 9.33.1; Apollod. *Bibl.* 3.7.3.

dor scene.[52] It is almost as though an Enkidu-like séance has been superimposed upon a Gilgamesh-like journey to Utnapishtim's Faraway Land.

For futher hints to the history behind the *Nekyia* we must turn to Odysseus' "cover story": Odysseus feigning to be a Cretan narrates first to Eumaeus and then to Penelope a "false" tale concerning his journey to Thesprotia where he obtained news of Odysseus' whereabouts.[53] The tale in effect contains the essentials of the whole *Odyssey*. For whereas in Odysseus' real wanderings Alcinous saw to it that the Phaeacians in Scherie prepared treasure for Odysseus,[54] the "Cretan Odysseus" in the pretended wanderings tells how the Thesprotian king Pheidon showed him all the treasures that were stored for Odysseus.[55] And Pheidon is alleged to have sworn to him that a ship had been launched with a crew ready to convey Odysseus on the last stage of his journey to Ithaca, which matches the real journey in which Odysseus was ferried home from Scherie in a ship manned by the Phaeacians.[57] Pheidon's son even provides some of the services performed by Alcinous' daughter.[58] Finally, the Cretan Odysseus says that Pheidon informed him that Odysseus had just gone to consult the oracle at Dodona as to whether he should return to Ithaca openly or secretly,[59] which was the very question that was twice raised in the *Nekyia*.

Reports of a Thesprotian Oracle of the Dead, *nekyomanteion*, by the rivers Acheron and Cocytus and the Acherousian Lake[60] led

[52] Told in I *Samuel* 28.3—20; commentary by J. G. Frazer, *Folk-Lore in the Old Testament*, 2.517—554.

[53] *Od.* 14.199—359 esp. 316—333 (narrated to Eumaeus); *Od.* 19.165—307 esp. 287—299 (narrated to Penelope). W. J. Woodhouse, *The Composition of Homer's Odyssey*, 144ff. and Fernand Robert, *Homère* (Paris 1950), 171—5 are the best commentaries on these passages.

[54] *Od.* 11.340f.

[55] *Od.* 14.323—326 and 19.293—295.

[56] *Od.* 14.331—333 and 19.288—290.

[57] *Od.* 13.50ff.

[58] *Od.* 14.317—320.

[59] See at n. 31 above.

[60] The oracle is said by Herod. 5.92.7 to have been consulted by Periander of Corinth. Its location, possible connection with Argonautic saga, and certain associa-

Pausanias to suggest that Homer derived the names of his underworld streams from the Thesprotian rivers.[61] This has been doubted by some, among them Rohde, who believed instead that the names were fitted from Homer to the topography.[62] But the relevance of the Thesprotian theory to the *Nekyia* cannot be ignored. It is at the court of King Pheidon that the journey of the Cretan Odysseus and that attributed to Odysseus are alleged to cross. The two journeys are artificially dissociated in the cover story in order to deceive Eumaeus and Penelope, but they are in a sense one. Although Homer does not say that Odysseus visited the Thesprotian oracle, but only the oracle of Zeus at Dodona, the visit to Pheidon in this false *Odyssey* is perhaps a veiled reference also to his visit to the Thesprotian oracle of the dead. Pheidon, "He Who Spares", whose name would make a transparent euphemism for a god of the dead, is perhaps another Hades.[63]

Who, asks Robert, will believe that this *Odyssey* presented as false was entirely imagined by the author of the real *Odyssey?*[64] One answer might be, of course, that Odysseus is a skilled enough liar to incorporate so much of the truth that his lie is true in all the essentials except that of location. The Thesprotia version might therefore be a cover-story entirely invented by Homer. Telemachus' wanderings might be a similar invention for a different purpose. But an alternative answer is that there might once have existed an Odysseus-in-Thesprotia story and a Wandering-in-Far-Seas story which the author of the *Odyssey* amalgamated. Robert saw in the Thesprotia story a rival *Odyssey* which Homer partly derided (by putting it into the mouth of the lying Odysseus) and partly utilized to enrich his *Odys-*

tion with Theseus, Peirithous, Heracles, and Orpheus will be mentioned shortly below.

[61] Paus. 1.17.5. According to H. Wagenvoort, *Mnemosyne* 24(1971), 126, Thesprotia is one of the early territories "reserved" for souls, whose river Acheron was later transferred to the underworld, not the other way round. Cf. the view of K. F. Ameis-Hentze on *Od.* 10.513: "Die Züge des Bildes sind von der Oberwelt entlehnt."

[62] E. Rohde, *Psyche*⁸, 52. n. 73.

[63] As argued by F. Robert, *Homère*, 173. Cf. euphemisms like the "Eumenides". The fact that there was in Argos in the seventh century a real King Pheidon does not tell against this probability.

[64] *Ibid.* 172.

sey.[65] Professor Woodhouse regarded all Odyssean references to prophecies as developments from the oracle of the dead at Thesprotia and from the visit to the oracle at Dodona which he took to be the original saga-version of Odysseus' historical journey.[66]

This last supposition gains in significance from Dakaris' recent discovery, now to be considered, of an actual historical *nekyomanteion* with even the *mêchanê* for showing "ghosts" in Thesprotia near the juncture of the rivers Acheron and Cocytus just to the south of Mesopotamon. The existing building with its labyrinthine passageways dates only from Hellenistic times, but it shows traces of occupation from the Mycenaean period.[67] Here must have been the ancient town of Ephyra later renamed Cichyrus,[68] near which Thucydides[69] reports that the Acherusian Lake received the river Acheron just where the Thesprotian Oracle of the Dead is placed by Pausanias, Pliny, and others.[70] Ephyra-Cichyrus and the Oracle are, moreover, reached by the port *Cheimerion,*[71] with which Homer's "*Cimmerians*" or "*Cheimerians*" at *Odyssey* 11.14 might be connected (see p. 38 above). The vulgate reading *Κιμμερίων* was already felt to be strange in antiquity. This is indicated by an unusual number of variant readings, among them *Χειμερίων* "wintry people" attributed to the ancient scholar Proteas Zeugmatites. Furthermore, the vulgate reading, if it is taken to refer to the historic Cimmerians of the Euxine,[72]

[65] *Ibid.*

[66] W. J. Woodhouse, *The Composition of Homer's Odyssey*, 144.

[67] The excavation was begun by S. Dakaris in 1958. For the fullest reports see his "The Dark Palace of Hades", *Archaeology* 15(1962), 85—93 and "Das Totenorakel bei Ephyra", *Antike Kunst*, Beiheft 1(1963), 35—55. See also N. G. L. Hammond, *Epirus* (Oxford 1967), esp. 64—66 and 314f. For a review of the literature see T. B. L. Webster, *Lustrum* 11(1966), 9.

[68] As we know from Strabo 7.7.5, p. 324.

[69] 1.46.3—4.

[70] Paus. 1.17.5; Pliny, *N.H.* 4.1.2—4 with commentary by N. G. L. Hammond, *Epirus*, 444—458; Photius *Lex.* s.v. *Θεοὶ Μολοττικοί*; and Eustathius on *Od.* 1667. 46ff.

[71] Thuc. 1.46.3—4; Strabo 7.7.5, p. 324; Pliny *N.H.* 4.1.2—4 (where it is called *Chimera*).

[72] This is the traditional interpretation. Its elaborate defence by J. B. Bury, "The Homeric and the historic Kimmerians", *Klio* 7(1906), 77—88, is to my mind unconvincing.

seems to be quite incongruous in the midst of Odysseus' western wanderings. Huxley, even before the excavation of the Oracle, neatly resolved the puzzle by advocating *Χειμερίων*[73], or it should be *Χειμεριῶν*, that is *Χειμεριέων* scanned by a common synaloephe, signifying the people of the Thesprotian port *Χειμέριον*, by which the Oracle at Ephyra is approached. That the origin of the enigmatic Cimmerians was actually the obscure Cheimerion would explain Proteas' reading and is presumably what Pausanias read in his text of the *Odyssey*. If, as seems to be the case, the Oracle excavated by Dakaris (who accepts Huxley's reasoning) dates ultimately from the Mycenaean period, knowledge of it could have been current in Mycenaean tradition, though conceivably Homer's implied knowledge of it might be due to the reoccupation of the area by the Greeks from Elis in about 700 B.C.[74]

The Thesprotian hypothesis can be taken one step further. Since a *nekyomanteion* is a place not for a descent, but for an evocation of a single ghost, to supply not supernatural prophecy nor oracular advice, but natural information which the dead person had carried to the grave (as we know from the description by Herodotus of Periander's consultation of his wife Melissa's ghost at the Thesprotian Oracle), it is tempting to believe that an original saga in which Odysseus visited Thesprotia was modified by Homer for his own first version of the *Nekyia* which told how Anticleia alone was evoked to give Odysseus natural information about his wife and son and the affairs of his kingdom in Ithaca; the poet then grafted on to it the consultation of the Theban prophet (borrowed as argued above from a recent Theban Epic rather than an agelong Mycenaean tradition) and a

[73] G. L. Huxley, "Odysseus and the Thesprotian Oracle of the Dead", *P.P.* 13(1958), 245—248. It is interesting also to see how near Eustathius got to this solution at *Od.* 1667. 41ff.

[74] Worth mentioning *à propos* of Thesprotian tradition is the further possibility raised by G. L. Huxley, *Greek Epic Poetry* (London 1969), 67 and 72 that Medea in the Argonautic tradition of Eumelos spoke to the dead seer Idmon in a *nekyomanteia* and that she may have been associated with the Thesprotian oracle of the dead in the epic *Naupactia*. There are, however, no firm facts to go on. See also K. Meuli, *Odyssee und Argonautika* (Berlin 1921), 115, and N. G. L. Hammond, *Epirus*, 366 n. 4. For a different interprepation of the evidence see V. J. Mathews, "Naupaktia and Argonautika", *Phoenix* 31 (1977), 191 and 197.

Descent into the Underworld which has been transported to the far western edge of the world, by or beyond the streams of Ocean, where the fusion of disparate elements seems less contradictory.

The process of conflation that has been suggested here, whereby a place for the evocation of a ghost merges with a place for a descent, can be illustrated by a further story associated with Thesprotia. Like the Thesprotian Oracle of the Dead, which on account of the changing territorial boundaries between Thesprotia and Molossia is sometimes linked with Molossia,[75] this story is also associated in some accounts with Molossia. Its beginning is preserved in two short notices in the anonymous *Brevis Expositio* on Vergil's *Georgics* 1.39.[76] We read firstly that "the King of the Molossians seized Proserpine, and when Ceres came knocking at his door her daughter refused to go to her, on account of her love for the place." And secondly that "Ceres descended into the lower world in the attempt to recover her daughter, but Proserpine was unwilling to follow her mother." Both notices are evidently a rationalization of the canonical myth of the abduction of Proserpine by Hades-Aidoneus, except that in the canonical myth (to be considered more fully in chapter 3) it is rare that Ceres (or Demeter) descends, as she does here, to fetch her daughter, and Proserpine's (or Persephone's) unwillingness to leave the Underworld is equally rare.[77]

[75] The oracle's Thesprotian connections have already been outlined above. For its link with Molossia see Photius *Lex.* s.v. *Θεοὶ Μολοττικοί· οἱ χθόνιοι, ἐπεὶ ψυχοπομπεῖον ἦν ἐν Μολοττοῖς.* Moreover at *Nem.* 7.36.39 Pindar says that Neoptolemus came to "Ephyra" (where the oracle was located, n. 68) and "ruled in Molossia".

[76] In *Servii Commentarii* ed. G. Thilo and H. Hagen (Leipzig 1878—1902), III. ii. 213: "*Rex Molossorum Proserpinam rapuit et Ceres ostia cum cantatoribus multis pulsavit nec veniebat ad eam filia eius pro loci amore*" and "*In infernum descendit Ceres, ut filiam reciperet; illa matrem sequi noluit.*"

[77] Demeter's descent does, however, occur in Orphic tradition (Orph. *Hymn.* 41.5, cf. Hyginus *Fab.* 251, also Ovid, *F.* 4.611ff., *M.* 5.533 (?), Claud. *R.P.* 3.107f.), and Proserpine's refusal to return is met with in Vergil, *Georg.* 1.39 *nec repetita sequi curet Proserpina matrem,* and possibly in Columella, *Rust.* 10.272 and Lucan, *Phars.* 6.698 and 739, on which see R. Förster, *Der Raub und die Rückkehr der Persephone* (Stuttgart 1874), 45, 59ff. Förster surmised that the source which Vergil followed was probably Philochorus (see next n.), but G. Zuntz, *Persephone*, 401 argues that Vergil is more likely to have been inspired by the myth, no doubt a

The continuation of the story, which illustrates the conflation, is told apparently in the second book of Philochorus' *Atthis* as well as in three versions by Plutarch, Pausanias, and Aelian.[78] These tell how the catabatic heroes Theseus and Peirithous journey to Thesprotia or Molossia and grapple with the King's watchdog Cerberus seeking to steal either Persephone or Kore, cast respectively as the wife and daughter of King Aidoneus (as the ruler of the land is now called). These versions evidently narrate in a rationalized form the Descent of Theseus and Peirithous in the hope of abducting the Underworld Queen from the Netherworld. And since in this rationalized version of the Descent the two heroes are said to have been caught not in Hades nor in Tartarus, as in the canonical version, but in Cichyrus or Ephyra (where Theseus is further said to be detained with Peirithous until Heracles intercedes for his release) it is evident also that not only the land of Thesprotia, but the very site of the Thesprotian Oracle of the Dead has come to be assimilated to the Underworld. The rationalization of the Ruler of the Underworld into a Thesprotian or Molossian King serves, moreover, to illustrate the point claimed earlier by Robert, namely that the Thesprotian King Pheidon in Odysseus' false tale might likewise be a rationalized Hades-figure. At 9.30.5—6 Pausanias, no doubt confused by Homer's mixture, again conflates a "Descent into the Underworld", this time Orpheus', with the Thesprotian *Nekyomanteion*, and by speaking of "the Avernus in Thesprotia" (*τὸ ῎Αορνον... τὸ ἐν τῇ Θεσπρωτίδι... εἶναι γὰρ πάλαι νεκυομαντεῖον αὐτόθι*) he further conflates the Thesprotian Oracle of the Dead with the alleged Oracle of the Dead on the shore of

poem, that lay behind the rationalistic perversion of the kind reported in the *Brevis Expositio*. In the canonical myth of the Homeric *Hymn to Demeter* 334—386 Hermes descends into the Underworld and leads up Persephone, now full of joy, to her mother Demeter in the Upperworld. And in another version (see Callim. fr. 466 Pfeiffer *ap.* schol. on *Theocr.* 2.12) Hecate descends to look for Persephone and in art assists at the Anodos of Persephone, see Beazley, *A.R.V.*[2] 1012.1 and *Paralip.* 440, and cf. generally on Hecate's role in connection with Persephone *N. J. Richardson's* references in *The Homeric Hymn to Demeter* (Oxford 1974), 155f. and 295.

[78] Philochorus, *F. Gr. Hist.* 328F18; Plut. *Thes.* 31.4 and 35.1—2; Paus. 1.17.4f., 1.18.4, 2.22.6, 3.18.5, 5.14.3; Ael. *Var. Hist.* 4.5. Cf. also J. Tzetzes, *Chiliades*, 2.406ff. On the version rationalized see further ch. 5 *ad init.* and ch. 7 n. 104 below.

Lake Avernus in Italy, where Odysseus' descent was also located in tradition.

Side by side, indeed, with the Thesprotian location of the Homeric *Nekyia* is the Italian localisation to which I have just drawn attention. Here is the original location of the *Nekyia* according to Victor Bérard, who holds that the western setting of Odysseus' Wanderings is original and derived from a Phoenician handbook.[79] But despite Bérard's ingenious defence of this view on the ground that the legends of a *Nekyomanteion* on the shore of Lake Avernus near Cumae in Italy were narrated before the historic period of colonisation and were incorporated in a pre-Homeric *periplus* which has influenced the *Odyssey*, the evidence is far from convincing for reasons we shall shortly see.

The oldest extant testimony to the location of Odysseus' *Nekyia* in these parts is perhaps the lost play of Aeschylus which represents a chorus of "Ghost-Raisers", honouring Hermes as their ancestor, "around a lake", possibly Avernus.[80] At any rate Daeira, who is mentioned in the same play, appears subsequently in Lycophron's *Alexandra* 710 as the name of his Persephone near Avernus, which lake, he says, was sacred to Persephone (698); and with this last point Diodorus 4.22.1 agrees. Lycophron's description of Teiresias as a necromancer (*νεκρόμαντιν*, 682) in the Plain of the Departed, moreover, implies the presence of a *Nekyomanteion*, which was presumably near the "Lake Avernus" in Campania (704); and although Lycophron's date is comparatively late, much of his knowledge of the historical and geographical traditions of the West comes, like Strabo's much later, from the third century writer Timaeus of Tauromenium.[81]

[79] V. Bérard, *La Resurrection d'Homère* (Paris 1930), 134: "Le text est grec; la source est phénicienne"; and for the *Nekyia* at Avernus, *id. Les Phéniciens et l'Odyssée* (Paris 1927), II. 313ff.

[80] Aeschylus, *Psychagogoi* fr. 277 (ed. Nauck) *ap*. Aristophanes, *Frogs*, 1266 with schol. *ad. loc*. There may, of course, be much more parody of the play by Aristophanes than we know.

[81] For the reconstruction of Timaeus' writings from various sources see esp. J. Geffcken, *Timaios und die Geographie des Westens* (Berlin 1892), and cf. F. Jacoby, *F. Gr. Hist*. 566. vol. iiib. 538—546 and T. S. Brown, *Timaeus of Tauromenium* (Berkeley 1958).

The earliest specific mention, however, of an Oracle of the Dead on the "Avernus lake" (near Cumae) is found in the Attic dramatist Sophocles, whom the almost unknown poet Python seems to be parodying in his satyr drama *Agen*, which also deals with a conjuring up of the dead at something designated as *ἄορνον*.[82] The passage by Sophocles is reported in the *Συναγωγὴ λέξεων χρησίμων*. I quote it fully here, with only minor orthographical changes, from I. Bekker's edition *Anecdota Graeca* (1814), 413f.: *"Αορνος λιμήν περὶ Τυρσηνίαν. φησὶ δὲ καὶ ἐν Κύμῃ τῇ Χαλκιδικῇ "Αορνον λίμνην εἶναι, περιπεφυκότων δὲ πολλῶν δένδρων μηδὲν εἰς αὐτὴν ἐμπίπτειν τῶν ἀποπιπτόντων φύλλων. εἶναι δὲ καὶ νεκυομαντεῖον ἐν τῇ Τυρσηνίᾳ λίμνῃ Σοφοκλῆς ἱστορεῖ.* A. C. Pearson in his edition of the fragments of Sophocles no. 748 reads the second word *λιμήν* as *λίμνη* and so does H. Erbse in his *Untersuchungen zu den attizistischen Lexika* (1950), α 127 where in other respects too a different text is printed. The notice is still not assigned to any play with certainty: Holzinger supposed it to belong to Sophocles' lost *Euryalus;* Pearson to his *Odysseus Akanthoplex;* Phillips plausibly connects it with another fragment in which Sophocles speaks of the Cerberians, meaning Cimmerians.[83]

The Sophocles passage is worth quoting fully, as I have done, both for the considerable light it throws upon Odysseus' Italian tradition and because of a current misinterpretation of it. Phillips in the article just cited says that "Pearson doubts whether Cumae was meant by Sophocles, however later writers took the allusion." This, however, is to obscure the main argument of Pearson's that Sophocles must have introduced the name *"Αορνος* alluding to the Cumaean lake but without mentioning Cumae itself. When the Cumaean Avernus became famous, he argued, the absence of a specific reference to Cumae by Sophocles made it seem that Sophocles intended a different lake, which the compiler of the passage, Aelius Dionysius or another (perhaps the Atticist Pausanias, as Erbse suggests), called the "Tyrrhe-

[82] Cf. Bruno Snell, *Scenes from Greek Drama* (Berkeley 1967), 105ff. where, too, a good case is made for 326 B. C. as the year of performance.

[83] See C. von Holzinger, *Lycophrons Alexandra* (Leipzig 1895), 346; A. C. Pearson, *The Fragments of Sophocles* (Cambridge 1917), 3.10; and E. D. Phillips, "Odysseus in Italy", *J.H.S.* 73(1953), 56 n. 29 referring also to the Cerberians passage in *Et. Magn.* 513.45 = Sophocles fr. 957 Nauck, 1060 Pearson.

nian". However, Sophocles himself would probably not have distinguished "Tyrsenia" from Campania, as he apparently does not in fr. 598 cf. Vergil, *Georgics* 2.164; hence there is no need to suppose, as the compiler imagines, that a second Avernus existed on the west coast of Italy in Tyrrhenia. Nor is there need to delete the word *λίμνη* as Dindorf wished, since the words *ἐν τῇ Τυρσηνίᾳ λίμνῃ* are probably the compiler's and not Sophocles'. Sophocles, then, must have said that there was a *νεκυομαντεῖον ἐν τῇ ἀόρνῳ λίμνῃ περὶ Τυρσηνίαν* or words to this effect.[84]

Substantially the same extract but without the attribution to Sophocles is preserved in two other places. These two are worth quoting partly because they throw some light upon the text for this tradition concerning Avernus. In the *Etymologicum Magnum* we find (in T. Gaisford's edition), p. 115 the entry *Ἄορνος: Λίμνη (λιμήν D. Va) περὶ Τυρσηνίαν. Φασὶ δὲ καὶ ἐν Κύμῃ τῇ Χαλκιδικῇ Ἄορνον λίμνην εἶναι, περιπεφυκότων (δὲ) πολλῶν δένδρων μηδὲν τῶν ἀποπιπτόντων φύλλων ἐμπίπτειν εἰς αὐτήν. Εἶναι δὲ καὶ νεκυομαντεῖον.* Eustathius on the *Odyssey* p. 1667 likewise preserves the tradition thus (Stallbaum's edition): *Ἐν δὲ ῥητορικῷ λεξικῷ εὕρηται καὶ ταῦτα· Ἄορνος, λιμὴν περὶ Τυρσηνίαν. καὶ ἐν Κύμῃ δέ φησι τῇ Χαλκιδικῇ Ἄορνος λίμνη. περὶ ἣν πεφυκότων πολλῶν δένδρων μηδὲν τῶν ἀποπιπτόντων φύλλων ἐμπίπτειν εἰς αὐτήν. εἶναι δὲ καὶ νεκυομαντεῖον ἐκεῖ.* Substantially the same tradition is suggested also by the lexicographer Hesychius who explains *Ἄορνος* as *λιμὴν ἢ λίμνη* and by the *Lexicon Zonarae*, in which we find the first part of the alternative explanation *Ἄορνος: Λιμὴν περὶ Τυρσηνίαν.*[85] The collective value of these reports lies in the fact that they indicate that in their source Avernus was reported to be a "harbour" (*λιμήν*) as well as a "lake" (*λίμνη*), a fact well attested by Strabo and other writers.[86] This in turn suggests that Pearson and Erbse in all probabil-

[84] A. C. Pearson, *The Fragments of Sophocles*, 3.9f.

[85] Ed. J. A. Cramer, *Anecdota Graeca E Codd. Manuscriptis Bibliothecae Regiae Parisiensis* (Oxford 1841), 4.115.

[86] Strabo 5.144, *Ἄορνος… λιμένος καὶ μέγεθος καὶ φύσιν ἔχων.* Strabo goes on to mention the possibility of sailing into Avernus and the alterations to the area made by Agrippa and his architect and engineer L. Cocceius Auctus, whose signature is found in the temple of Augustus at Puteoli (*C.I.L.* 10.3707). Avernus was,

ity were wrong in suspecting λίμνη for λιμήν in the Συναγωγή above. Likewise we may feel that successive editors of Hesychius have also erred when they suspect the words λιμὴν ἢ in the alternative explanation given by Hesychius. His recent editor K. Latte (Copenhagen 1953) in bracketing these words merely follows M. Schmidt, who in turn quotes Schow, "verba λιμὴν ἢ sunt ab haesitante librario, qui cum ambigeret, utrum verius esset, cum vocem λίμνη obscurius forte scriptam reperiret, utrumque scripsit." And Gaisford, who rejects the reading λιμήν by two good manuscripts *D* and *Va* (respectively the Bodleian MS D'Orville 2 =Auct. X.1.1.2. and the Leiden MS Voss. Gr. Q 20 f.7) merely repeating F. Sylburg's note of 1594 "Pro λίμνη in vulg. ed. est λιμὴν, errore satis manifesto", is also mistaken.[87]

I have quoted these passages for another reason too. They indicate the very curious "no leaves" tradition associated with Avernus, which exists beside the popular etymology of Avernus as meaning "no birds" (*A-ornos*). And this last has been perpetuated by the folklorist explanation that it was impossible for birds to fly across the lake because of the poisonous odours which rose up from it.[88]

in fact, linked with Lake Lucrinus and the sea to form for Octavian the *Portus Julius*, which was eulogised by Vergil at *Georgics* 2.161—164. For the fullest account see Dio Cassius 48.50f. The construction was undertaken of three great tunnels connecting *Portus Julius* by land with the Cumaean acropolis and the sea. One tunnel to the south of Avernus, the "Grotta della Sibilla" of local legend (for which see further my article cited in ch. 6 n. 1 below), is the House of Hades to which Odysseus came, according to V. Bérard, *Les Phéniciens*, II. 321.

87 *Pace* Sylburg it is far from clear that λιμήν is an error. For the MSS see F. Madan, *A Summary Catalogue of Western Manuscripts in the Bodleian Library at Oxford* (Oxford 1897), vol. IV p. 38 no. 16880 and K. A. De Meyier, *Codices Manuscripti VI: Codices Vossiani Graeci et Miscellanei* (Lugduni Batavorum 1955), p. 120 respectively.

88 For this see e.g. Heraclides *ap. Paradoxographus Vaticanus Rohdii*, XIV, and *ap.* Antigonus *Hist. Mirab.* 152 (168)=fr. 128a—b Wehrli, Timaeus *ap. id. ib.*, Ps. — Aristotle, *Mirab. Auscult.* 102 (108) in *Paradoxographi Graeci* ed. A. Westermann, Strabo 5.244, Lucretius, *De Rer. Nat.* 6.738ff., and Vergil, *Aen.* 6.239—242, cf. 201f. with Servius *ad loc.* Despite the absence of a mention of Aornos, Plutarch's myth of Thespesios at *de ser. num. vind.* 563—568 seems also to be based on the Campi Phlegraei insofar as the souls, like birds, go around the chasm to avoid flying across it. The "no birds" tradition is also narrated of the

In the light of the early evidence so far reviewed the question can now be put whether these and subsequent passages can legitimately be said to preserve, as Bérard claims, a memory of the Oracle of the Dead operating at Avernus from time immemorial. And to begin with, an important modification to Bérard's Phoenician thesis has already had to be made by Phillips, who although persuaded by many of the geographical and topographical — but not etymological — points in Bérard's argument contends that the supposed pre-Homeric *periplus* which has allegedly influenced the *Odyssey* and given to the *Nekyia* its Avernus-setting would need to be earlier than the period of Phoenician expansion itself. He himself argues that Minoan or Mycenaean voyages are a more likely source for the passages of the *Odyssey* that suggest a real acquaintance with the West, and these places, he suggests, the early colonists carrying Homer with them then rediscovered for themselves.[89]

This argument carries a certain appeal and does not contradict recent archaeological research, which confirms the impression gained from Homer that, for the late Mycenaean period, Sicily and the east coast of Italy were the western limits of the known world. This does make it possible that Italy could have been regarded before the period of colonisation as a world of the dead and the supernatural. However, this is of no account for the *Nekyia* unless it can be shown that a *Nekyomanteion* is likely to have existed there in early times on the shore of Avernus. And the probability from what can be made of the scattered references to the Oracle is against this. The correct inference, drawn recently by Colin G. Hardie[90], seems to be that the Oracle of the Dead beside Avernus in Italy never existed in cult practice as distinct from the literary tradition that introduced Odysseus' *Nekyia*

λίμνη of Eridanus by Apollonius Rhod. *Argon.* 4.599—603. And Lucian at *De Luctu* 3 nicely parodies the motif by suggesting that if live birds cannot cross the Lake in the Upperworld then dead birds cannot fly over Lake Acheron in the Underworld. For the chthonic meaning of Avernus see further discussion of the etymology by F. Ribezzo, *Riv. Indo-greco-italica*, 12(1928), 98 and V. Pisani, "Miscellanea etimologica", *Rend. Accad. Lincei*, 8(1932), 337—357 para. 69.

89 *J.H.S.* 73(1953), esp. 63f.

90 I summarise below from C. G. Hardie's excellent discussion of the Avernian testimonia in the Appendix to his "The Great Antrum at Baiae", *P.B.S.R* 37(1969), 32f.

to the West. At any rate Aeschylus and Sophocles are hardly evidence of cult practice. And Cicero, whose villa, the "Academia", lay just to the east of Lake Avernus, and who might be expected to have first-hand knowledge, quotes an old poet for the traditional localisation of the evocation of ghosts in his *Tusculanae Disputationes* 1.16.37: "*inde in vicinia nostra Averni lacus,*

> *Unde animae excitantur obscura umbra opertae ex ostio,*
> *Altae Acheruntis, salso sanguine, imagines mortuorum.*"

But this, as Hardie points out, need be no more than a reference to the literary tradition in which Vergil was later to work. Similarly Maximus of Tyre's description at 14.2 of the rite by which to summon a ghost from the Underworld Entrance at Avernus is evidence for no more than a literary tradition of Odysseus' evocation. And the passage in Livy 24.12.4, often quoted as proof of cult practice, referring to Hannibal's coming to the Lake from Capua in 214 B.C. on the pretence of sacrificing there, really in hope of springing a surprise attack on Puteoli ("*Inde Numidis Hispanisque ad praesidium simul castrorum simul Capuae relictis cum cetero exercitu ad lacum Averni per speciem sacrificandi, re ipsa ut temptaret Puteolos quodque ibi praesidii erat, descendit.*") does not identify the cult, still less say that there was an Oracle of the Dead or place of descent at Avernus.[91] Ephorus of Cume, who visited Cumae about 360 B.C. and is quoted by Strabo 5.244f., is thought by many to support the existence of a prehistoric Oracle.[92] But the historian, who was looking for the Oracle-centre of Homer's Cimmerians at Avernus and saw other underground dwellings which he mysteriously describes as "clay pits", *ἄργιλλαι*, was told only the not too credible story that it was destroyed by a king and was then transferred "to another place", where it "still

[91] The Lake of Avernus is said to be sacred to Persephone (p. 64 above), and Dio Cassius 48.50.4 speaks of the Lake as dedicated to "Calypso" whose statue, or that of some other heroine, sweated when Agrippa was building his naval base (cf. Serv. on Verg. *Georg*. 2.162). But Ephorus (see below) is evidence enough that the Oracle, if it ever existed, was no longer visible on Avernus' shore in Hannibal's time.

[92] E.g. by E. Norden, *P. Vergilius Maro Aeneis Buch VI* (Leipzig 1903 and 1926), 117—118 and E. D. Phillips, *J.H.S.* 73(1953), 63.

survives". The inference is that he sought for, but could not find the Oracle of the Dead, only the report that it had been suppressed. And this corresponds to Strabo's own view, since he reports that the cutting down of the forest around Avernus by Agrippa during the construction of a naval base in 37—36 B.C. has proved all earlier stories about the existence of the Oracle to be mere fable (*loc. cit.*). That an Oracle of the Dead was said to have existed on Avernus' shore and that it was destroyed is mentioned also by Diodorus 4.22.1—2 who, like Strabo, probably draws on Ephorus here, though he also draws on Timaeus in close context. Timaeus, we may presume, agreed with Ephorus over the disappearance of the original Oracle. At any rate Antigonus *Historiae Mirabiles* 152 (168), just before mentioning the no-leaves tradition found in the later *lexica* already referred to above, reports Timaeus as denying the story of Avernus' effect on birds. Presumably Timaeus had been there. All this suggests that the alleged prehistoric Oracle was "the bookish notion of mythographers and historians who had not been there,"[93] and that Avernus was chosen as the location of the *Nekyia* when Odysseus was taken to the west, though the real Oracle of the Dead which influenced the *Odyssey* was at Ephyra in Thesprotia.

As for Ephorus if he was shown an alleged new site of the Oracle, the possibility that he was shown a Cave rediscovered in 1962 at Campanian Baiae is also raised by Hardie.[94] The cave seems to have been a cult-centre datable to about 500 B.C., when Aristodemus was tyrant of Cumae and when mystery cults were being introduced in South Italy and Campania, and being a place for some kind of descent, not for the evocation of ghosts, it is the nearest thing to an underground dwelling now to be found in the vicinity.[95] All this did

[93] C. G. Hardie, *P.B.S.R.* 37(1969), 33.

[94] Hardie, *loc. cit.* cites in favour of this possibility Scymnus, *orb. descr.* 236, which uses the present tense: "at Cumae, where an underground oracle is shown, a 'Kerberion' (or place of Cerberus)". The passage should not be taken to refer to the Sibyl's cave on the Cumaean acropolis, which is a place for prophecy and is not a Kerberion, or entrance to the lower world.

[95] For the possibility that this Cave was built by Aristodemus as part of his religious policy, see Hardie, *op. cit.* 14—33, where it is further argued with good reason that the tyrant built the Sibyl's Cave at Cumae too. A. G. McKay in his

not, of course, put an end to the belief in the existence of an Oracle of the Dead beside Avernus in Italy, for in due course it was taken over by the Roman poet Naevius and then by Vergil as the setting for Aeneas' consultation of the dead. Hellanicus says that Aeneas came into Italy from the land of the Molossians with Odysseus,[96] and this is another link between Thesprotia and Italy.

It is also worth considering Odysseus' Corinthian connections. For if not originally a Corinthian hero, Odysseus was soon adopted by Corinth and was even given a Corinthian genealogy, exploited by Aeschylus, Euripides and Sophocles, by virtue of being made the son of the Corinthian trickster Sisyphos.[97] And from a comparison of Odysseus' wanderings with the topography of the Saronic gulf, Mireaux suggests that there might have existed a proto-Corinthian periplus in the Corinthian waters around the Isthmus, Attica, and the Argolid which was transferred in the seventh century to the waters of the west where Corinth under Cypselus was expanding her interests.[98] If Odysseus' journey does reflect the diplomatic policy of a

excellent book *Ancient Campania* (Hamilton 1972), 1.141f. and 150f. accepts the first of these possibilities, but concerning the Sibyl's Cave inclines to his earlier view argued in "The Greeks at Cumae", *Verg. Dig.* 3(1957), 7—10 (offering the first and, until Hardie, only explanation of it) that it may have been built by captive or enlisted Etruscan masons after the naval battle off Cumae in 474 B. C. For a factual account of the Baian Cave see the report given by its excavator R. F. Paget, "The 'Great Antrum' at Baiae", *P.B.S.R.* 35(1967), 102—112 and cf. his more interpretative book *In the Footsteps of Orpheus* (London 1967).

[96] *F. Gr. H.* 4F84=Dionys. Hal. 1.72.

[97] For the similarities between the two figures see Rhys Carpenter, *Folk Tale, Fiction and Saga in the Homeric Epics*, 122ff. It is, of course, extremely unlikely that Sisyphos in Corinthian legend was represented as one of the damned, as he was in the *Nekyia* of Homer.

[98] E. Mireaux, *Les Poèmes Homériques* (Paris 1948), 2.81—100, where Scylla is identified with Cape Scyllaeon, Circe's tomb is located on one of the Pharmacusae Islands, and the Cyclopes are said to represent Corinthian industrialists on the Corinthian Isthmus. See also n. 101 below. The *Nekyia* is not located by Mireaux, who perhaps considered it not to be part of this early periplus. It is, however, said by Rhys Carpenter, *Folk Tale, Fiction and Saga*, 124—127 to have Corinthian connections on the (to my mind slender) basis that Odysseus' descent was modelled upon that of Sisyphos, who, like Palaimon and Salmoxis (figures in the Bearson theory n. 46 above), was buried on the Isthmus. For other attempts to find the original location of the *Nekyia*, see L. G. Pocock, *Odyssean Essays* (Oxford 1965), 42ff.

Cypselid Corinth in western waters, it is thus given topicality. The amalgamation of an Odysseus-in-Thesprotia story and a Wandering-in-Far-Seas story might then have been effected under Corinthian influence. Corinthian activity around the gulf of Ambracia would at least explain how the Thesprotian location got into the story. And a Corinthian (or, indeed, a Boeotian or Thesprotian) Odysseus need not be inconsistent with a contemporary "Ithacan" if, as I am inclined to believe, "Ithaca" was derived from the cult-title of Odysseus *Ithacesios* or *Ithacos*, which was localised and applied to Odysseus' island-home (rather than the other way round) in much the same way as the topography of the Phlegraean Fields in Campania was given names of underworld geography or as Ascension Island, Easter Island, or Natal received their names.[99] And since an "Ithacan" might exist in any locality, there was no need for Thomson to assume (see pp. 54f. above) that a Boeotian Odysseus preceded an Ithacan, and then postulate a number of migrations.

Finally, in the true and false tales Odysseus sails home from Scherie and Thesprotia respectively. The name of the Phaeacians, who convey him from Scherie, Welcker derives from *φαιός*, "grey", "dusky", and supposes that the Phaeacians are the mythical ferrymen of the dead who inhabit the borderland of the world.[100] The supposition is somewhat fanciful, since Homer scarcely conceived Scherie with its idealized earthly life as a world of the dead. Nevertheless the Phaeacians are described by Alcinous as no longer having relations with mortals (*Od.* 13.180f.), and Odysseus is conveyed home in a sleep "most like to death", *θανάτῳ ἄγχιστα ἐοικώς* (*Od.* 13.80). The ship

and 69ff., and E. Bradford, *Ulysses Found* (London repr. 1971), 104ff., who locate it respectively in and beyond the strait of Gibraltar.

[99] Acusilaus *ap.* schol. on *Od.* 17.207 (*F. Gr. Hist.* 2F43) states that Ithaca was named after Ithacos — *καὶ ἐκ μὲν τοῦ Ἰθάκου ἡ νῆσος ἐπωνομάσθη Ἰθάκη.* Cf. A. B. Cook, *Zeus* (Cambridge 1914—1940), 1.327f. with refs., and H. W. Stubbs, "Troy, Asgard, and Armageddon", *F. L.* 70(1959), 440—459, for Odysseus' connections also with Prometheus *Ithas* or *Ithax.*

[100] F. G. Welcker, "Die Homerischen Phäaken und die Inseln der Seligen", *Rh. Mus.* 1(1833), 219—283. See also K. J. Beloch, *Griechische Geschichte* (Berlin 1924), I. i. 194f., J. A. K. Thomson, *Studies in the Odyssey*, 96f., and (for objections raised against the theory) A. Shewan, *Homeric Essays* (Oxford 1935), esp. 259—268.

that brought him from Scherie, moreover, is as mysterious as the pilotless ship that took him to the misty land of the Cimmerians: "The Phaeacians have no pilots nor any steering-oar such as other ships have. The ships themselves know men's thoughts and minds, and they know the cities and fruitful fields of men everywhere, and most swiftly do they cross the gulf of the sea, hidden in mist and cloud" (*Od.* 8.557ff.). Poseidon's punishment of the Phaeacians for having ferried Odysseus back to Ithaca, which Mireaux takes as a condemnation of the Corcyraean traitors to Corinth and a lesson for the new Corinthian foundation on Ithaca-Leucas which Corinth was developing as a compensating interest,[101] is moreover akin to the malediction of Urshanabi and Charon for having taken Gilgamesh and Heracles respectively across the waters of death. Each is a way of suggesting that the journey cannot be repeated. Homer seems thus to have treated the entire wanderings of Odysseus as a journey in unchartered waters. If there ever was an Odysseus-in-Thesprotia story, Scherie might have been an invention by the poet which has been further enriched with the description of a Terrestrial Paradise[102] and the story of Nausicaa's broken romance.[103] If Calypso can give Odysseus a raft and Leucothea a magic veil to take him to Scherie,[104] why not a ship and magic aid to get him home? In any event, the fact that the prophetic consultation is narrated in the cover-story strongly supports the findings in the first part of this chapter that the *Nekyia* belongs to the original conception of the *Odyssey*.

[101] On *Od.* 13. 146—183 see E Mireaux, *Les Poèmes Homériques,* I. 96—98, who assumes for this thesis that Scherie is Corcyra (an ancient identification defended at length by A. Shewan, *Homeric Essays*, 268—292) and that Ithaca, after Dörpfeld, is Leucas (arguments for and against are assembled by Shewan, *op. cit.* 1—102).

[102] *Od.* 7.114—132. Cf. A. Shewan, *Homeric Essays*, 264—266.

[103] For the folklore adaptation of Nausicaa's romance see W. J. Woodhouse, *The Composition of Homer's Odyssey*, 54—56. The theme resembles the Egyptian tale of Sinuhe the Shipwrecked Sailor (on which see C. H. Gordon, *Before the Bible*, 102ff., 111) with further parallels collected by A. Shewan, *Homeric Essays*, 244f.

[104] *Od.* 5.333ff.

3. *The Nekyia as Catabasis*

It has been argued above that necromantic and catabatic elements are inextricably intertwined in the *Nekyia*. This assumption is not shared by the scholiast and his followers to whom lines 568—627 appear to be an interpolated passage within a *nekyomanteia*.[105] It is necessary therefore to examine further the catabatic significance of Odysseus' journey described in the *Nekyia*.

The picture we gather from the trench-scene is that Erebos is below ground — for the souls come up out of Erebos, *ὑπὲξ 'Ερεβέυς* — and Odysseus is sitting in the upperworld at the edge of the *bothros*. The scene is well represented in art,[106] though Odysseus in Polygnotus' painting of the *Nekyia* is depicted crouching over the pit upon his knees (*ὀκλάζοντα ἐπὶ τοῖς ποσίν*).[107] This ritual, which resembles a necromantic séance, is perhaps derived from a ghost-cult. But the belief that the *Nekyia* is a *νεκυομαντεία* and not a *κατάβασις* is, to my mind, mistaken. We have already described how Odysseus had first to cross Ocean to Persephone's groves, where the rivers Pyriphlegethon and Cocytus flow into Acheron. Although Odysseus in Book Eleven is not said to have reached the "halls of Hades and Persephone" in the literal sense, the full significance of this journey needs to be shown. To this end Anticleia's greeting of her son is revealing:

> *Τέκνον ἐμόν, πῶς ἦλθες ὑπὸ ζόφον ἠερόεντα*
> *ζωὸς ἐών; χαλεπὸν δὲ τάδε ζωοῖσιν ὁρᾶσθαι.*
> *μέσσῳ γὰρ μεγάλοι ποταμοὶ καὶ δεινὰ ῥέεθρα,*
> *'Ωκεανὸς μὲν πρῶτα, τὸν οὔ πως ἔστι περῆσαι*
> *πεζὸν ἐόντ', ἢν μή τις ἔχῃ εὐεργέα νῆα.*
>
> (*Od.* 11.155—9)

"Hard it is", she says in effect, "for the living to cross Ocean and the great rivers and dread streams that are between and to behold these

[105] See p. 53 above.

[106] Particularly noteworthy is the famous Attic pelike dated *c.*440 B.C.,on which see L. D. Caskey, "Odysseus and Elpenor on a Pelike in Boston", *A.J.A.* 38(1934) 399f. with plates. For related representations see J. E. Harrison, *Myths of the Odyssey* (London 1882), 93—145.

[107] Paus. 10. 29.8.

regions of darkness".[108] The "darkness" in the phrase *ζόφον ἠερόεντα* perhaps denotes the western darkness rather than the darkness of Erebos, for Odysseus is not below the earth for his conversation with his mother. Nevertheless Anticleia greets her son as though he were already come to the Land of the Dead. And inasmuch as Odysseus interviews his mother's ghost and the ghosts of the other dead in what may be called their own country in the far off west, the scene in the *Nekyia* is distinguishable from regular necromantic evocations of the dead in the land of the living such as Periander's consultation of Melissa at the Thesprotian oracle of the dead. In this sense Lobeck's denial of necromancy altogether to the Homeric poem[109] is justified.

The surprise element in Anticleia's greeting is also worth noticing: "My child, how did you manage to come here, being still alive?" Much the same question had already been asked of Elpenor by Odysseus when he observed his comrade's ghost in Hades. "How did you manage to come here, Elpenor?", he asked. "You got here quicker on foot than I in my black ship":

> *Ἐλπῆνορ, πῶς ἦλθες ὑπὸ ζόφον ἠερόεντα;*
> *ἔφθης πεζὸς ἰὼν ἢ ἐγὼ σὺν νηῒ μελαίνῃ.*
>
> (*Od.* 11.57f.)

Taken literally these words have a comic effect and might have been the object of Aristophanes' parody in the *Frogs* in the scene where Xanthias, Dionysus' slave, ran around the lake of Acheron instead of being ferried across like Dionysus.[110] We can see in the *Frogs*, moreover, that there are two parts to the mechanism of reaching the Underworld. Dionysus, who learnt the way below from Heracles, must first cross the lake of Acheron before he can find Pluto's gate.[111] By making Charon call out "Who's for the Cerberians?" at line 187, as Dionysus is about to be ferried across the Acherousian lake, Aristophanes undoubtedly serves to make another link with Heracles'

[108] Lines 157—159 are obelized, but without good reason. See L. G. Pocock, *Odyssean Essays*, 70f.

[109] C. A. Lobeck, *Aglaophamus* (1829, Darmstadt 1968), 316; accepted by E. Rohde, *Psyche*[8], 37.

[110] Aristoph. *Frogs*. 191 cf. 136.

[111] *Ibid.* 161ff., 431ff.

Descent to fetch Cerberus — and these Cerberians, like the later Tartars of Tartarus, might even have seemed to a seventh century audience far more frightening than any three-headed Cerberus. But the parody seems to reflect also the stages of Odysseus' journey in the *Nekyia* since these Cerberians evidently correspond to the Cimmerians whom Odysseus is supposed to have met on the far shore of Ocean. Indeed among the variants for the Cimmerians at *Odyssey* 11.14 are the *Κερβερίων* viz. "Cerberians" read by Crates and *Κερβερέων* by Aristarchus.[112] Thus with a little help from Aristophanes, the force of Anticleia's earlier question becomes clearer. She thinks that Odysseus has crossed both Ocean and the dread rivers between. Her surprise at how Odysseus managed to cross *being still alive* suggests that she regards Ocean and these rivers as a frontier between the living and the Land of the Dead. The conflation between Ocean and the Waters of Death has already been traced in the *Epic of Gilgamesh.* For all imaginative purposes the *Nekyia*, too, describes Odysseus as having gone on a Journey of the Dead.

But still Odysseus is not yet below ground. It has been thought that the change of formula from "then up came the ghost of...", as each ghost approaches the pit, to "next I saw (the ghost of)..." itself marks the transition from waiting above ground to wandering about in the world below.[113] However there is nothing in the formula to suggest this, for we are expressly told that the Women whom Odysseus saw came to him — "for grim Persephone sent them forth" (*Od.* 11.226). There is no reason in fact to suppose that Odysseus is below the earth until immediately after his meeting with Achilles, when he seems, if not to be below ground already, at least to be peering through the front door into the interior of the Underworld. "The soul of swift Achilles", says Odysseus, "went off with long strides across the asphodel meadow, rejoicing in that I said his son was illustrious" (*Od.* 11.538—540). And while Odysseus thus stares into the underground habitation of the ghosts and gazes after Achilles, the ghost of Ajax appears. For a while it looked resentfully at Odysseus, who implored forgiveness for

[112] These are to be added to the list of variants already mentioned on pp. 60f. and 65 above. Cf. S. Eitrem, *R. E.* 11.283 s.v. "Kerberos".

[113] W. F. Jackson Knight, *Vergil: Epic and Anthropology*, 163.

the wrong he had inflicted in the world above. But the unforgiving ghost stood apart and then without a word made off to join the other ghosts in Erebos. Immediately afterwards, from Minos onwards up to line 627, we find Odysseus deep within the interior of the Underworld. We are, then, to assume perhaps that at 563 Odysseus followed Ajax into the Underworld.[114] At any rate the gradual yielding of the evocation to the descent may explain why the anomalous blood-motif was fading out. There is, finally, no evidence that Odysseus was walking around the Underworld rather than simply looking around. The whole scene could have been taken from tapestry.

That Odysseus made a Journey of the Dead is borne out by the rest of the *Odyssey*. "What hardihood", says Circe, "to have descended into the house of Hades alive. You will be twice dead when other men die but once" (*Od.* 12.21—22; cf. 10.490). Equally significant is Odysseus' own account to Penelope of his experience "on the day when I descended into the house of Hades":

ἤματι τῷ ὅτε δὴ κατέβην δόμον ''Αϊδος εἴσω.

(*Od.* 23.252)

Circe's remark shows that Odysseus, as a result of his experience, will be unlike other men. In heroic mythology a *catabasis* may happen once in a lifetime at the most. This further distinguishes the catabatic journey from a necromantic consultation.

Finally the *catabasis* may be associated with an attractive conjecture, that Homer's description of the events on Circe's isle is itself a rationalized account of an initiation ceremony with Hermes as guide. Mireaux regards the sacrifice, potent drinks, turning of men into pigs, and union with Circe as evidence of a "véritable rituel, celui d'une cérémonie très semblable sans doute à un épisode des grands mystères, lesquels se célébraient à Eleusis, avant les semailles, au début de l'automne".[115] And might not the eager prancing of Circe's tame wolves

[114] M. van der Valk, *Beiträge zur Nekyia* (Kok, Kampen 1935), 118—121.

[115] E. Mireaux, *Les Poèmes Homériques*, 1.243—251 esp. 247. *A propos* of the passage quoted in chapter I n. 43 above Circe has also been compared to the Babylonian Ishtar, who changed her lovers into animals. D. L. Page, *Folktales in Homer's Odyssey*, 60 remarks: "this point of resemblance between the *Odyssey* and the *Epic of Gilgamesh* is perhaps not fortuitous. Babylonian Ishtar may well be

and mountain lions correspond to Hesiod's Cerberus, who fawns but permits no visitor to escape?[116] Moreover Mireaux points out that the initiation of second degree at Eleusis which includes a "descente symbolique au pays des morts" takes place one year after that of the first degree, and that by a striking coincidence Odysseus' visit to Hades took place one year after the first meeting with Circe.[117] According to this interpretation Circe is both the goddess in the theogamy and the hierophant who prescribes the rituals for Odysseus' Journey of the Dead. Circe and Teiresias are accordingly distinguishable from each other as hierophant and prophet respectively. Teiresias is the prophet of destiny in this world and not, with the reservation noted earlier, a guide through the lower world. In the next chapter we shall turn from Odysseus to consider Heracles' Descent into the Underworld and his initiation into the Eleusinian Mysteries.

the prototype of Homeric Circe." Circe's ability to transform humans into pigs may be a special instance of her bewitching powers which have been adapted to fit the ritual.

[116] See pp. 86f. below. This likewise suggests the adaptation of an earlier, more general story (see previous n.).

[117] E. Mireaux, *Les Poèmes Homériques*, 1.249f.

CHAPTER III

HERACLES, CERBERUS, AND ELEUSIS

No fullscale epic survives, as it does for Gilgamesh and Odysseus, celebrating the Descents of Heracles or Theseus or Orpheus into the Underworld.[1] Nevertheless the catabatic journeys of all three have made a lasting impact on Vergil's *Aeneid* and on world literature at large. The early catabatic exploits of these and other catabatic figures will be considered in this and the following two chapters. In this chapter we begin with Heracles.

Early authors portray Heracles' adventures as a rising crescendo of heroic achievement. In some of them Heracles may be thought of as having sought for immortality in a disguised form. We shall select Heracles' Descent to fetch Cerberus, the Hell-hound who guards the entrance to the lower world, to illustrate this point and to show how this is but one manifestation of a common theme which assumes many forms. The changes as Heracles sheds his archaic violence and becomes a more spiritualized hero will also be considered.

Heracles' descent into the House of Hades dates from high antiquity. Cerberus is known by name to Hesiod (*Theogony* 311), but Hesiod does not say that Heracles went to fetch him. Homer, although he nowhere names the dog, twice refers to Heracles' descent to fetch him, once (*Il.* 8.357—369) with Athene as guide and once (*Od.* 11.620f.) with Athene and Hermes as guides. The descent must also have formed the theme of Stesichorus' poem *Cerberus*, but this early work is unfortunately known only from a brief notice by Pollux.[2]

[1] Our knowledge of epic *catabaseis* generally is extremely fragmentary; see Ganschinietz s.v. "Katabasis", *R.E.* (1919) 10. esp. 2401—2, supplemented for specific descents in various places below.

[2] Pollux *Onom.* 10.152: *ἀρύβαλλος δὲ ἐπὶ τοῦ συσπάστου βαλαντίου... ἐν τῷ Στησιχόρου Κερβέρῳ.* The interpretation urged by J. Vürtheim, *Stesichorus' Fragmente und Biographie* (Leiden 1919), 21—3 that the "wallet" implies a comic

Further fragments of the Cerberus-descent will be mentioned presently in this chapter.

Chief among the exploits to be considered with Heracles' descent to capture Cerberus is his wounding of Hades. Homer, without giving the occasion, says that Heracles "smote him in Pylos", or as is sometimes preferred, "in the Gate[3] among the dead, giving him over to pains", *ἐν Πύλῳ ἐν νεκύεσσι βαλὼν ὀδύνῃσιν ἔδωκεν* (*Il.* 5.397). Professor Rose thinks it probable that in the original story Heracles "set forth to conquer death and win immortality, and succeeded in doing so. But to later ages this was too incredible, ... and reasons had to be found for such a prodigious venture".[4] Unfortunately we have little means of telling whether the view favoured by Rose is correct, that Heracles' quest for Cerberus is a later tale added to Heracles' combat with the God of Death in order to motivate it, or whether the battle with Hades was originally an integral part of Heracles' adventure to fetch Cerberus, or even Alcestis, as Leaf was inclined to believe.[5] What seems clear in either case is that Heracles' combat with Hades must have taken place at the Entrance to the Underworld[6] and

figure comparable to Aristophanes' Heracles (and perhaps to Sophocles' in the satyric *Ἡρακλῆς ἐπὶ Ταινάρῳ*) because Dionysus in Aristophanes' *Frogs* 111f. enumerates all that money can buy in the next world has been adequately met by C. M. Bowra, *Greek Lyric Poetry*² (Oxford 1961), 94.

[3] For the disputed meaning in antiquity of *ἐν Πύλῳ κτλ.* see Walter Leaf, *The Iliad* (London 1886—1888), *ad loc.* The scholiast who says *'Αρίσταρχος τὸν πύλον ἀκούει κατὰ μεταπλασμὸν ἀντὶ τοῦ τὴν πύλην* clearly understood that Aristarchus took *Πύλῳ* as a common noun meaning "gate"—and cf. the Homeric epithet of Hades *πυλάρτης* or Gate-warder, and the terminology (*Il.*5.646) of passing between the Gates of Hades to express death—but *πύλος* is not elsewhere used as a synonym for *πύλη* and furthermore Homer always uses the plural *πύλαι*. The scholiast's statement could of course rest on a misunderstanding of Aristarchus, who might have explained Pylos as the Gate of the Underworld and not as a synonym for it.

[4] H. J. Rose, *A Handbook of Greek Mythology*⁶ (London 1958), 215f.

[5] W. Leaf on *Iliad* 5. 393—400.

[6] Wilamowitz, *Die Ilias und Homer*² (Berlin 1920), 208 suggested that the name Pylos (see n. 3 above) might have originally designated the Entrance to the Underworld, then the western part of the Peloponnese, and finally a definite place whose exact location was not however agreed upon. M. P. Nilsson, *The Mycenaean Origin of Greek Mythology* (Cambridge 1932), 87—89 and 203—4 disputes this development but agrees that the myth was transferred from the Nether to the Upper World.

celebrates at least temporarily Heracles' victory over Death. Heracles seems also on another occasion to have raided Nestor's Pylos and to have wounded also other deities.[7] There was also instituted a cult of Hades at Elean Pylos[8] in gratitude for that god's assistance against Heracles' attack there, which lends some further support for the view that Pylos was somehow regarded as the Entrance to the Underworld.

For the version which Leaf had in mind of Heracles' wrestling with Hades in order to recover Alcestis, our earliest source is Euripides' *Alcestis*. The story is not referred to by Homer, but a mention of Alcestis in the Iliadic Catalogue (2.715) shows at least that he knew her family, as did Hesiod (fr. 37 ed. Merkelbach and West). Such scanty evidence does not prove, of course, that Heracles belongs to the oldest Alcestis-saga. Lesky holds that he does; Robert that he does not.[9] But since early evidence does not exist, it is obvious that either opinion may be maintained with equal confidence and with the absence of conflicting testimony.

No literary proof survives for Leaf's alternative suggestion either, namely that in the early form of the myth Heracles fought with Hades in order to capture Cerberus. That this was so is indicated by the scholiast on the Pylos passage of *Iliad* 5, who associates the wounding of Hades with Heracles' attempt to carry Cerberus off, and also

Legendary names are sometimes applied to newly founded places, for instance Avalon and Brazil to various places in mediaeval and modern times, Phasis and other infernal names to various topographies in antiquity.

[7] The raid is known to Homer *Il.*11.690f. For the wounding of various deities see Hes. *Shield* 359—367, Pindar *Ol.* 9.29—35, and the judicious discussion of these and other sources by J. H. Molyneux, "Two Problems concerning Heracles", *T.A.P.A.* 103(1972), 301ff. esp. 307ff. A non-Homeric story about Heracles' purification from bloodshed is told by the scholiast on the Iliadic passage, which may be an *αἴτιον* to explain the nature of the Lesser Mysteries, cf. Diod. 4.14.3 and shortly below.

[8] See Paus. 6.25.2—3. The fact that Nestor's Pylos has recently been located in Epano Eglianos, about six miles to the north of the Pylos in Messenia, does not invalidate the belief held by the inhabitants of Elean Pylos that Heracles attacked their Pylos.

[9] A. Lesky, "Alcestis, der Mythus und das Drama" (*Sitzungsberichte der... Akademie der Wissenschaften in Wien*, 1925), 54ff. Cf. Carl Robert, *Griechische Heldensage* (Berlin 1920), 1.32. For further discussion of the myth see also the following chapter.

apparently by the scholiast on line 46 of Pindar's ninth Olympian Ode, who further states that Pindar wrongly took Homer's phrase *ἐν Πύλῳ κτλ.* to mean Nestor's Pylos instead of its real meaning of "in the gate of Hades", (*ἐν πύλῃ τῇ τοῦ Ἅιδου*). But neither scholiast gives proof of having drawn on any very early evidence.

When we turn to art we find a number of revealing versions of Heracles' descent to fetch Cerberus. The oldest surviving representation of the theme appears on a Middle Corinthian kotyle from Argos datable about 590—580 B.C.[10] Hades turns away from behind his throne, and in front of it a goddess, identified as Persephone or more likely Athene,[11] stands preventing Heracles from attacking him. Behind Heracles are Hermes and a single-headed, prancing Cerberus. A single column indicates the palace of Hades. The margin between a threat and a fight with Hades is perhaps thin. But it is quite conceivable that the kotyle, with its representation of an intervening goddess, depicts a toning-down, possibly under Eleusinian influence,[12] of an earlier legend. It seems likely, therefore, that the combat with Hades was integral to a pre-Eleusinian descent to fetch Cerberus. Boardman in an important study of the Heracles iconography in the time of Peisistratos sees the earliest evidence for Heracles in a definite Eleusinian setting on a fragment in Reggio datable about 540 B.C. and attributes to Eleusinian influence the variant of the common myth in which Heracles offers no violence to Cerberus, who responds calmly to Heracles at the invitation of the underworld deities, especially

[10] H. G. Payne, *Necrocorinthia* (Oxford 1931), 127 fig. 45c and p. 130; F. Brommer, *Herakles. Die zwölf Taten des Helden in antiker Kunst und Literatur* (Köln 1953), pl. 24b. Scenes of Heracles' capture of Cerberus are listed in fuller detail by Brommer, *Vasenlisten zur griechischen Heldensagen*³ (Marburg 1973), 91ff. and cf. also esp. E. Kunze, *Archaische Schildbänder* (*Olympische Forschungen*, II. Berlin 1950), 110—112.

[11] The identification of the goddess as Persephone is accepted by C. M. Bowra, *Greek Lyric Poetry*, 92. In the first edition *loc. cit.* Bowra made so bold as to suggest that the artist followed Stesichorus whose Heracles may have attempted to defy Hades with his bow, but in the second edition p. 94 he dropped the suggestion. The goddess is now taken, however, to be Athene; see e.g. J. Boardman p. 7 in his article cited to n. 13 below.

[12] For the Eleusinianization of Heracles see shortly below, esp. p. 90 referring to Diodorus 4.25f., who says that after Heracles was initiated at Eleusis he succeeded in obtaining the dog through the intercession of Persephone herself.

Persephone. Instances of this variant, which exists side by side with the traditional version showing Heracles dragging the dog, already collared, in threatening manner, are found only on Athenian vases and from about 530 B.C. until the beginning of the fifth century.[13] But all this does not preclude the possibility as Rose saw it, that in a yet more primitive form of the myth Heracles wounded Hades before Cerberus provided the reason for the descent. There is no evidence on the other hand to support the contrary view advocated by Wilamowitz, that Heracles fought with Cerberus before he fought for Cerberus.[14]

Consideration may be given also at this point to a Labour, non-Homeric but known to Hesiod, which although not an underworld adventure provides in several ways an arresting parallel to both Heracles' quest for Cerberus and the fight with Hades. In this Labour Heracles fights with Geryon, his herdsman Eurytion, and the dog Orthus, on the Island of Erytheia ("Red Island") in the stream of Ocean in order to take possession of Geryon's cattle and bring them back to

[13] J. Boardman, "Herakles, Peisistratos and Eleusis", *J.H.S.* 95(1975), 1—12 and plates I—IV, esp. I*a* for the Eleusinian scene on the Reggio fragment 4001 from Locri (which also shows on the amphora's neck Heracles leading the dog, and Athene and Iolaos going before them, *A.B.V.* 147.6, illustrated in *Arch. classica* 4(1952), plates 30.1,31—32 and H. Metzger, *Recherches sur l'imagerie athénienne* (Paris 1965), plates 1.2,2); II*a*—*c*, III*a* and IV*a* (=respectively Moscow Hist. Mus. 70, *A.B.V.* 255. 8; Boston 28.46, *A.B.V.* 261. 38; Vatican 372, *A.B.V.* 368. 107; Amiens 3057.225.47a, *A.B.V.* 384.25; Purrmann Coll., Montagnola, J. D. Beazley, *Paralipomena* (Oxford 1971), 141.5) for the variant; I*b*—*c* (=Würzburg 308, *A.B.V.* 269.19; Boston 01.8025, *A.R.V.*[2] 163.6) for instances of the traditional version. Boardman also includes a version (III*b*=Leningrad, *A.B.V.* 364.59) combining the dragging of the dog with the pre-capture appeasement. The literary version of Euripides' *Hercules Furens* on pp. 91f. below perhaps corresponds to this representation and to similar scenes recently studied by C. Sourvinou-Inwood, "Three Related Cerberi", *Antike Kunst* 17(1974), 30—35.

[14] U. von Wilamowitz-Moellendorff, *Euripides Herakles* (Berlin 1889), 2.138 on line 612 says, "Die etappen der entwickelung sind (1) kampf mit dem Tode in gestalt des höllenhundes (2) kampf um den hund mit dem Tode in gestalt des titanen Menoitios oder des *ianitor orci*, der seit Kritias Aiakos heisst (3) kampf unter genehmigung der guten götter des jenseits (4) gnade dieser götter." The third and fourth stages are due to Eleusinian influence to be discussed shortly below. There is nothing, however, to show that the belief under (1) above was current in antiquity. See also below p. 87.

Greece.[15] No hint is given by Hesiod as to the geographical location of this fabulous island, despite J. Bérard's contrary claim that, even before the discovery of Iberian Tartessus by the Phocaeans, the Iberian location of Geryon's "Terre de Couchant" was implied by Hesiod at *Theogony* 287ff.[16] This setting in fact belongs to subsequent mythographers following the western expansion of the Greeks. That Heracles reached as far west as Tartessus is thus reported by Stesichorus in his *Geryoneïs* — and the Iberian localisation has prevailed in spite of Hecataeus' attempt to bring it back inside the Pillars of Ambracia on the western coast of Greece.[17] These rival claims attest to the popularity of the myth and nicely illustrate how the various traditions of the Greek colonisation movements have become incorporated in myth.[18]

Heracles, moreover, is said in the epic poem *Heraclea* by Peisander to have journeyed across the Ocean in the Sun's "cup", which he borrowed for the voyage.[19] The crossing is specifically linked with the Geryon myth in Stesichorus' *Geryoneïs*[20] and may have as its forerunner some such tale as Gilgamesh's Ocean-crossing in Urshanabi's boat, a journey which only the Sun-god had made before. We are not told, to be sure, that Heracles, like Gilgamesh, quested for immortality either in this Labour or when on another occassion he journeyed westward to harry the Garden of the Hesperides. But we may presume

[15] Hes. *Theog.* 287—294. The fullest account survives in Apollod. *Bibl.* 2.5.10 and for other versions see references in Frazer's note *ad loc.* Geryon is sometimes called Geryoneus or Geryones; Orthus is sometimes Orthrus.

[16] J. Bérard, *La Colonisation Grecque de L'Italie Méridionale et de la Sicile dans L'Antiquité*[2] (Paris 1957), 404.

[17] Stesichorus *ap.* Strabo 3.2.11, p. 148; Hecataeus *ap.* Arrian *Anab.* 2.16.5.

[18] J. H. Croon, *The Herdsman of the Dead* (Utrecht 1952), 35—66 has suggested that the Geryon-myth was originally the property of the Chalcidian traders at Cumae from whom their allies the Phocaeans of Massalia took it to Gades in the seventh century B.C. Stesichorus' location coincides with the Chalcidian colonisation-area, whereas Hecataeus represents the Corinthian tradition. For a parallel instance of the influence of discovery upon the location of a myth see above p. 35 and n. 51.

[19] *Ap.* Athenaeus 469—470 where the versions of Panyassis and Pherecydes are reported also.

[20] *Ibid.* 871D. For Stesichorus' version of the myth see now D. L. Page, "Stesichorus: The Geryoneïs", *J.H.S.* 93(1973), 138—154.

that the Golden Apples which he plucked from the dragon-guarded tree at the world's end are the talismans of immortality taken from the Tree of Life in that Garden of Paradise.[21] It has likewise been supposed by analogy that behind the theft of kine in the Geryon myth lies a true Harrowing of Hell.[22] This last supposition requires to be modified, but modified as follows it may be accepted.

Geryon's island, as we have affirmed, is not an Underworld. But belief in a World of Souls across Ocean has already been mentioned in the chapters on Gilgamesh and Odysseus.[23] The island may, therefore, be a mythical variant for the Underworld which Heracles visited on his descent to fetch Cerberus. It is significant in this context that Geryon's dog Orthus is related to Hades' Hell-hound Cerberus;[24] that Geryon himself has features in common with Cerberus;[25] and that Vergil even locates Geryon or his shade at the entrance to the Underworld.[26] This does not prove, as Nilsson warns,[27] that Geryon is actually a figure of the Underworld and his dog Orthus identical with Cerberus. For Cerberus and Geryon may have been two versions of a "conflict with monsters" theme, in which the one adversary may have developed into an underworld figure while the other simply

[21] This myth is believed to be of Minoan origin; see M. P. Nilsson, *The Minoan-Mycenaean Religion*², 627f. How the apples, which belonged originally to Hera, came to be planted in the Garden of the Hesperides is explained by A. B. Cook, *Zeus*, 2.1020f. and 3.1064.

[22] G. Weicker, *R.E.* 7.1290 s.v. "Geryoneus". In J. H. Croon's, *The Herdsman of the Dead*, 47, 67—74, Geryon is said to have been the "Herdsman of the Dead" and Admetus of Pherae is thought to have been a parallel figure in origin. This is rightly repudiated by H. J. Rose, *A Handbook of Greek Mythology*, 160 n. 14.

[23] We may recall especially in this context the conflation of the Underworld and the World of the Dead beyond Ocean in the name Cerberians as used by Aristophanes; see pp. 75f. above.

[24] Hes. *Theog.* 308—311.

[25] Geryon is three-headed (Hes. *Theog.* 287) or three-bodied (Verg. *Aen.* 6. 289); Cerberus, though he is fifty-headed in Hes. *Theog.* 312, is three-headed in the canonical form represented by Verg. *Aen.* 6. 417—421. Moreover if Cerberus can be connected with Sanskrit Çarvari (on which see S. Eitrem, *R.E.* 11.283 s.v. "Kerberos"), so perhaps can Ger-y-oneus. But on this see E. Rohde, *Psyche*⁸, chap. 7 n. 6.

[26] *Aen.* 6. 286—289.

[27] *The Mycenaean Origin of Greek Mythology*, 215.

resembles one. Moreover it is certain that in a pastoral tradition, especially in Mycenaean times when cattle were a royal attribute and *pecunia* itself, cattle-raiding such as we find in the Geryon-myth must have been a common occupation. It is therefore likely that the Geryon-myth as such was not originally a Harrowing of Hell but rather a cattle-raid which has been fitted into a catabatic framework.[28] Heracles' Journey to the Far West to wrest the cattle from Geryon thus appears as a mythical variant of his *catabasis* to overcome Hades and steal Cerberus from the Underworld. The Garden of the Hesperides is not a Land of the Dead, but by analogy and association with a western Hades the Greeks also frequently located their Paradise in the West. All three adventures comprising Cerberus, Geryon, and the Apples of the Hesperides thus appear as variants of the one theme, the conquest of Death.[29]

A remarkable conflation between the myths of Geryon and Cerberus with a further parallel to Heracles' fight with Hades occurs in a curious underworld encounter between Heracles and Menoites told by Apollodorus (*Bibl.* 2.5.12). Menoites in Stesichorus' *Geryoneïs* seems to pasture the cattle on Erytheia, but in Apollodorus' version of Heracles' descent to fetch Cerberus he is the guardian of Hades' kine in the Underworld[30], and he challenged Heracles to wrestle. Heracles promptly seized him and cracked some of his ribs before Persephone interceded. Though Heracles killed one of the kine, he took none back with him on this occassion, presumably because he had ostensibly come for Cerberus.

Heracles' descent to fetch Cerberus has so far been viewed as a primitive quest for immortality in a disguised form which at one stage seems to have involved a fight with Hades. A peculiar aspect of this feat is revealed in the description of the dog by Hesiod, who says that he welcomes visitors to the Underworld but devours whosoever

[28] Cf. Croon in n. 22 above. Ghost-driving (note the herdsmanlike manner in which Hades drives the souls in Pind. *Ol.* 9. 33—35) is probably an allegorization to cattle-driving rather than vice-versa.

[29] Cf. H. J. Rose, *A Handbook of Greek Mythology*, 214ff.

[30] Hades' underworld cattle are most odd. However Margaret Murray quotes a story of "elf-bulls" kept under a fairy hill in *The God of the Witches* (London 1933), 52, so they are not entirely unparalleled.

tries to leave.[31] It has accordingly been suggested that Cerberus is the embodiment of the all-devouring Empire of Death, Hell being frequently depicted in Near Eastern literature and Medieval art as a monster that swallows the dead;[32] but the Hesiodic passage is no evidence that such a belief was current with regard to Cerberus in Classical antiquity.

Rose thought of Cerberus in like terms, as the savage "devourer of the dead" not unfamiliar in Pacific mythology; [33] but if, as is likely, Rose had in mind the Pacific female guardian of the Underworld Temes-Savsap, who devours any ghost that is unable to complete the path of the labyrinth which she has in part drawn before the entrance to the Abode of the Dead,[34] the parallel is inexact. For the Pacific ghost-devourer, like the Egyptian dog depicted in the vignettes of the Egyptian *Book of the Dead,*[35] devours the unjustified dead before or as they enter the Underworld whereas Cerberus admits all and devours only those who attempt to leave. The Cerberus who inspires terror in those who enter Hades is a conception of later ages.[36]

The Hesiodic description of the Hell-dog as the devourer of all who try to leave the Underworld gives grounds for wondering whether his removal from the Underworld might not once have had cult significance and celebrated the release of ghosts as was wont to happen on the annual All Souls' Day of the Athenian Anthesteria. Presumably when the dog was restored, the ghosts were chased back again. Heracles' cult-connections with Athens itself are not very strong, but a cult elsewhere might have connected the two themes of Ghost's Holiday and Removing the Dog.[37] Admittedly the tradition that

31 Hes. *Theog.* 769—773; at 311 Cerberus is said to eat raw flesh.

32 For instances of both see chap. 1 nn. 52—57.

33 H. J. Rose, *A Handbook of Greek Mythology*, 31, where attention is drawn also to the death-devourer Eurynomos in Polygnotus' famous picture of the Underworld described by Paus. 10.28.7.

34 See W. F. Jackson Knight, *Vergil: Epic and Anthropology* 150—152.

35 See, for instance, the Judgement Scene reproduced by E. A. Wallis Budge, *The Book of the Dead* (London 1898), frontispiece.

36 The development is documented in E. Rohde, *Psyche*[8], chap. 7 n. 6.

37 Heracles fetches up Cerberus at Taenarum in Laconia (Soph. fr. 233 ed. Pearson, *The Fragments of Sophocles*, 1.167f.; Eur. *Her. Fur.* 23—5; Sen. *Her. Fur.* 807ff.; Apollod. 2.5.12; cf. Stat. *Theb.* 2.32f; Strabo 8.5.1, p. 363), or at the

Heracles is a Hell-Harrower has left few traces in the canonical story, but it would explain why Heracles is qualified to resurrect Alcestis. At all events Heracles' fight with Cerberus can be said at least to have despoiled the efficacy of Hades' realm, while his battle with Hades lays emphasis directly on the wounding of Death.

Many of Heracles' other labours and *parerga* are perhaps crude simplifications of the same type of prodigious venture. Heracles' quests for Big Game in the west or at Hades-Entrances are further variations of the combat theme. Whatever significance these tasks might once have had is lost and in their present form they are simply marvellous exploits in which the marvellous is emphasized with the use of folktales to increase Heracles' heroic stature. That Heracles is a death-defying figure is however remembered by Diodorus, who says that at the end the gods decided to reward Heracles for his labours with immortality.[38] Here Heracles' victory over Death is replaced by his apotheosis.

So far Heracles has been studied as a hero hallmarked by brute force, *βίη Ἡρακλείη*. But he is subsequently transformed into a more spiritual hero, the marks of which appear in other versions of his descent to fetch Cerberus. Although Heracles' descent is not celebrated in any surviving epic, as we have already remarked, there exists a number of remarkable similarities between certain passages in Bacchylides, Aristophanes, Vergil, and Apollodorus from which Eduard Norden supposed that there must once have existed an early epic poem of the Descent of Heracles, to which he gave the name *Ἡρακλέους κατάβασις*. This epic, Norden argues, was drawn upon either directly or indirectly by the authors just named.[39] The suppo-

Acherusian Chersonese near Heraclea Pontica on the Black Sea (Xen. *Anab.* 6.2.2; P. Mela 1.103), or at Troezen (Paus. 2.31.2; Apollod. 2.5.12), or at Mount Laphystius in Boeotia (Paus. 9.34.5), or at Hermione in Argos (Paus. 2.35.10; cf. Eur. *Her. Fur.* 615). Pausanias' suggestion that the sanctuary of Hades at Elean Pylos was opened yearly because men die only once (6.25.2) seems like a wild guess but whether there was an All Souls' Day cannot be ascertained.

[38] Diod. 4.10.7: *τοῖς θεοῖς δέδοκται... καὶ τοῦτο* (i.e. the task of all twelve labours) *πράξαντα τεύξεσθαι τῆς ἀθανασίας*. Cf. Hom. *Od.* 11.602—4.

[39] The catabatic features which Norden traces in these authors and, with less persuasion, in Sophocles are discussed in various places indicated in note 2 on page 5 of his commentary *P. Vergilius Maro: Aeneis Buch VI*³. The tenacity with

sition that Vergil was influenced by this epic furthermore enabled Norden to solve certain apparent inconsistencies in the *Αἰνείου κατάβασις* which had puzzled Servius and other ancient scholiasts commenting on the Descent of Aeneas into the Underworld. Norden's discoveries are therefore particularly relevant to our purpose. And quite recently Norden's claims have received fresh confirmation from an unexpected source.

A newly discovered fragment of lyric poetry preserved in *P. Oxy.* 2622 and commented on by *P.S.I.* 1391 tells of Heracles' initiation at Eleusis by Eumolpus and of his encounter with Meleager in the Underworld. The theme of Heracles' underworld encounter with Meleager during his quest for Cerberus was treated also in Bacchylides' fifth *Epinician* 50ff., where Heracles asks Meleager if he has a surviving unwedded sister whom he could make his bride. The same subject is narrated also by the scholiast on Homer *Iliad* 21.194, except that Meleager here at his own suggestion requests Heracles to marry his sister Deianeira; and after returning to the Upperworld Heracles hastens to Aetolia, where he successfully rescues Deianeira from the River Achelous, who was wooing her.[40] Since the scholiast on the Homeric passage attributes the story to Pindar, Wilamowitz believed it to have been told in a Pindaric dithyramb which was composed in dactylo-epitrite entitled K]*ạτ̣ά̣[βασις] Ἡρακλέ̣ο̣υ̣[ς] ἢ Κέρβερος*.[41] And it now seems reasonable to agree with the first editor of *P. Oxy.* 2622[42] that the story occurred in this poem too, which being also composed in dactylo-epitrite may be part of the same dithyramb or is perhaps a

which certain catabatic motifs adhered together during their transmission in these versions is shown further in my "Two Virgilian Similes and the *ʽΗΡΑΚΛΕΟΥΣ ΚΑΤΑΒΑΣΙΣ*", *Phoenix* 24(1970), 244—55. For further discussion on the Descent of Heracles in connection with Aeneas' descent see below pp. 212ff.

[40] Schol. on Hom. *Il.* 21.194=Pindar fr. 70b Snell³ (1964). Heracles often wrestles with shape-shifting water-gods as in this myth, cf. also chap. 4 n. 6 below. In turn, Deianeira has a marked penchant for being assaulted, wooed, and threatened by such river-deities.

[41] *P. Oxy.* 1604=Pindar fr. 61 Bowra=70b Snell³, on which see Wilamowitz, *Pindaros* (Berlin 1922), 314 n. 1 and 341—348. Turyn, however, refers the Homeric scholion to the paean which mentions Achelous, fr. 71 Turyn=233 Bowra=70+249b Snell³.

[42] E. Lobel, *Oxyrhynchus Papyri* 32 (London 1967), 63—65.

separate poem. Finally with brilliant insight Professor Hugh Lloyd-Jones completes the picture by making it highly probable on several counts that Pindar, almost certainly the author of the present fragment, drew on the same *῾Ηρακλέους κατάβασις* as did Bacchylides, Aristophanes, Vergil, and Apollodorus.[43] The composite nature of Heracles' Eleusinian *catabasis* has still not been sufficiently analysed, but discussion of this and related matters will be postponed until pp. 218ff. below, at which point the influence of the Heracles descent on the underworld journey of Aeneas will be taken up. Suffice it to notice here the development in the character of Heracles himself.

Even before the publication of *P. Oxy.* 2622 and the commentary upon it, Heracles was known to have been initiated at Eleusis or at the Lesser Mysteries at Agrae. In the fullest account of this by Apollodorus, whose *Bibliotheca* 2.5.12ff. seems to combine two distinct but not inherently contradictory traditions, Heracles is said to have come to Eleusis wishing to be initiated, but this was not lawful for "foreigners" and he was, moreover, impure from the blood shed during his slaying of the Centaurs. He was therefore adopted by an Athenian called Pilius and purified by Eumolpus before being initiated (so Plutarch, *Theseus*, 33.2 and the scholiast on *Iliad* 8.368). And his initiation by Eumolpus took place immediately before his descent to fetch Cerberus. Heracles' purification, adoption, and initiation are the chief elements of this story, and these elements are referred to separately by other authors. Diodorus says at 4.14.3 that Demeter founded the Lesser Mysteries in Athens for the very purpose of purifying Heracles from the blood of the Centaurs, and at 4.25f. that he was initiated by Musaios, not Eumolpus, at Eleusis in preparation for the labour; the scholiast on Aristophanes, *Plutus* 845, reports that the Lesser Mysteries were founded so that Heracles could become an adopted Athenian and then be initiated; the pseudo-Platonic *Axiochus* seems to hint simply at his initiation both at the Lesser Mysteries and at Eleusis before making the descent into the lower world.[44] But the

[43] Hugh Lloyd-Jones, "Heracles at Eleusis: P. Oxy. 2622 and P.S.I. 1391", *Maia* n.s. 19(1967), 206—209.

[44] 371E, *καὶ τοὺς περὶ ῾Ηρακλέα τε καὶ Διόνυσον κατιόντας εἰς ῞Αιδου πρότερον λόγος ἐνθάδε μυηθῆναι, καὶ τὸ θάρσος τῆς ἐκεῖσε πορείας παρὰ τῆς ᾽Ελευσινίας ἐναύσασθαι.* The *ἐνθάδε* seems to refer to the Lesser Mysteries at Athens. For Hera-

discovery of the recent fragment, with a suggestion that he was the first "foreigner" to be initiated at Eleusis and that the person who initiated him was as in the Apollodoran narrative Eumolpus, places a far greater emphasis on Heracles' connection with the Eleusinian Mysteries than hitherto. In fact the "Eleusinianized" Heracles — and here we are anticipating certain conclusions about the nature of the fragment — represents a significant modification of the old defiant Heracles in a variety of ways.

As an initiate Heracles descends less by brute force than by virtue of possessing the right credentials. An official guide is added under Eleusinian influence. And instead of barging his way through the Underworld in a lawless manner Heracles receives an initiate's welcome from Persephone, who, according to Diodorus 4.26, intervenes on his behalf in order that he might take Cerberus. The frequent appearance of both Hermes and Persephone and the changes in style of the Cerberus-scenes on the vases described above (pp. 82f.) also indicates Eleusinian influence. Wilamowitz, indeed, even before the discovery of either Bacchylides' fifth *Epinician* or the new Heracles *catabasis*, in each of which Persephone is mentioned, connected the Diodorus passage with Heracles' Eleusinian initiation and further associated with it the Euripidean passage of the *Hercules Furens* in which Amphitryon asks Heracles if he had captured the dog Cerberus by a fight, or had received it as the goddess' gift.[45] If Persephone's intercession on Heracles' behalf is an Eleusinian innovation, as now seems highly probable, and the hand to hand fight with Hades was the regular pre-Eleusinian version, Amphitryon's question in effect elicits a parody on the two versions. By making Heracles answer that he obtained the dog "by a fight — but I had the luck to see the *orgia*

cles as initiate see also Lycophr. 1328 and Tzetz, *Chil.* 2. 394. Lloyd-Jones, *Maia* 19(1967) 212 n. 8 refers also to *P.R.I.M.* 20. col. 1. 18f. (1996 Pack²), a speech apparently spoken by Heracles when refused initiation.

[45] U. von Wilamowitz-Moellendorff, *Eur. Herakles*², 2. 138 on *H.F.* line 612, and cf. lines 610—613.

'Αμφ.: ἦλθες γὰρ ὄντως δώματ' εἰς "Αιδου, τέκνον;
'Ηρ.: καὶ θῆρά γ' ἐς φῶς τὸν τρίκρανον ἤγαγον.
'Αμφ.: μάχῃ κρατήσας ἢ θεᾶς δωρήμασιν;
'Ηρ.: μάχῃ· τὰ μυστῶν δ' ὄργι' εὐτύχησ' ἰδών.

of the initiates", Euripides gives the further impression that his hero had the best of both worlds. He had the privilege of an initiate with the enjoyment of a good fight as well.

After the Eleusinianization of Heracles in the sixth century, it was not a very great step for him then to be moralised. And in the fifth century the sophist Prodicus did just this. Heracles was presented with the choice between the rigours of virtue or the temptations of pleasure. Heracles chose the former and his transition from a figure of lawless *vis* into one of virtue was complete. The story is preserved by Xenophon,[46] but despite the later treatment by the Stoics in which Heracles is a model for Stoic kingship and service to mankind,[47] this idea never caught on in the popular imagination.

It is noteworthy, too, that the Eleusinian catabatic pattern with which Heracles' descent is conflated represents in itself a fusion of disparate elements in that the pre-Greek Goddess of Death, Persephone, seems to have been identified with a disappearing and returning Maiden, Kore, who is the Daughter-goddess of the corn-Mother Demeter. The two are unified, but not completely, through the myth of Kore's abduction by the Lord of the Underworld, Aidoneus or Hades, whose bride she becomes.[48] According to the earliest version told in the Homeric *Hymn to Demeter* (398—400 and 445—447) Persephone spends one third of every year with Hades in the Underworld and two thirds with her mother Demeter above ground. According to a modern explanation suggested by Cornford and advocated

[46] Xen. *Mem.* 2.1.21—34; essentially confirmed by the schol. on Aristoph. *Clouds* 361.

[47] H. J. Rose, *A Handbook of Greek Mythology*, 205 is rather tough on the Stoic Heracles, who is a type of wise man in e.g. Seneca, *De constant. sap.* 2, and a benefactor to mankind *ib. De beneficiis* 1.13. For this and other significant adaptations of Heracles in various roles from Homer to the present day see further G. Karl Galinsky's excellent study *The Herakles Theme* (Oxford 1972).

[48] The evidence is collected and discussed afresh in a brilliant study by Günther Zuntz, *Persephone* (Oxford 1971), Part II, 70—178. On p. 77 Zuntz observes that the unification between Persephone and Kore was never complete: "The realm below could never really be without its queen, and she who returned to be with the Mother was the Maiden, the Daughter: this was *τὰ τῆς Κόρης μυστήρια*. No farmer prayed for corn to Persephone; no mourner thought of the dead as being with Kore".

by Nilsson, Persephone's descent represents the storage after harvest in the underground silos (*θησαυροί*) of the grain, which stays in Pluto's ("Wealth's") realm until the sowing. Since the Eleusinian Mysteries, so the argument goes, were celebrated in the month of Boedromion, i.e. September/October, the time of sowing in Athens, the vegetation deity Persephone-Kore must therefore be envisaged as being above ground during the eight months from the time of sowing until the corn is reaped in May and threshed in June and as below the earth during the other four months. It is further suggested that Theseus' name may be derived from *θησαυρός* meaning "One who puts the corn down" (cf. Latin *Conditor*), which would make Theseus virtually a death-figure.[49] (For the myths connecting Theseus with Persephone see pp. 129ff. below.) According to the *Hymn* (401ff.) itself, however, Kore's return is said to occur in spring when the earth begins to bloom, and her reappearance is closely followed by the growth of corn and other plants too (453ff. and 417ff.). Later antiquity accordingly refers Persephone's time of absence in Hades to winter, when the corn-seed is beneath the soil after the autumn-sowing, and on this interpretation her rape is envisaged as taking place in the autumn.[50] If this correctly represents the early significance of the Greek myth, it provides a contrast to the Near Eastern and Egyptian fertility pattern in which the deities were thought to disappear in summer, at the time when the seed-corn is stored for the following season or when the vegetation is parched by the summer-heat.

But if the Eleusinian descent is an agrarian rite it also has eschatological significance. For we are told that whosoever sees the mysteries

[49] See F. M. Cornford, "The *'Απαρχαί* and the Eleusinian Mysteries", in *Essays and Studies presented to Sir W. Ridgeway* (Cambridge 1913), 153ff. and M. P. Nilsson's expanded view in *A.R.W.* 32(1935), 105ff.; cf. *The Mycenaean Origin of Greek Mythology*, 171 n. 29, *Greek Popular Religion* (New York 1940), 50—52, and *Geschichte der griechischen Religion*, I³. 472ff. The chief support for this view seems to be Diodorus 5.4.6 saying that Kore's *Καταγωγή* at Syracuse was celebrated when the corn was ripe. But *Καταγωγή* here may refer either to her descent or to the "bringing-in" of the corn. For this and other "descents" of Kore see L. R. Farnell, *The Cults of the Greek States* (5 vols. Oxford 1896—1909), 3. 87—89 and *The Evolution of Religion* (London 1905), 34—36 (for Kore at Alexandria).

[50] References to this arrangement and variations are collected together in N. J. Richardson, *The Homeric Hymn to Demeter*, 284f.

is happy and that he who is uninitiated will not share in them after death.[51] Eschatological insight is thus imparted to the Eleusinian initiate in a ritual which promises new life. The double significance of the ritual is seen in the seed-corn which, it seems, was treated as a prototype of human immortality. Rubensohn long ago argued that this "spiritual twist" to the agrarian descent occurred at Eleusis itself, but this view has been rightly rejected as resting on very slender evidence indeed.[52] It is worth noting how the analogy of human immortality to the sowing of grain appears also in the Pauline doctrine of the resurrection of the body, and this in turn reflects Christ's parable of the necessity for the wheat-grains to die before they produce abundantly.[53] There is of course no suggestion of this analogy being indebted to the Eleusinian Mysteries. And an actual suggestion made by Pfister that the Gospels have been "Heracleanized" has been answered on every score by Rose.[54]

[51] Cf. the *Homeric Hymn to Demeter*, 480—483, *ὄλβιος ὃς τάδ' ὄπωπεν ἐπιχθονίων ἀνθρώπων· / ὃς δ' ἀτελὴς ἱερῶν, ὅς τ' ἄμμορος, οὔ ποθ' ὁμοίων / αἶσαν ἔχει φθίμενός περ ὑπὸ ζόφῳ εὐρώεντι*, which is the source of many similar passages, e.g. Pindar fr. 121 ed. Bowra, and Sophocles fr. 837 Pearson= 753 Nauck. See also N. J. Richardson's note *ad loc.*, pp. 310—314, on the wording and meaning of this formula and cf. further my pp. 218f. below.

[52] See L. R. Farnell, *The Cults of the Greek States*, 3.143f.

[53] I *Corinthians*, 15.35ff.; cf. *John*, 12.24.

[54] H. J. Rose, "Herakles and the Gospels", *H.T.R.* 31(1938), 113—141; an answer to F. Pfister, "Herakles und Christus", *A.R.W.* 34(1937), 42—60.

CHAPTER IV

ORPHEUS AND DIONYSUS

Orpheus is depicted in the Sixth Book of the *Aeneid* at lines 119—120 among those catabatic figures who made the journey to the World of the Dead before Aeneas. The story of Orpheus' Descent is told, moreover, in considerable detail already by Vergil in the Fourth Book of the *Georgics*. We have therefore for the study of Orpheus' Descent into the Underworld in the *Aeneid* something that is not available to us for other catabatic myths, namely Vergil's own version of the story. It is fitting that we begin with this version, and then re-examine the chief variants of the Orphic myth with a view to showing that it was Vergil's method of *mythopoeia* to borrow from a variety of sources and to alter and combine versions together, as opposed to the view that he merely versified an existing tradition.

The telling of Orpheus' Visit to Hades in the *Georgics* is touching, all the more so for its being narrated within the framework of the Descent of Aristaeus, elsewhere in antiquity the patron-deity of apiculture,[1] but here the mortal son of an immortal nymph Cyrene. He inexplicably lost his bees and so descends to his mother's underwater palace beneath the river Penëus in Thessaly, to complain to her of his misfortune. She, being at a loss to explain the cause of his calamity, refers him to the sea-god Proteus, who makes it known that the wrath of Orpheus is responsible for what has happened. Orpheus' wrath, Proteus tells him, was incurred by Aristaeus himself, when he brought about the death of Orpheus' wife, Eurydice. She received a fatal bite from a venemous snake while fleeing from Aristaeus' lustful embraces: "*dum te fugeret*" (457). In the hope of recovering his beloved from the World of the Dead Orpheus descended, through the cavern of Taenarum, to the very depths of Orcus. During the descent he charmed all with his lyre, and even persuaded Proserpine

[1] See Ap. Rhod. *Argon.* 4.1132ff., Diod. 4.81, and Ovid, *Ex Pont.* 4.2.9.

to release her, on condition that he did not look back until they reached the upperworld. But, alas, having almost succeeded in bringing his beloved back, he turned around to look upon her as she followed behind, and so lost her forever. Thereafter he mourned her loss for seven months until the Thracian Bacchants, piqued by his single-minded devotion, tore him to pieces. At this point in the story Proteus plunges into the sea without stopping to suggest how Aristaeus might recover his bees. But Cyrene, now that she is acquainted with Orpheus' wrath, knows what to do to expiate it. And forthwith the bees of her son are recreated.

The story of Aristaeus' descent, notable in its own right, is unknown before Vergil. It is an exquisite example of the type of concise narrative poem or "epyllion" developed by the Alexandrians, which Vergil seems to have created out of numerous motifs selected from Greek literature, especially Homer, and embellished with Alexandrian techniques. The nymphs in Cyrene's underwater cave, for example, are an elaboration from the list at *Iliad* 18.39ff. of those in Thetis', and the welcome given to Aristaeus is comparable to the scenes which Athene and Telemachus witness at *Odyssey* 1.144ff., and which Telemachus enjoys at *Odyssey* 4.39ff. Furthermore the appeal of Aristaeus to his mother Cyrene upon losing his bees evokes a reminiscence of how Achilles had twice appealed to his mother Thetis after losing first his girl Briseis at *Iliad* 1.348ff. and then his ward Patroclus at *Iliad* 18.35ff. But whereas Thetis on both occasions rises from the waves of Ocean to greet Achilles in the *Iliad*, Vergil makes Aristaeus actually descend beneath the river to his mother's home. It has been suggested that the idea for Aristaeus' descent may have come from Theseus' submarine descent to his mother Amphitrite in Neptune's underwater palace[2] — a version known both through art and Bacchylides.[3] This may well be an additional source of inspiration, but parallels for underwater descents exist in Homer too. Iris goes down to Thetis' submarine home at *Iliad* 24.83ff., and still better, Dionysus

[2] E. Norden, "Orpheus und Eurydice", *Sitz. Berl. Akad. d. Wissensch. Phil.-histor. Kl.* (1934), 638.

[3] *Odes* 12. xvi. For fuller discussion of the descent see pp. 142ff., and on the question whether Bacchylides was known in the Augustan age see chapter 7 n. 79 below.

descends into the sea to be met by Thetis after persecution by Lycurgus with the loss of all his Bacchanals (*Iliad* 6.135ff.).

Not only does the outline of Aristaeus' descent, moreover, ring with Homeric echoes reworked by Vergil in minute detail in the Hellenistic manner,[4] but the consultation by Aristaeus of the sea-god Proteus has been admirably adapted from the description of his capture and questioning by Menelaus at *Odyssey* 4.351—570. Robert Graves' objection that by dragging Proteus into the story from Egypt, when there was an oracle of Apollo at Tempe which Aristaeus could have consulted, Vergil is guilty of an "irresponsible use of the myth"[5] is purely captious. There seems to have been a tradition whereby information or immortality is obtained from shape-shifting sea-deities — Menelaus himself receives from the sea-god both information (as to the way home) and an oracular assurance of immortality.[6] Proteus is thus introduced aptly into this story, which ends appropriately enough with the recreation of Aristaeus' bees.

A special difficulty in the story has been detected in Cyrene's re-appearance after Proteus' narrative to tell Aristaeus how to atone. The conclusion frequently drawn from this is that if Cyrene is able to advise Aristaeus on how to do this, Proteus is, after all, otiose. Wilkinson, whose detailed analysis of the episode is conducted with masterly skill, defended Cyrene's re-emergence on the ground that it was "dictated by the [epyllion] form" of Hellenistic poetry.[7] But again Vergil seems to have looked towards Homer, modelling the

[4] Cf. further Brooks Otis, *Virgil: A Study in Civilized Poetry*[2] (Oxford 1966), 196ff., and L. P. Wilkinson, *The Georgics of Virgil* (Cambridge 1969),1 13—117, and esp. 213—222 for the Hellenistic embellishments.

[5] R. Graves, *The Gk. Myths*, 1.280.

[6] Ch. 2 n. 20. Similarly Heracles learns from Nereus the way to the Garden of the Hesperides, where grew the Golden Apples, talismans of immortality (Pherecydes *ap.* schol. Ap. Rhod. *Argon.* 4.1396, Apollod. *Bibl.* 2.5.11; cf. p.85 above). It is a cardinal part of Peleus' capture of the sea-goddess Thetis, even, that he will become the father of a kind of Messiah-figure. Jacob's wrestle with the strange adversary at the ford of Jabbok leading to a blessing and a change of name (*Genesis* 32.22—32, cf. *Hos.* 12.4) may perhaps belong to a similar class of myths. On the origin of the Greek sea-deities see the discussions noted in J. H. Croon, *The Herdsman of the Dead*, 58.

[7] L. P. Wilkinson, *The Georgics of Virgil*, 116.

framework of Aristaeus' descent this time upon that of Odysseus' Visit to Hades in Books 10—12 of the *Odyssey*. Circe, we recall, could tell Odysseus nothing without the clue furnished by Teiresias that his route homeward to Ithaca was to be by way of Thrinakie. Similarly Cyrene was unable to advise Aristaeus what to do until the wise old man Proteus supplied the clue to the cause of his misfortune. Only then could Cyrene tell him how to appease the wrath that had led to the loss of the bees. Her re-appearance is required, therefore, by the logic of the episode. And if the roles assigned to Proteus and Cyrene are in fact modelled upon those of Teiresias and Circe, the Homeric seer and hierophant respectively (see pp. 42ff. and 78 above), incidental support may also be lent to an attractive theory advanced by Scazzoso that the whole Aristaeus-episode ultimately reflects the Mystery Religions, in which Cyrene is the hierophantic guide.[8]

The question of whether Orpheus' descent into the lower world in quest of his wife Eurydice also reflects any Mystery Religion is harder to answer. For unlike Persephone's descent, which is central to the Eleusinian Mysteries, Orpheus' Visit to the Land of the Dead has no known relation to any Orphic Mysteries. Instructions to Orphics relating to their reception in the Hereafter are recorded as early as the fourth century B.C. on Gold Leaves discovered in graves in various parts of southern Italy and Crete.[9] But if the descent itself has any mystical significance, it is, with the exception of one late hint, concealed from us. I shall argue presently in the light of this hint that it is most probable that the descent in fact once had such significance. But the argument is complicated by the problem that we do not know for certain whether there was a *ἱερὸς γάμος* or "ritual marriage" in the Underworld, or even whether Orpheus failed (as

[8] P. Scazzoso, "Riflessi misterici nelle 'Georgiche' di Virgilio", *Paideia* 11(1956), 5—28.

[9] These have received a definitive new edition and interpretation by G. Zuntz, *Persephone*, 275ff. Furthermore the instructions on the Gold Leaves from Petelia, Pharsalos, and Eleutherna are thought (*ib*. 376—393) to be derived from a poem by Pythagoras giving the geography of the Underworld and incorporating the most ancient Mesopotamian motifs. For Pythagoras' descent see also E. Rohde, *Psyche*[8], 598—601 and A. B. Cook, *Zeus*, 2.933f.

in the Vergilian version above) or succeeded originally in bringing Eurydice back from the dead.

According to the Greek historian Diodorus of the first century B.C., Orpheus acted "similarly to Dionysus" (παραπλησίως τῷ Διονύσῳ, 4.25.4) when the latter is reported to have brought back Semele from the Underworld. It would appear from this that Diodorus knew of a version in which Orpheus likewise succeeded in recovering Eurydice. Some light, in fact, upon the theme of Orpheus' quest may be afforded by further consideration of Dionysus' descent to fetch his mother Semele, which in the existing evidence bears a closer relation to cult-practice than does Orpheus' descent. In other respects, the two descents have much in common. Both are clearly of a different stamp from the descents already considered of Odysseus and Heracles. Insofar as they show primarily the devotion by a man and god to his wife and mother respectively, they exemplify the development of the love-interest in the catabatic pattern. And Diodorus shows that their roles are almost interchangeable. Before investigating the problems of Orpheus explicitly, let us then assemble and interpret the versions of Dionysus' descent, and even try to reverse Diodorus' comparison to see whether there exists any version in which the god ever returns without Semele, as Orpheus in Vergil's *Georgics* returns without Eurydice, and then go on to consider what evidence there may be for believing that Dionysus, despite his being a vegetation-deity and despite the love-interest, ever acquired wisdom in the World Below.

In Hellenic myths Dionysus is frequently coupled (as just mentioned) with Semele, an earth-goddess with a Thraco-Phrygian name. In his original home it appears that he was united in the world below with a goddess known locally by such names as Bendis or Brimo.[10] That he is in such myths a "divinity of Nature renascent" is well documented; and a striking instance of his association particularly with the increase of fruit-trees is provided by Pindar.[11] Fertility implications

[10] See L. R. Farnell, *The Cults*, 5.101. Semele, as her name shows, can scarcely, *pace* Farnell here, be called a "Hellenization" of anything.

[11] Fr. 140 ed. Bowra. The custom of hanging Dionysus' mask or image on trees has also been interpreted as a vegetation-rite, see L. R. Farnell, *op. cit.* 5.194—196 and M. P. Nilsson, *The Minoan-Mycenaean Religion*², 530f. Compare also the myth

may also once have been prominent in the god's marriage annually to the Queen Archon in the Cattle-Stall on the Acropolis at Athens, but his marriage in this instance seems to have acquired political overtones largely expunging the agrarian.[12]

The question whether Dionysus is essentially a god of the Underworld as distinct from a divinity of "Nature renascent" has been much debated, especially in the light of Heraclitus' statement that "Aides [that is, Hades] and Dionysus are the same". I am inclined to accept as valid the argument that Heraclitus is here stating a "paradox fraught with recondite meaning" offering no proof, therefore, that Dionysus is to be literally equated with Hades, the god of the Underworld.[13] But to assert that he is in no sense "infernal" seems to be going too far. Evidence of his "catabatic nature" can be inferred from a vase as early as the sixth century B.C. depicting his resurrection apparently with Semele (certainly with her if the inscriptions labelling Dionysus and Semele on the vase are genuine)[14], and from various literary passages describing his descent into the world below from Aristophanes' *Frogs* onwards.

In this play produced in 405 B.C., providing the earliest extant literary *κατάβασις Διονύσου*, Dionysus is dressed like Heracles and is made to descend into the Underworld, but for another purpose than to fetch up his mother Semele. It becomes evident from the events of the play that Dionysus' Journey into the Underworld has been model-

of how the Sumerian goddess of fertility was first turned into a corpse and then hung from a stake for three days (p. 16 above).

[12] *Ibid.* 5.217—219. The ceremony is described in Ps.-Arist. *Athen. Const.* 3.5 and other sources assembled by M. P. Nilsson, *Studia de Dionysiis Atticis* (Lund 1900), 156 and seems to have taken place on the twelfth of Anthesterion (see esp. Thuc. 2.15.4 and Aristoph. *Frogs*, 215ff.).

[13] G. Zuntz, *Persephone*, 409 on Heraclitus fr. 15 ed. Diels-Kranz, *ὡυτὸς δὲ 'Αίδης καὶ Διόνυσος, ὁτέῳ μαίνονται καὶ ληναΐζουσιν.*

[14] Fig. 128 in J. E. Harrison, *Prolegomena*³ (Cambridge 1922), 406 = Naples No. 172, *A. B. V.* 203, 1. G. Zuntz, *op. cit.* 407—411 (though something seems to have gone wrong with the reference on p. 409 n. 5) is sceptical of all the "Anodos" vases as evidence that Dionysus is "chthonic", i.e. infernal. For some judicious remarks regarding the interpretation of females represented with Dionysus, see further L. R. Farnell, *The Cults,* 3.252ff. and 5.245ff. And for the most recent, illustrated treatment of these vases see C. Bérard, *Anodoi* (Suisse 1974), esp. 143 on this vase PL. 3 fig. 8.

led upon Heracles' *catabasis,* except that Dionysus is not bent on stealing the Hell-dog Cerberus, but hopes to fetch back a poet, the newly deceased Euripides. By a comic reversal of the plot Euripides is outclassed in a contest by his older rival Aeschylus, and so Dionysus returns unexpectedly with this poet instead. On the journey below, Dionysus, although he does not actually meet Persephone on stage, after witnessing the hymning of the great Eleusinian deities by the mystic chorus (324ff.) is invited inside the House of Pluto, where "Phersephassa" (that is, Persephone) resides with her underworld lord (669ff.). Furthermore the very hymning during which the hierophant bids the chorus to summon forth the Eleusinian god Iacchus (394ff.) resembles the ritual calling forth of Dionysus at his own Lenaean festival,[15] where indeed the play was performed; and although Aristophanes sharply differentiates between Dionysus and Iacchus,[16] an Athenian audience in 405 B.C. might easily have identified the two.[17] Heracles' Eleusinian descent to fetch Cerberus is thus dovetailed with Dionysus' traditional descent to fetch Semele into a neat jigsaw, so that Dionysus both experiences an initiation and fetches up Aeschylus. To broaden still further the comic effect of the journey — several

[15] According to the scholiast on Aristophanes, *Frogs* 480 the Torchbearer in the Lenaean *agones* says "Call ye the god" (*καλεῖτε θεόν*), and all present respond with the ritual cry, "Son of Semele, Iacchus, Wealth-Giver" (*Σεμελήι' Ἴακχε πλουτοδότα*). For other links between the Lenaea and Eleusis see now L. Deubner, *Attische Feste*², (Hildesheim 1966), 125f.

[16] Dionysus was dressed, after all, as Heracles and was actually witnessing the scene. Moreover he himself, with comic effect, shouts "I've done it: call the god" (*ἐγκέχοδα· κάλει θεόν*) at *Frogs* 479 (for the formula cf.n.15 above), thereby showing that he was not the god.

[17] Dionysus and Iacchus are identified in the cult of the Lenaea (n.15 above) and elsewhere in Attic tradition (see e.g. C. P. Segal, "The Character and Cults of Dionysus and the Unity of the Frogs", *H.S.C.P.* 65(1961), 218f.). But the fact remains that Dionysus was not an Eleusinian divinity; see e.g. G. E. Mylonas, *Eleusis and the Eleusinian Mysteries* (Princeton 1961), 276—278 and *id. Arch. Eph.* 1960 (1965), 68—118. There is some evidence that not only at Lerna but also at Corinth Dionysus was associated with Demeter; see A. D. Ure, "Demeter and Dionysos on Acrocorinth", *J.H.S.* 89(1969), 120f. But the identification between Dionysus and Iacchus, as H. J. Rose, "Demeter and Dionysus", *J.H.S.* 72(1952), 121 affirms, seems to rest on no better reason than that Dionysus' other name "Bacchus" sounds like Iacchus.

comic poets, it might be mentioned here, regarded the Descent into Hades as a theme to be parodied[18] — Aristophanes draws also on several other motifs familiar from the old class of *καταβάσεις εἰς αἴδου*, his parody of Odysseus' descent having already been mentioned on pp. 75—76 above.[19] Thus Aristophanes seems to be the first to have coupled Dionysus and Heracles as initiates.[20] It is tempting also to credit Aristophanes with suggesting an original syncretism between Dionysus and the Eleusinian Iacchus, but it is extremely unlikely that any suggestion made by one slapstick comedian would have caught on as official doctrine.

Dionysus' *catabasis* was enacted also at the *καταγώγια* at Priene;[21] and similar performances were probably given by the thiasos of Maenads known as *καταβάται*.[22] According to F. Schwenn's widely favoured treatise,[23] Semele's periodic *ἄνοδος* or *ἀναγωγή*, "bringing up", was celebrated also at Delphi, Samos, Troezen, Athens, and Lerna. The evidence, though not abundant, is largely corroborative and may be briefly summarized as follows. At Delphi Semele's return (*ἀναγωγή*) rests chiefly upon Plutarch's inference from a drama festival held every eighth year.[24] Plutarch also describes[25] how Thespesius

[18] In addition to those discussed at various places in the book, attention may be drawn here to Pherecrates' *Hell's Pennies* (*οἱ Κραπαταλοί*), the scene of which was set in Hades, and *The Miners* (*οἱ Μεταλλῆς*), which represented, it seems, the mines at Laurium as the Entrance to Hades and depicted a woman returned from Hades who extolled the Utopian existence there, and to Aristophanes' own play *Gerytades* (*Γηρυτάδες*), in which a delegation of three poets was sent to Hades. For these see J. M. Edmonds, *The Fragments of Attic Comedy*, I.236—243, 246—249, and 617——625 respectively.

[19] The *Frogs* was considerably influenced also by Euripides' play *Peirithous*, as D. L. Page, *Greek Literary Papyri* (London 1950), 122f. recognizes.

[20] For a later passage associating the two (not earlier than the fourth century B. C.), see Ps.-Plato, *Axiochus* 371E already quoted in chapter 3 n. 44 above.

[21] See L. R. Farnell, *The Cults*, 5.313 (R 105a).

[22] *Ibid.* 5.298 (R.68a). For other descent rituals see ch. 3 n. 49 above. Aphrodite's *Καταγώγια* at Eryx is analogous to the spring trireme-celebration at Smyrna where the goddess "returned" in the sense of "putting to shore" (*ibid.* 5.191f.).

[23] *R.E.* 2nd. ser. 2.1343 s.v. "Semele".

[24] *Quaest. Graec.* 293C—D, *ἐκ δὲ τῶν δρωμένων φανερῶς Σεμέλης ἄν τις ἀναγωγὴν εἰκάσειε.*

[25] *De Ser. Num. Vind.* 565F—566A.

during his otherworldly vision was shown the route by which Dionysus ascended (*ἀνελθεῖν*) and then brought up (*ἀναγωγεῖν*) Semele — up presumably from Hades, as commentators on the passage commonly assume citing Diodorus and Apollodorus (see n. 30 below) in support. At Samos, according to a rationalizing version recorded by the scholiast on Aristophanes' *Frogs* at line 330, Dionysus is said to have brought back not his mother, but his mother's soul (*ψυχή*).[26] But usually Semele herself is fetched up. The belief that this took place at Troezen is recorded by Pausanias, even though he personally doubted that Semele ever died (2.31.2). And that it took place at Athens seems to be celebrated in a Pindaric fragment (63 ed. Bowra) which describes how at the Athenian spring festival of Bromius, possibly at the Anthesteria,[27] the dancing chorus "approaches the diadem-wreathed Semele" (*οἰχνεῖ τε Σεμέλαν ἑλικάμπυκα χοροί*).

But Pindar elsewhere makes it clear that Semele was struck by a thunderbolt and now lives among the Olympians.[28] This is at variance with the notion that she dwells below in Hades. It is, of course, conceivable that in his cryptic manner Pindar simply omitted the stages between Semele's death and ascension, which told of her descent to Hades and subsequent recovery. But the natural meaning of the passage is that Semele ascended to Olympus *immediately* upon being

[26] According to the scholiast's version Hades agrees to send up Semele's soul on condition *τοῦ Διονύσου τῶν μάλιστα τερπόντων αὐτῷ ἀντίψυχον ἀντ' ἐκείνης πέμψαντος· τὸν δὲ Διόνυσον πυθόμενον τὰ παρὰ τῶν κάτω θεῶν ἐπεσταλμένα σοφίσασθαι πρὸς ταῦτα καὶ τριῶν ὄντων αὐτῷ μάλιστα ἠγαπημένων, τοῦ τε κισσοῦ καὶ τῆς ἀμπέλου καὶ τῆς μυρσίνης, ἀποστεῖλαι τοῖς κάτω θεοῖς αὐτήν. δηλοῖ δὲ καὶ 'Ιοφῶν ὁ τραγικός*. The scholiast makes it clear in the note earlier that *αὐτήν* refers to myrtle such as initiates wear. Having sent down myrtle Dionysus may be presumed to have Diddled the Devil. There thus appears a hint of vicarious sacrifice in this story, with which Prosymnus' death (p. 105) and the offering of a lamb (p. 105) may be compared. Compare also Inanna-Ishtar's substitute and Admetus' need to find a substitute at Euripides, *Alcestis* 13f., which on Robert's thesis (p. 81 above) would be a pre-Orphic vicarious sacrifice.

[27] Compare e.g. Jane E. Harrison, *Themis*, 418. L. R. Farnell in *The Cults*, 5.193 mistakenly connects the ode with Thebes.

[28] *Ol.* 2.25—27, *ζώει μὲν ἐν 'Ολυμπίοις ἀποθανοῖσα βρόμῳ κεραυνοῦ τανυέθειρα Σεμέλα*; cf. also Pind. *Pyth.* 11.1. C. M. Bowra, *Pindar* (Oxford 1964), 65 inexplicably asserts that Semele is in the Isles of the Blessed.

struck,[29] in which case her resurrection from Hades and her ascension by lightning would appear to be two versions, which in some later accounts have been conflated.[30]

When we turn to Lerna, however, the accounts are more puzzling. For although Dionysus is said to have made the descent there in order to fetch up his mother, not a shred of evidence exists to show that she was ever in fact resurrected. While the danger of an argument from silence must be recognized, it must be pointed out also that the evidence is fairly consistent in emphasising Dionysus' return only. The possibility that Semele was not brought back by Dionysus in this instance — and it is only a possibility — is therefore worth considering.

Dionysus' descent through the Alcyonic Lake at Lerna in quest of the goddess Semele — we have already referred on p. 97 above to a descent by Dionysus into the sea at *Iliad* 6.135f. — is an Argive tale related at some length by Pausanias (2.37.5—6),[31] from whose description of the event it appears that Dionysus was shown the way down by Polymnus, a local hero better known as Prosymnus. Pausa-

[29] E. Rohde, *Psyche*[8], 581f., in his appendix "Death by Lightning", takes this to be the primitive lightning-version which is also preserved by late writers e.g. Charax *ap.* Anon, *de Incred.* xvi, p. 325.5ff. (West), *κεραυνοῦ κατασκήψαντος ἠφανίσθη· ἐκείνην μὲν οὖν, ὁποῖα ἐπὶ τοῖς διοβλήτοις λέγεται, θείας μοίρας λαχεῖν φήθησαν.*

[30] Semele's death, resurrection, and ascension, as found in Apollod. *Bibl.* 3.5.3. and Diod. 4.25.4, is virtually regarded nevertheless as the canonical version (see e.g. H. J. Rose, *A Handbook of Gk. Mythology,* 150). Her ascension is explained by J. E. Harrison, *Themis*, 420 as an Olympianisation of the old ritual of the Bringing up of Semele: "Semele, Earth, never could or did go to heaven, but she rose up out of earth." Her status as a goddess (Hesiod's statement that Semele bore Dionysus *ἀθάνατον θνητή· νῦν δ' ἀμφότεροι θεοί εἰσιν* at *Theog.* 942 reverses the historical development) would, of course, suffice to explain Pindar's allusion to her as dwelling on Olympus. She was an earth-goddess before she became a mortal princess; see p. 99 above and the evidence assembled to show this by E. R. Dodds in his Commentary *Euripides: Bacchae*[2] (Oxford 1960), 62—64 on lines 6—12. Her integration into the Theban royal family as one of Cadmus' daughters at Pind. *Ol.* 2.22ff. and fr. 63 ed. Bowra is another variant in the Theban tradition.

[31] *εἶδον δὲ καὶ πηγὴν 'Αμφιαράου καλουμένην καὶ τὴν 'Αλκυονίαν λίμνην, δι' ἧς φασιν 'Αργεῖοι Διόνυσον ἐς τὸν ῞Αιδην ἐλθεῖν Σεμέλην ἀνάξοντα, τὴν δὲ ταύτῃ κάθοδον δεῖξαί οἱ Πόλυμνον. … τὰ δὲ ἐς αὐτὴν Διονύσῳ δρώμενα ἐν νυκτὶ κατὰ ἔτος ἕκαστον οὐχ ὅσιον ἐς ἅπαντας ἦν μοι γράψαι.*

nias himself refrains from divulging the nature of the rites which, he says, were performed annually at night by the lakeside in honour of Dionysus. However, something of their nature can be gleaned from Clement[32] and Arnobius[33] who — although these do not mention Lerna — say that Prosymnus promised to show Dionysus the way to the Underworld in return for sexual gratification. Dionysus agreed to this proposal, but found upon his return that Prosymnus was dead and buried. Dionysus nevertheless fulfilled his part of the bargain by using a fig stick on the dead man's grave.

Further hints concerning the ritual are to be found in the scholiast on the *Iliad* who remarks that Perseus flung the dead Dionysus into the Lernaean lake,[34] and in a passage by Plutarch who tells how the Argives summoned Dionysus back again out of the water with the call of trumpets, throwing "into the depth" (*εἰς τὴν ἄβυσσον*), presumably the Lake Alcyonia, a lamb for the Gate-Keeper.[35] On the basis of these hints and a second passage by Plutarch in which the god is said to sleep in winter and awake in the spring,[36] Farnell supposed that Dionysus' dead or decaying image was thrown into the lake at an autumn or winter ceremony and that in the spring Dionysus was

[32] Clement, *Protrepticus* 2.29—30.

[33] Arnobius, *Adversus Gentes* 5.28=*P.G.* ed. Migne. 5.1140—3. Here Dionysus is made to see Cerberus, Styx, the Furies and all the traditional sights seen by visitants to the Underworld. The god, it is worth noting, met and charmed his way past Cerberus, as Orpheus is regularly reported to have done, in Horace, *Carm.* 2.19.29—32.

[34] Schol. T. *Il.* 14.319: *[Περσεὺς] Διόνυσον ἀνεῖλεν ἐς τὴν Λερναίαν λίμνην ἐμβαλών.* Cf. Aug. *civ. dei* 18.13, Cyril. *adv. Iul.* 1.10, p. 341.

[35] J. Gwyn Griffiths in his Commentary *Plutarch: Isis et Osiris* (Cardiff 1970), p. 433 on the relevant passage 364F reminds us that the Argives also used trumpets in a Bacchic festival described by Plutarch at *Quaest. conv.* 4.6.2, 671E, and that a trumpeter took part in the festival of the Anthesteria at Athens, where Dionysus is depicted as being drawn in a ship-carriage. For the blowing of trumpets in seasonal mysteries see also Th. H. Gaster, *Thespis*², 75 n.5, 458, and L. R. Farnell, *The Cults* 5.185. The imagery survives into Christian thought, since the dead will arise on the Last Day at the sound of a trumpet (I *Cor.* 15.52; I *Thess.* 4.16). The lamb here seems to be a propitiation of the gate-keeper of Hades for Dionysus' return (cf. n. 26 above). On the "bottomless" lake cf. schol. Pind. *01.* 7.60.

[36] Plut. *Isis et Osiris* 378E—F. M. J. Vermaseren, *The Legend of Attis in Greek and Roman Art* (Leiden 1966), 33 would make the passage refer to Attis.

resurrected "bringing with him Semele back into the light."[37] For this last statement, however, there exists no evidence whatever. The constant emphasis on Dionysus' return from Hades to the exclusion of Semele suggests rather that, like Moses on Sinai who left his followers wondering what was happening and came back with a revelation from the Deity,[38] Dionysus disappeared through the lake and later returned reinvigorated after a mystical experience with the goddess who remained in the Underworld after all. The drama, which perhaps "touched on the secrets of the ghost-world",[39] was no doubt part of the cult secret. But the possibility is real that the version in which Semele is brought back by Dionysus and ascends to Olympus, and the version in which she stays below are two simultaneous but separate variants.

Both Orphic and Dionysiac descents look like rationalizations of visits to fetch an underworld goddess (with the important proviso that Eurydice, unlike Semele, was perhaps not in origin an earth-goddess),[40] the former in the form of a widower trying to rescue his

[37] *The Cults*, 5.182—5 and 192—4 (for the whole reconstruction). Farnell contrasts the autumn/winter ceremony with Attis' *catabasis*, which he believes on the strength of Macr. *Sat.* 1.21.7 took place only a few days before his resurrection in the spring (see now, however, chap. 1 n. 9 above). Hyacinthus, who had a pre-Greek cult at Laconian Amyclae, and Hippolytus might seem similarly to have had but a short residence in the Underworld; for references to these see H. J. Rose, *A Handbook of Gk. Mythology*, 142 n. 17 and 140 n. 13.

[38] Strabo 16.2.38f., p. 762 has already spoken of Moses in relation to Orpheus, Amphiaraos, Trophonios, Minos, Lycurgus and others, but not Dionysus.

[39] L. R. Farnell, *The Cults*, 5.184.

[40] No reliance should be placed on the meaning of her name "The Wide-Ruling One" — she is also called Agriope "Wild-eyed" or Argiope in a version by Hermesianax (p. 108 below) — since Eurydice seems in fact to be a stopgap name. Even Aeneas' wife was called by this name in the *Cypria* fr. 22 (ed. Allen), and since her spectre, too, fades from her husband, O. Gruppe wondered whether Orpheus' Eurydice was named after her (Roscher's *Lexikon* 3.1162). This particular conjecture is not without its own difficulties. These aside, the name of Orpheus' wife is not found in early literary sources, but even so may have been current in the fifth century B.C.; see n. 68 below. The idea that Eurydice was actually an earth-goddess comparable to Semele and Kore-Persephone (as distinct from her role being assimilated to one) was advocated by e.g. Jane E. Harrison, who supposed that her loss in the Vergilian version was a rationalization of a Kore's need to return to the Underworld that has been telescoped. She says: Orpheus "fails, because she must perennially return to Hades that she may rise again next spring" (*Themis*, 420 and

wife, the latter a son piously trying to rescue his mother. That each on occasion apparently fails to rescue the female is a seemingly awkward ending, but not necessarily, as we have seen in Dionysus' case, an unhappy one. If, as was once thought, there ever existed behind the myths of this kind a Frazerish ritual in which the king is himself sacrificed and stayed in the Underworld,[41] it must be fully admitted that all vestiges of the original have disappeared. Orphic and Dionysiac descents are rather to be contrasted with than likened to the Near Eastern descents of Inanna and Ishtar, who sent below their respective lovers Dumuzi and Tammuz as substitutes for themselves. On the other hand the myth in which Semele is regained could be the product of a ritual (which on Frazer's interpretation would belong to a later development), in which the king descends into the Underworld in order to fetch up the Queen with whom he emerges as the divine consort. Dionysus' sexual activity on the dead man Prosymnus' tomb seems to represent a kind of *hieros gamos* which might originally have taken place with a goddess; though in its present form it serves as an explanation of the phallic ritual in Dionysiac mysteries.[42] If a story of this type were influenced by similar, but unrelated, stories of underworld consultations and the gaining of spiritual enlightenment — Gilgamesh's and Odysseus' underworld consultations were after all current well before the sixth century B.C. — the two myths might merge and the re-ascent of the Queen be forgotten. How and when the amalgamation might have arisen at Lerna is not easy to see, but if the Argive Dionysus had a mystical experience in the Underworld, it may be presumed that he consulted his mother below. One tentative suggestion is that the Argives, because of their interest in filial piety,[43] have turned a story about a son who consulted (the ghost of)[44] his mother into that

cf. 529 n. 2). Eurydice is sometimes said to be a Dryad or Nymph, see Servius on Verg. *G.* 4.459 and 534.

[41] This stage would presumably correspond to the period when the Kore, according to Jane E. Harrison, *op. cit.* 420, 503, returned from the Underworld alone.

[42] The aetiological purpose of the myth is discussed by A. B. Cook, *Zeus*, 2. ii. 1022.

[43] As exemplified in the Argive story of the filial devotion of Cleobis and Biton; Herodotus 1.31, the *locus classicus*, and other sources are discussed by A.B. Cook, *op. cit.* 1.447—451.

[44] Compare the Samos version at n. 26 above.

of a son who tried to bring her back, but without altering the tradition that she stayed below.

We have concluded so far then, that there is a good possibility that in at least one representation Dionysus returns without Semele, as Orpheus returns without Eurydice. But if Dionysus' return without Semele is represented as a radiant success, the failure of Orpheus to recover Eurydice in Vergil's fourth book of the *Georgics*, depicting as it does a poignant, tragic catastrophe for Orpheus, is in striking contrast. This prompts two further questions. First, was there ever a time in the development of the myth when Orpheus' apparent failure to recover Eurydice was not represented as tragic? And secondly, how is the existence of two separate traditions of the Orphic myth, in the one of which Orpheus fails while in the other he succeeds in recovering his wife, to be explained? These two questions we shall try to answer while endeavouring at once to provide a survey of the main outlines in the development of the descent-tradition of Orpheus down to Vergil.

In answering the second of these questions we should begin on solid ground if we knew at what date the earliest success-story of Eurydice's recovery was circulating. Diodorus, as we have noted (p. 99) above, apparently knew of such a version, writing as he was in Vergil's lifetime. But much earlier than this, we find that Hermesianax in the third book of the *Leontion* represents Orpheus as having "brought back Thracian Agriope from Hades (*ἀνήγαγεν... ʽΑιδόθεν*), having equipped himself with his lyre. He sailed to the foul, relentless place where Charon silently herds the souls of the dead into his bark, while the current of the lake as it flows out through the tall reeds echoes afar. Orpheus journeying alone over the flood dared many things as he played his lyre, and all manner of gods he charmed. Lawless angry-browed Cocytus he withstood and also the gaze of dread Cerberus pointing in fire his voice and in fire his cruel eye, an eye bearing terror on three-fold head. There by his song he persuaded the mighty lords to let Agriope receive back the spirit, *πνεῦμα*, of her tender life."[45] The importance of this text lies in showing that Orpheus,

[45] Translated (after Dronke) from O. Kern, *Orphicorum Fragmenta* (Berolini 1922), *test.* 61=*ap.* Athenaeus 13.597b, but reading Herwerd's *ἀκέων* (Charon "silently" herds) where Kern prints † *ἀκοὴν*. Cf. Wilamowitz *ἀκέην*, Hiller *μικρὴν*. See also chapter 7. n. 17.

at least from the early third century B.C., was regarded as having succeeded in bringing back his wife. The aorist *ἀνήγαγεν* is decisive in ruling out the possibility that Orpheus lost her before she regained the upperworld. Her name Agriope (or Argiope if Zoëgma's emendation is preferred) in Hermesianax's version shows, furthermore, that the tradition concerning the name of Orpheus' wife was once fluid,[46] and that more than one version therefore was circulating about her.

The success-version, measured in terms of Orpheus' recovery of his wife from Hades, can be put still earlier if pseudo-Heraclitus' *De incredibilibus* (21) belongs to the late fourth century; and even earlier than this if the comparison by the orator Isocrates at *Busiris* 11.7—8 (written 391—390 B.C.) between Busiris, who used to eat shipwrecked sailors, and Aeolus, who used to send them back safely to sea, and Orpheus, who would bring back the dead from Hades (*ἐξ Ἅιδου τοὺς τεθνεῶτας ἀνῆγεν*), is in fact based on the story of Orpheus' recovery of his wife. The imperfect tense and plural object in this passage have been taken as a clear indication that Orpheus regularly harrowed Hell and therefore brought back souls other than Eurydice's.[47] But since Aeolus is known only once, and that in the *Odyssey*, to have sent back sailors, Isocrates seems to be generalizing; therefore the imperfect *ἀνῆγεν* and the plural *τοὺς τεθνεῶτας*, if success is implied at all, might in the context mean only that Orpheus, having once recovered his wife, was the sort of man to bring back the dead.

Earlier than this, however, there exists no certain evidence of a success-version, although lately a growing number of scholars[48] have inclined to the view that the conventional, archaic story did in fact end with Orpheus' successful recovery of his wife. Let us therefore consider the early evidence pertaining to Orpheus' Descent into Hades

[46] See n. 40 above.

[47] Peter Dronke, "The Return of Eurydice", *C. & M.* 23(1962), 206 n. 21.

[48] Among them W.K.C. Guthrie, *Orpheus and Greek Religion* (London 1935), 31; I. M. Linforth, *The Arts of Orpheus* (Berkeley 1941), 16ff.; C. M. Bowra, "Orpheus and Eurydice", *C.Q.* 2(1952), esp. 119; P. Dronke, *op. cit.* 201f.; M. Owen Lee (see p. 118 below); H. A. Khan, "Horace's Ode to Vergil on the Death of Quintilius: I,24", *Latomus* 26(1967), 114 n.1, the subject of this whole article 107—117 being of interest in showing how Horace allegedly reprimands Vergil for his excessive grief by instancing the futility of Orpheus' attempt to bring Eurydice back from the dead; and now L. P. Wilkinson, *The Georgics of Virgil*, 116f.

and the basis on which this conjecture (which I find unconvincing) as to the outcome of the archaic version is made.

Orpheus, whose name written as *ΟΡΦΑΣ* first appears on a sixth century B.C. metope at Delphi,[49] is not for the most part a Messianic figure with whom one identifies, but a Thracian priest and Cadmus-type culture-hero who discovered and taught men arts and science, and is especially renowned for his musical powers.[50] The earliest reference to his Descent is, however, much later than the sixth century. Names of poets who wrote early *καταβάσεις*, which may have been Orphic, are known to us, but little or nothing is known about either them or their poems. One such name is Prodicus of Samos, to whom Clement of Alexandria writing in the second century A.D. ascribes a *Descent into Hades* of Orpheus;[51] and it used to be thought[52] that this Prodicus was the same person as the Prodicus of Phocaea who is said by Pausanias at 4.33.7 to have composed the *Minyas*. The theory claimed to take us far, since Polygnotus, the painter of the celebrated mid-fifth century mural at Delphi showing in one scene Orpheus in the Underworld, is also said by Pausanias (10.28.2) to have used the *Minyas* as a source for his painting; and the assumption therefore was made that Polygnotus drew for the Orphic scene from Prodicus' *Minyas*, also called *Descent into Hades*. Furthermore the two Prodici were identified also with Herodicus of Perinthus, to whom (along with Orpheus of Camarina, a poet who was evidently named after Orpheus) the *Suda* ascribes a *catabasis* of Orpheus.[53] The entire theory, however, has been discredited, not merely on account of the precarious identifications, but because Pausanias made his suggestion that Polygnotus might have borrowed from the *Minyas* with reference to anoth-

[49] *Test.* 1 (Kern). The reference to ὀνομακλυτὸν Ὀρφήν in a lost poem by Ibycus of Rhegium (*test.* 2) shows furthermore that he was already celebrated in poetry in the sixth century B.C.

[50] Discussed by e.g. I. M. Linforth, *The Arts of Orpheus*, 15f. and 32ff. referring to the most important *testimonia* esp. 123 and 46—55 (Kern) respectively.

[51] *Stromateis* 1.21,131 = *test.* 222 (Kern).

[52] K. O. Müller, *Orchomenos und die Minyer*² (Breslae 1884), 18, cf. 212. The argument was advocated in different degrees also by Wilamowitz, *Homerische Untersuchungen* (Berlin 1884), 222—226, C. A. Lobeck, *Aglaophamus*, 360, cf. 373, and C. Robert, *Die Nekyia des Polygnot*, 79.

[53] S.v. *Ὀρφεύς* = *test.* 176 and 199 (Kern).

er underworld scene, not the Orphic scene described in great detail by Pausanias at 10.30. 3—5, in which Eurydice seems to be conspicuously absent and Orpheus is said to be not playing the lyre, but holding it in his left hand while touching a willow-tree with his right. Add to this the fact that what fragments of the *Minyas* do survive do not point to Orphic connections,[54] and the whole suggests that, whatever the *Minyas* may or may not have contained, Polygnotus depicted in the Orphic scene not the Visit to Hades by Orpheus while alive in search of his wife, but rather his appearance in the Afterworld after his death. The distinction is important and is recognized by Vergil, who describes both the descent of Orpheus during his lifetime in the *Georgics* and the appearance of Orpheus in the Afterworld visited by Aeneas during this hero's descent in the *Aeneid,* at which time Orpheus is virtually a choir-leader who even after death teaches the power of the lyre.[55] Finally, as Clement in the same passage also tells us,[56] an Orphic *Descent into Hades* was attributed, by the Alexandrian scholar Epigenes, to Cercops the Pythagorean; but apart from the fact that this work is the *Orphicum Carmen* known to Cicero,[57] its author, like the others just mentioned, remains but a shadowy witness from whom nothing definite can be inferred for our purpose.

The earliest known evidence for Orpheus' descent is, then, Euripides *Alcestis* produced in 438 B.C. And here the reference is tantalizingly brief. Admetus informs his wife Alcestis, as she is about to die on his behalf, of his own unwillingness to venture into the lower world to fetch her back. "If", he says, "I had the tongue and music of Orpheus so as to charm with my songs Demeter's daughter or her lord and win you from Hades, I would go below and neither Pluto's Hound nor Charon at his oar, the ferryman of souls, would stay me before I restored your life to light":

[54] See chap. 5 n. 2.

[55] *Aen.* 6.645—647. Here Orpheus is referred to by the sobriquet "*Threicius longa cum veste sacerdos*" according to the convention, which makes a historical understanding of Orphism so contentious, of refraining from mentioning him by name. (Wilamowitz and Linforth, but not Nilsson, accept as primary evidence for Orpheus only those documents sealed with his name; see Linforth, *The Arts of Orpheus*, xiii and n.1.)

[56] *Test.* 174 (Kern).

[57] *N.D.* 1.107.

εἰ δ' Ὀρφέως μοι γλῶσσα καὶ μέλος παρῆν,
ὥστ' ἢ Κόρην Δήμητρος ἢ κείνης πόσιν
ὕμνοισι κηλήσαντά σ' ἐξ Ἅιδου λαβεῖν,
κατῆλθον ἄν, καί μ' οὔθ' ὁ Πλούτωνος κύων
οὔθ' οὑπὶ κώπῃ ψυχοπομπὸς ἂν Χάρων
ἔσχον, πρὶν ἐς φῶς σὸν καταστῆσαι βίον.

(357—62)

The very brevity of the allusion to Orpheus in this passage seems to presuppose the existence of an earlier version of the *κατάβασις Ὀρφέως* with which Euripides' audience was expected to be familiar. But it is not at all clear from the allusion whether Orpheus in the earlier story succeeded in bringing his wife back from Hades or not.

Plato's treatment of the myth in the *Symposium*, the next to survive after Euripides', is hardly trustworthy evidence (as will be readily seen) for the elucidation of this problem. In this dialogue Phaedrus exploits the contrast raised in Euripides' play and relates how the gods rewarded Alcestis, who died for love of her husband, by sending up her soul, *ψυχή*, from Hades, whereas Orpheus, despite his braving the terrors of Hell while questing for his dead wife, the gods "sent empty (*ἀτελῆ*) away from Hades, showing him only a phantom, *φάσμα*, of the woman for whom he had come. They did not give up her real self (*αὐτὴν δὲ οὐ δόντες*) because he seemed to be a coward, minstrel that he was (*ἅτε ὢν κιθαρῳδός*), and to lack the courage to die as did Alcestis for the sake of love, contriving instead to enter Hades alive. They therefore punished him for this and arranged his death at the hands of women" (179D).

Plato in this passage has evidently retouched the myth to show Orpheus in a highly unflattering light. Had Orpheus been viewed through more favourable eyes, he might have been seen as at least surpassing Admetus in bravery. After all, Admetus not only accepted his wife's offer to die, but having refused to face the terrors of Hell himself, allowed Heracles instead (as we know from Euripides) to descend on his behalf. But to Phaedrus, suppressing this comparison, Orpheus' reliance on song was a sign of weakness and his descent was a piece of effrontery representing an attempt at avoiding a lover's death, for which he deserved to be given, in lieu of his wife, a phantom, and to meet afterwards with a humiliating kind of death.[58] Yet if we suppose, as is most probable, that in the archaic version of the myth the daring manner in which Orpheus charmed his way through the Underworld was emphasised, the notion of Orpheus' weakness as a musician was in all probability not raised. Once the issue of his courage was raised, however, by the comparison between the characters of the two descent stories, Phaedrus was prepared to introduce a number of false antitheses, by shifting uneasily from Orpheus to Alcestis, to demonstrate that Orpheus was completely devoid of this virtue. This interpretation, which is indubitably prejudiced against Orpheus, seems to have been Phaedrus' invention[59] and perhaps reflects Plato's scorn of the Mysteries. This passage may even be itself the origin of the tradition that Orpheus was a "weak" character — a tradition which bothered the scholiast on Apollonius of Rhodes' *Argonautica* (1.23), who asked why Orpheus, being weak (*ἀσθενὴς ὢν*), was included among the Argonautic heroes, and concluded that Orpheus must have been needed to ensure a safe passage past the Sirens.

The issue, then, must be taken back to Euripides and the question to be asked is: can we assume that the *Alcestis* passage presupposes a version in which Orpheus successfully brought his wife back from Hades or not? Gruppe,[60] after careful examination of all early Orphic *catabaseis,*[61] concluded that if we were not familiar with the conven-

[58] Orpheus' hideous death was the subject also of several Attic vase-paintings of the first half of the fifth century and of Aeschylus' *Bassarae.* Cf. Dionysus' dismemberment, for which see E. R. Dodds, *The Greeks and the Irrational* (Berkeley 1951), 155f.

[59] Plato's presentation of the Alcestis myth may not be completely reliable either. It has been argued (Wilamowitz, *Isyllos von Epidauros* [Berlin 1886], 57ff.; Wentzel, *R. E.* 1.377ff. s.v. "Admetos") that Apollodorus *Bibl.* 1.9.15, which reports that Alcestis' soul was sent up by Kore, preserves the original. But this version may equally well have derived from the passage in Plato in which the gods give back her soul. For the original versions conjectured by Robert and Lesky see above p. 81.

[60] 0. Gruppe s.v. "Orpheus in der Unterwelt" in Roscher, 3 esp. 1157—1165.

[61] Classical versions of the *κατάβασις 'Ορφέως* and the older commentaries upon them are given in O. Kern, *Orphicorum Fragmenta, testimonia* 59—75 and *fragmenta* 293—296 and in K. Ziegler, *R.E.* 18A, 1268—1281 s.v. "Orpheus (0. u. Eurydike)", while important recent commentaries are referred to in this chapter. See also next note.

tional story (as he called it) in Vergil, we might easily deduce that he did: but, he argues, with the exception of *ἀνήγαγεν* in Hermesianax (to which we might add *ἀνῆγεν* in Isocrates), early texts do not directly contradict the conventional story and there is no indication that at any identifiable period the story actually changed.

Now, more than seventy years later, this view seems to have been entirely reversed, and, as indicated (at. n. 48) above, Orpheus' bringing Eurydice back to earth is regarded as the original and conventional version. No verdict on this matter is likely to be regarded as final until surer evidence can be brought to light.[62] But I believe for a variety of reasons that we should remain sceptical of the currently favoured interpretation and of the conflicting hypotheses advanced to explain the alleged transition from Orpheus' successful recovery of Eurydice to one of failure. The fragility of the evidence may be illustrated with reference to three separate hypotheses in particular.

The view that there is much greater point to Admetus' speech if the archaic pre-Euripidean version had had a successful outcome has been strongly argued for by Dronke, in the belief that it would have been well-nigh absurd to reinforce a wish for success by reference to a well-known failure; and he takes the logical point of Admetus' speech to be: "If I could *succeed* as Orpheus did, I too would go down to fetch you back."[63] The fact that the archaic version told of Orpheus' successful recovery of his wife is clinched, he continues, by the scholiast on Euripides, who says that "Orpheus descended when his wife Eurydice had died from a snake, and having cast a spell over Pluto and Kore he led her back out of Hades."[64] And, finally, it is suggested that the successful ending was twisted into a failure by Plato: Eurydice's *φάσμα* in the Platonic version is taken to be a cari-

[62] The recently discovered Orphic descent on a Bologna papyrus — for the text see esp. R. Merkelbach, "Eine orphische Unterweltsbeschreibung auf Papyrus", *Mus. Helv.* 8(1951), 1—11, whose specifically Orphic character is strenuously maintained by R. Turcan, "La catabase orphique du papyrus de Bologne", *R.H.R.* 150(1956), 136—172 — is too fragmentary to assist our argument here: but see p. 171 below.

[63] P. Dronke, *C. & M.* 23(1962), 201f.

[64] *'Ορφέως γυνὴ Εὐρυδίκη, ἧς ἀποθανούσης ὑπὸ ὄφεως κατελθὼν καὶ τῇ μουσικῇ θέλξας τὸν Πλούτωνα καὶ τὴν Κόρην αὐτὴν ἀνήγαγεν ἐξ ᾄδου* (ed. E. Schwartz, ii. 227).

cature of the archaic pre-Euripidean version represented by Hermesianax, in which Orpheus succeeded in having his wife's πνεῦμα restored.

This is an attractive hypothesis, but ultimately unsatisfactory. It is of course difficult to escape from a kind of circular argument — the notion that Plato is responsible for twisting success into failure already presupposes, for the validity of this theory, that a successful recovery of Eurydice underlies the *Alcestis* passage. And the scholiast's notice that Orpheus recovered his wife in the original story is in fact practically worthless, except in showing that Dronke's reasoning was anticipated in antiquity. For its author could easily have read back into Euripides what might have been learnt from later versions, and he does not tell us from what source he took the name Eurydice for Orpheus' wife, who is anonymous in Euripides, as in Plato and Isocrates. But, without going further, has not too much been read into the *Alcestis* passage? Admetus refers to the arts which enabled Orpheus to overcome the obstacles Cerberus and Charon merely to indicate that he himself has the will, but lacks the means to descend among the dead, and his point is simply that, if only he had Orpheus' means to make the journey, nothing would prevent him from bringing Alcestis back. The unspoken implication, which the playwright was not obliged to spell out, might well be that Admetus would then be achieving more than Orpheus. Nothing in the Euripidean version at any rate suggests that Orpheus *was* successful in his mission to bring back his wife from Hades.

The distinction should be carefully drawn in any case between success in making the journey to the lower world, on which all versions of Orpheus' descent are agreed, and the possible failure to achieve the purpose for which the journey is made. Vergil may have recognized the distinction for the *Aeneid* since his Orpheus, having failed in the *Georgics* to recover Eurydice, was cited by Aeneas, in the passage noted at the head of this chapter, among the heroes who had already succeeded in accomplishing the Journey into the Underworld before him. We need not, contrary to the usual view,[65] suppose from this that Vergil necessarily had two versions of the *κατάβασις 'Ορφέως* in

[65] See most recently L. P. Wilkinson, *The Georgics of Virgil*, 203n.

mind, since it would have sufficed for Aeneas' purpose that Orpheus had visited his dead wife in the Underworld and returned. Orpheus' failure to recover Eurydice may in this respect be compared to the experience of Gilgamesh, who while still alive journeyed into the Otherworld, and thereby performed more than ordinary mortals, but ultimately failed in his mission to bring back the secret of immortal life. But on any interpretation, the emphasis on Orpheus' *deserved* failure of purpose in Plato's myth makes it read like a hostile version (which Euripides' Orphean allusion is not) and the point of discredit in Plato seems to be directed against Orpheus in his capacity as a minstrel-player of the *κιθάρα*.

The existence at any date of these two separate traditions of the Orphic myth is of course hard to explain. Linforth had already attempted to dispose of the possibility that Plato twisted a successful recovery of Eurydice into a failure on the ground that "Plato could not have said bluntly 'Orpheus failed', *'Ορφέα... ἀτελῆ*, without explanation or apology, unless this version of the story too were already abroad"; and he believed that two separate traditions were already current by Plato's time.[66] This, as we have seen, was doubted by Dronke. And it was doubted also by Bowra, who supposed that it was easier to understand how the Euripidean version (which he too thought ended successfully) was later transformed (by a Hellenistic poet, to whom I shall return presently) into a tragic failure if one could postulate the intermediary existence of a Protesilaus-like version, perhaps known to Plato from some Attic tragedian,[67] in which Orpheus successfully regained Eurydice for a short time at the end of which he has to give her back to Hermes. The existence of such an intermediary version was conjectured by Bowra on the basis of his interpretation of the famous fifth-century sculptured Attic relief of Hermes, Orpheus, and Eurydice as representing the moment when Eurydice, having been successfully brought to the upperworld, has to return to Hades under the guidance of Hermes.[68] And he takes two

[66] I. M. Linforth, *The Arts of Orpheus*, 19.

[67] The Protesilaus-Laodamia story was known to Euripides whose *Protesilaus* (schol. Aristid. p. 671 ed. Nauck *T.G.F.* 563) tells how the dead hero was allowed by the gods of the Underworld to revisit his wife Laodamia for a single day.

[68] *C.Q.* 2(1952), 121. The original (*c.* 430—400 B.C. acc. to Sir John Beazley)

passages by Plutarch[69] and Lucian[70] as also supporting the conjecture. Both these writers in the Graeco-Roman period imply that Orpheus may have recovered his wife, and Orpheus is furthermore associated in these passages not only with Alcestis, but with Protesilaus too. However, even if the discovery of new fragments should lead to the confirmation of a version in which Orpheus enjoyed "limited success", this would still fall short of proving that the original version ended with Eurydice's recovery. Plato could still have reverted to the archaic version with a vengeance, in which case Hermesianax or his predecessor would have been the innovator by dropping the Protesilaus-like restriction that Eurydice's recovery was only temporary.

Nevertheless despite the doubts I have raised as to the development of the Orphic myth in the forms already alleged, the modern tendency to suspect that, in the sixth and fifth centuries B.C., Orpheus as a central figure in a new movement with poems attributed to him must have succeeded in whatever his quest was thought to be, seems surely to be well placed. But the question arises: what kind of success should we look for?

That Orpheus acquired knowledge about the afterworld is clear from the Orphic *Argonautica* (40—42), where Orpheus speaks of what he saw and learnt when he made the descent to Hades for love of his wife:

has not survived and is known only through copies. Three are complete, in the Museo Nazionale at Naples, the Louvre at Paris, and the Villa Albani at Rome, and two others exist in fragmentary state. For more detailed documentation see Heinze Götze, "Die Attischen Dreifigurenreliefs", *Röm. Mitt.* 53(1938), 189—280 and cf. Evelyn B. Harrison, "Hesperides and Heroes: A Note on the Three-figure Reliefs", *Hesperides* 33(1964), 76—82. The names of the figures are inscribed on the best copy at Naples, but since the original has not survived there is no way of knowing whether or not the inscriptions are an addition.

[69] Plut. *Amatores* 17: *εἰ δή πού τι καὶ μύθων πρὸς πίστιν ὄφελός ἐστι, δηλοῖ τὰ περὶ Ἄλκηστιν καὶ Πρωτεσίλεων καὶ Εὐρυδίκην τὴν Ὀρφέως, ὅτι μόνῳ θεῶν ὁ Ἅιδης Ἔρωτι ποιεῖ τὸ προσταττόμενον.*

[70] In Luc. *Dial. Mort.* 23.3 Protesilaus appeals to the precedents set by Orpheus and Alcestis and begs Pluto to allow him too to return to his wife: *ἀναμνήσω σε, ὦ Πλούτων· Ὀρφεῖ γὰρ δι' αὐτὴν ταύτην τὴν αἰτίαν τὴν Εὐρυδίκην καὶ τὴν ὁμογενῆ μοι Ἄλκηστιν παρεπέμψατε Ἡρακλεῖ χαριζόμενοι.*

ἄλλα δέ σοι κατέλεξ' ἅπερ εἴσιδον ἠδ' ἐνόησα
Ταίναρον ἠνίκ' ἔβην σκοτίην ὁδὸν ''Αιδος εἴσω,
ἡμετέρῃ πίσυνος κιθάρῃ δι' ἔρωτ' ἀλόχοιο.

Norden was convinced that this source, though late, was derived from an early *κατάβασις 'Ορφέως* known also to Vergil and used by him in the Sixth Book of the *Aeneid.*[71] And from the fact that Orpheus here acquired knowledge about the afterworld during his Visit to Hades, Bowra further deduced that this descent, though inspired by love for his dead wife, was connected with Orphic mysteries in which Orpheus' wife may not necessarily have had pride of place, but may have been a means to explain why Orpheus visited the Underworld and so was able to reveal its mysteries.[72] Bowra himself did not enlarge upon this inference, but it clearly raises the issue whether there might not have existed an early version of the descent in which Orpheus, like Dionysus at Lerna, received a mystical experience in the Underworld, before his quest became the familiar tale of rescue.

The assumption that such a version existed in the fifth century is hinted at separately by Lee, who reinterprets the Attic relief mentioned above (p. 116) as a momentary concession granted to Orpheus in Hades where Eurydice is brought to him by the psychopompos Hermes, and Orpheus by lifting up his wife's veil glimpses into her face and so learns the secrets of the afterlife.[73] Lee himself classes all extant versions of Orpheus' descent as "Euripidean" or "Vergilian" according to whether they end in success or tragedy. But Orpheus' recovery of his wife may not have been an essential tenet in such a version for the followers of a legendary founder of the mysteries — sufficient for his culture-hero activities that he returned with mystical knowledge. The versions of Eurydice's recovery, on the other hand, as well as her subsequent loss, resemble the more familiar patterns of vegetation-deities, with which they have been doubtless at least partially contaminated[74] — the Vergilian version became assimilated still

[71] E. Norden, *Aeneis Buch VI*³, on lines 119—120.

[72] *C.Q.* 2(1952), 122—124.

[73] M Owen Lee, "Orpheus and Eurydice: Myth, Legend, Folklore", *C. & M.* 26(1965), 406.

[74] See at n. 40 above.

more completely to the Persephone myth when Aristaeus was identified with Pluto.[75] And in the literary treatments of Orpheus' descent the original acquisition of mystical knowledge has evidently been sacrified to the romantic element, leaving Orpheus' success to be judged solely by whether or not he returned with Eurydice. Similarly in the eleventh century of our era Orpheus again brings back his beloved, this time under the influence of the Christian tradition of Christ as the Victorious Orpheus.[76] But as Our Lord Himself conquered death and harrowed Hell but brought nobody back to earth (Lazarus was brought back on a different occasion), so Orpheus need not originally have brought back his wife, if he returned from his quest with mystical knowledge ensuring a future life to initiates.

If the assumed pre-Euripidean version were of this kind, the point of Admetus' reference to Orpheus would be perfectly intelligible. The subsequent tale of his wife's recovery with a happy ending may even owe its impetus to the association in Euripides' play of Orpheus with the fairy-tale version of Alcestis rescued by Heracles. The telling by Plato of not so much a failure as a duped success, in which Orpheus recovers only Eurydice's "phantom" (*φάσμα*), may be modelled in part, as Bowra suggests,[77] on stories like that of the phantom Helen, in which Helen's *εἴδωλον*, but not herself, went to Troy. This story, which no doubt conceals a distinction between a goddess and her image,[78] was certainly known to Plato through Stesichorus and possibly through Hesiod and Euripides as well,[79] and "has all the marks of genuine myth."[80] Yet, even so, might not Plato have picked

[75] See on this point the versions indicated e.g. by P. Dronke, *C. & M.* 23(1962), 209.

[76] *Ibid.* 206—210.

[77] *C.Q.* 2(1952), 120.

[78] Compare the numerous stories of abductions of divine statues in the Near East, as instanced by W. F. Jackson Knight, *Vergil: Epic and Anthropology*, 296ff. A link between Helen and stories of this kind is possible, for Helen seems originally to have been a goddess (see pp. 128—131 below). For her cult-image see Herodotus 6.61, and for the abduction of an image in Greece see n. 80 below.

[79] Stesichorus *ap.* Plato, *Rep.* 586C; Hesiod fr. 266 (Rzach); Eur. *Helen*, 44ff.

[80] As Gilbert Murray, *The Rise of the Greek Epic*³ (Oxford 1924), 205 observes. Murray further compares the regular carrying off and replacement of Hera's Image in the feast called Tonaia in Samos.

up the hint for Eurydice's phantom (*φάσμα*), which is somewhat different from a cult-image, from the *Alcestis* itself, where Admetus is incredulous as to whether he had received back his real wife or "some phantom (*φάσμα*) from the shades"?[81] Furthermore, in the *Alcestis* passage immediately preceding the allusion to Orpheus, Admetus says that since he cannot have his real wife he will cherish an "image" of his dead wife.[82] Admetus does not mention Protesilaus directly here, but Euripides' use of Protesilaus-like imagery (the Protesilaus-Laodamia story was known to him)[83] in this passage[84] surely anticipates the association of both Orpheus and Alcestis with Protesilaus by Plutarch and Lucian and renders less likely Bowra's assumption that these later writers drew the association from an early Protesilaus-like poem of Orpheus.

And so let us return to Vergil's tale of Orpheus' tragic love in the *Georgics*, with which we began. It is, as we have seen, quite unlike any other version we have so far considered. Here Orpheus is not content merely to visit his wife in the Underworld, nor does he win his wife back alive, nor is he tricked into receiving his wife's phantom, but he loses Eurydice through neglecting to observe the single condition of her release laid down by the goddess Persephone: *Immemor heu! victusque animi respexit* (491). This story is told also, with minor divergencies, by many of the later Latin poets[85] and by the Greek

[81] *ΑΔ.: ὅρα γε μή τι φάσμα νερτέρων τόδ' ᾖ.*
ΗΡ.: οὐ ψυχαγωγὸν τόνδ' ἐποιήσω ξένον.

(1127f.)

[82] *σοφῇ δὲ χειρὶ τεκτόνων δέμας τὸ σὸν*
εἰκασθὲν ἐν λέκτροισιν ἐκταθήσεται,
ᾧ προσπεσοῦμαι καὶ περιπτύσσων χέρας
ὄνομα καλῶν σὸν τὴν φίλην ἐν ἀγκάλαις
δόξω γυναῖκα καίπερ οὐκ ἔχων ἔχειν·
ψυχρὰν μέν, οἶμαι, τέρψιν, ἀλλ' ὅμως βάρος
ψυχῆς ἀπαντλοίην ἄν. ἐν δ' ὀνείρασι
φοιτῶσά μ' εὐφραίνοις ἄν· ἡδὺ γὰρ φίλους
κἂν νυκτὶ λεύσσειν, ὅντιν' ἂν παρῇ χρόνον.

(348—356)

[83] See n. 67 above.

[84] D. M. Jones, "Euripides' *Alcestis*", *C.R.* 62(1948), 51 and 55; and A. M. Dale, *Euripides: Alcestis* (Oxford 1961), 79.

[85] Notably Ovid, *Metamorphoses* 10.1—73 and a lost poem fr. 7 ed. Morel;

mythographers Conon and Apollodorus.[86] It also underlies the rationalistic version of Pausanias 9.30.5—6, where it acquires a touch of the Periander and Melissa theme, and the allegorical interpretation of Fulgentius, *Mitologiae* 3.10. Pausanias, who turns the story into a hallucinatory experience on the part of Orpheus, has more than once confused a *catabasis* with a *nekyomanteion* and in this passage he makes Orpheus consult the Thesprotian Oracle of the Dead at *Aornum* (p. 63 above): Orpheus sensing that his wife's ghost was following turned, but saw nothing and so killed himself in grief.

As has been mentioned above, the Vergilian setting of Orpheus' descent within the descent of Aristaeus is also new, the very connection with Aristaeus being unknown in pre-Vergilian accounts. If Vergil was the innovator who introduced Aristaeus into the myth of Orpheus, the idea may have suggested itself perhaps from the legend that Aristaeus was born of a nymph on a Mount Orpheus[87] or from the legend that Orpheus after death was an angry demon until appeased by a sacrifice.[88] Vergil will in that case have been the inventor of the motif of Aristaeus' lust as the cause of Eurydice running upon the snake unperceived in the grass. This is, in fact, one of the divergences between Vergil's telling of the story and Ovid's, who says that Eurydice while wandering in the company of some Naiads was bitten by a snake soon after her wedding.[89] Even if we assume that Eurydice was imagined by Vergil to have been with the Naiads when she was pursued by Aristaeus,[90] the discrepancy between these two accounts

Horace, *Carm.* 1.24.13—18 and 3.11.15—24; and also the author of the *Culex* 268—295; Seneca, *Hercules Furens* 569—591 and *Hercules Oetaeus* 1061—1089; Statius, *Thebaid* 8.57—60; and perhaps Lucan in his lost *Orpheus ap.* Servius on Vergil, *Georg.* 4.492. (The extant fragments of Lucan's *Orpheus* are assembled by J. P. Postgate, *Corpus Poetarum Latinorum* [London 1905], 145.) The poet Manilius at *Astron.* 1.325—327 and 5.326—328 seems to be the exception to the Latin tradition.

[86] *Narrationes* 45.2 *ap.* Photius, *Bibl.* 186 (=*F. Gr. Hist.* 26F1, vol. i. pp. 207f.) and *Bibliotheca* 1.3.3 respectively.

[87] Nigidius Figulus *ap.* schol. Germanic. 154. 12 Breys.

[88] As F. Klingner, *Vergils Georgica* (Zürich 1963), 230—231 suggested, referring to Conon, *Narrationes* 45.

[89] *Metamorphoses* 10.8—10.

[90] As is supposed by J. Conington-Nettleship-Haverfield, *Vergili Opera* on *Georg.* 4.460.

of her death does not disappear. Of course, Ovid may have taken the story from Vergil (whose account he certainly knew) and altered it,[91] but the possibility presents itself that he followed more closely a lost Greek original associating Eurydice's death with her marriage, from which Vergil himself deviated when introducing the Aristaeus theme.[92]

Essential, moreover, to the Vergilian tale of Orpheus' love twice lost is the broken tabu. This does not survive in Greek poetry though it is referred to by the Greek mythographers just mentioned above. It must, then, either be part of the original story which somehow dropped out and is restored[93] (this supposition necessarily carries the implication that Eurydice was originally not regained completely), or an addition suggested perhaps by the manner in which underworld rites are performed without looking back.[94] That this tabu too was introduced into the story by Vergil so as to make Orpheus lose his half-regained Eurydice by looking back would not be altogether surprising. But here we are in a difficulty because we cannot date precisely the collection of myths by Vergil's Greek contemporary Conon, who in his *Narrationes* also speaks of Orpheus losing Eurydice a second time, in this version through breaking the conditions set not by the goddess alone (as in Vergil, *Georgics* 4.487) nor by her husband Pluto (as in Apollodorus' later account), but by both Pluto and Persephone (*ἀλλ' οὐ γὰρ ὄνασθαι τῆς χάριτος ἀναβιωσκομένης, λαθόμενον τῶν περὶ αὐτῆς ἐντολῶν*, 45.2), a version which Ovid too seems to have followed (10.46—47). Since we do know, however, that Conon dedicated his work to Archelaus Philopator, [95] the king of Cappadocia from 36 B.C. to A.D.17, and Vergil is said to have recited

[91] Gilbert Highet, *The Classical Tradition* (Oxford 1949), 601 n. 38.

[92] Advocated by C. M. Bowra, *C.Q.* 2(1952), 114.

[93] The case is argued by H. J. Rose, *A Handbook of Greek Mythology*, 255 thus: "To regard [the breaking of the tabu] as a late addition to the legend of Orpheus because it happens not to be mentioned by any very early author is most illogical. It is not a Greek story, so why should the Greeks tell it of Orpheus if it had not always formed part of his history?"

[94] Cf. Hom. *Od.* 10.528, Aesch. *Cho.* 97, Soph. *O.C.* 490, fr. 534, Theocr. 24.94, and Ap. Rh. *Argon.* 3.1040f. J. Heurgon, "Orphée et Eurydice avant Virgile", *M.E.F.R.* 49(1932), 46f. conjectured on insufficient evidence that the motif was known also to Pindar.

[95] Phot. *Bibl.* 186, p. 330^b 25.

the fourth *Georgic* to Octavian in 29 B.C., [96] there is a good chance that Vergil's is the earlier work. If the *Culex* were really Vergil's youthful work, the account which it contains of how Proserpine persuaded Pluto to grant Eurydice's release (286—287) and the subsequent breaking of the tabu described in lines 292—293 would be earlier than either. But there are too many difficulties in the way of this assumption for any conclusion to be drawn.[97] And so we are left with the problem: how are the divergencies between Vergil and Conon as to who gave the order not to look back to be explained? And would a Greek mythographer in any case have derived his information from a Roman poet?

Norden assumed that Vergil was following a mythological handbook, probably that used by Servius Auctus.[98] Bowra assuming similarly that Vergil was not inventing argued with great learning and ingenuity that Vergil drew on a lost Hellenistic poem (cf. already pp. 116 and 122 above), whose author introduced the tabu to emphasise the theme of tragic love and nature's lament for Eurydice's death. The contents of the lost poem he reconstructs by comparing Vergil's version with the accounts told by Ovid, the poet of the *Culex*, Seneca, Statius, Conon, and Apollodorus, all of whom he believed were indebted to this same poem. In particular he believed that the *Culex* provided the missing clue over the question of who gave the order to Orpheus not to look back. He inferred from it that in the lost poem Proserpine asks her husband to grant the release, and he consents, but adds the restriction about not looking back, which Proserpine delivers. This composition Bowra put later than the *Lament for Bion*, which he took to imply that the success-version still held sway at the beginning of the first century B.C., but before Conon's brief abstract which provides the *terminus ad quem*.[99] We are not, of course, obliged

[96] Donat-Suet. 27(42).

[97] See E. Fraenkel, "The Culex", *J.H.S.* 42(1952), 1—9; for a recent attempt to dispel the difficulties compare A. A. Barrett, "The Authorship of the Culex", *Latomus* 29(1970), 348—362.

[98] E. Norden, "Orpheus und Eurydice", *Sitz. Berl. Akad.* (1934), 653 and n.

[99] C. M. Bowra, *C.Q.* 2(1952), 116f. (for reconstruction of the contents) and 125f. (for date). O. Gruppe also suggested such a poem, in Roscher's *Lexikon* 3.1159. Cf. also W. K. C. Guthrie, *Orpheus and Greek Religion*, 31.

to accept the assumption that the theme of Eurydice's non-recovery was introduced at the same time as the tabu. Personally I believe that even after making every allowance for the variants, it is virtually unthinkable that Vergil or his Hellenistic predecessor should have flatly and at such length contradicted what would, presumably, never have ceased to be official doctrine and that other writers should not have commented on it. But then, the view that "from the fifth to the first century we have a series of testimonies to a story in which Orpheus succeeded in bringing his wife back from the dead"[100] has, in fact, very little to support it. It is more likely that Orpheus originally descended through the power of his song in quest of his wife, and having found her returned with mystical knowledge; and that the more uxorious elements of the story have been a gradual accretion to the aetiological explanation for why he went below in the first place. If the tabu is an addition to, rather than an original part of the story, the suggestion that Vergil might have preceded Conon and invented the tabu himself[101] is not unreasonable. But the distinct possibility remains that Vergil was using, if not a handbook, a recent poem which introduced the tabu. Vergil was writing strongly in the vein of Hellenistic *epyllia* and the addition of this motif lent a brilliant touch of poignant tragedy which caught on among the Latin poets and through them, despite the attempts to put an end to the myth by sceptics such as Pausanias, became the classic version for the modern world.[102]

[100] C. M. Bowra, *op. cit.* 120.

[101] As recently advocated by P. Dronke, *C. & M.* 23(1962), 201.

[102] For later versions of Orpheus' descent see, in addition to the works of Dronke, Highet, and Lee above, the full-scale treatments by J. B. Friedman, *Orpheus in the Middle Ages* (Camb. Mass. 1970), Walter A. Strauss, *Descent and Return: The Orphic Theme in Modern Literature* (Camb. Mass. 1971), and works mentioned in their bibliographies.

CHAPTER V

THESEUS, LABYRINTHS, AND THE UNDERWORLD

Theseus might almost be called the Attic Heracles. Not only had he a penchant for abducting females like Ariadne and Helen, whose myths will presently engage our attention insofar as they seem to be related to the catabatic pattern, but great deeds which rivalled the Labours of Heracles, including a Journey to the World Below, were attributed to him. Yet he, unlike Heracles, was never Eleusinianized.

His Descent, in effect, was imposed upon him at the insistence of his friend Peirithous. The latter had already helped Theseus to seize Helen from Sparta at Theseus' request, and now called for reciprocal assistance from Theseus. Accordingly the intention of the two heroes in going below was to carry off from the Underworld the goddess Persephone to be a bride for Peirithous. And extant Greek tradition is fairly consistent in regarding the venture as an outrageous act of impiety. Consequently both heroes were punished by Hades for their presumption and were set among the damned, though the precise form of their punishment varied.

Some say that the two friends were magically held fast on seats in the Underworld, the earliest witness to this being a scene on one of the Peloponnesian shield-bands datable to *c.* 600 B.C.[1] This is the version found also in the scene described by Pausanias at 10.29.9 from Polygnotus' famous mid-fifth century wall-painting in the Cnidian Lesche at Delphi. Pausanias at 10.28.2 seems to suggest that Polygnotus' underworld scene here may have followed the lost epic *Minyas*.[2]

[1] E. Kunze, *Archaische Schildbänder*, 112f., Beil. 7.4; K. Schefold, *Myth and Legend in Early Greek Art* (London 1966), 69 fig. 24.

[2] The central theme of the *Minyas* has not been established, but it certainly does not tell of a descent by Orpheus (see pp. 110—111 above). E. Rohde, *Psyche*[8], ch. 7 n. 3 took the passage in Pausanias to mean that the descent in the lost poem was that of Theseus and Peirithous, but F. G. Welcker, *Der epische Cyclus* I

But the version which dominates in early classical vase-paintings and is recorded by the epic poet Panyassis, who died before the middle of the fifth century B.C., represented the two growing to a rock on which they sat.[3] And here they would both have remained for ever had they not been discovered by Heracles, who happened to have been sent below shortly afterwards on the mission to fetch Cerberus.

According to the most familiar variant of the rescue, Heracles obtained the release of Theseus only, leaving Peirithous in the Underworld to suffer his fate. This variant makes its appearance in the fifth century, and in art may have been represented by no other than Polygnotus himself in a shrine dedicated to Theseus in the heart of Athens known as the "Theseion" (not the temple commonly so-called).[4] It is favoured also by Euripides in the *Hercules Furens* at 1170

(Bonn 1835), 239f. has speculated from the name *Minyas* that it might have contained Heracles' war against Orchomenos under Erginus and, therefore, Heracles' descent and his rescue of Theseus. Welcker's theory unfortunately lacks conviction, but it at least attempts to solve the awkward problem of how Theseus came to be connected with a poem of such a name. G. Kinkel assembles what scraps of the *Minyas* do remain in his *Epicorum Graecorum Fragmenta*, 215ff. These show that the contents of the *Minyas* included the death of Meleager and alluded to Heracles, Orion, Charon (this is the earliest mention of the ferryman in literature), and to the punishments of Amphion and Thamyris. For these last see especially Pausanias 4.33.7 and 9.5.8f.; and note that Polygnotus' mural according to Pausanias 10.28f. shows Charon, Meleager, and Thamyris. Other early *catabaseis* of Theseus and Peirithous existed, which are also lost. A Hesiodic *catabasis* of the heroes is referred to by Pausanias at 9.31.5. And Pausanias at 10.28.7 refers to yet another catabasis in the *Nostoi*, the details of which are lost. On these see J. G. Frazer's commentary on Pausanias *ad loc.,* and for the last see also A. Severyns, *Le Cycle Épique Dans L'École D'Aristarque* (Paris 1928), 385f.

[3] Panyassis *ap.* Paus. 10.29.9=fr. 9 Kinkel; and cf. the *Suda* s.v. *λίσποι*. For Panyassis' date, see W. MacLeod, "Studies on Panyassis — an Heroic Poet of the Fifth Century", *Phoenix* 20(1966), 95—110.

[4] The scene at any rate seems to be represented on the Niobid Painter's calyx-krater in the Louvre M.N.C. 511 (G. 341) *c.* 460—450 B.C. See for this *A.R.V.*[2] 601.22 and P. Arias-Hirmer-Shefton, *History of Greek Vase Painting*, plates 173—174. And this vase, as argued by J. Six, "Micon's fourth picture in the Theseion", *J.H.S.* 39(1919), 130—143 and with reinforcing evidence by J. P. Barron, "New Light on Old Walls: the Murals of the Theseion", *J.H.S.* 92(1972), 21—45 with plates, may well be a direct copy of the fourth mural (see Pausanias 1.17.2ff),

and is presupposed alike in the rationalized variants mentioned in chapter 2 above.[5] However, in the lost, doubtfully Euripidean play *Peirithous,* both the friends were rescued. Insofar as Theseus here makes out in the surviving conversation held with Heracles in the Underworld that his stay with his captive friend in the lower world had been voluntary, inspired, it seems, by the generous wish to share his fate or save him, the play may well have struck a new note in the myth. And from Heracles' reply it is evident that Theseus had attempted to strike a bargain with him. He offered assistance in capturing Cerberus in return for Heracles' help in freeing Peirithous.[6]

We can be sure that Vergil knew of the release of at least Theseus, since Aeneas refers to his Descent at line 122 of the Sixth Book of the *Aeneid* in a way that would have been inappropriate had Theseus stayed in the lower world. The Descent clearly rankled Charon, since at 393, when faced with Aeneas' attempt to cross the Stygian lake, he names Theseus and Peirithous among the earlier mortal visitors who had caused him trouble. Later still, when Aeneas has made the crossing and finds himself in the World of Shades proper, he learns from the Sibyl that Peirithous and Theseus are, after

which particular mural Barron for a number of reasons tentatively ascribes to Polygnotus, the colleague of Micon known to have painted the shrine's third mural (see p. 142 below).

[5] Pp. 62—63. Cf. also Diod. Sic. 4.63.4, Hygin. *Fab.* 79, Apollod. *Bibl.* 2.5.12 and *Epit.* 1.21, and the next paragraph for Vergil. For fuller evidence, literary and artistic, concerning the freeing by Heracles see H. Herter in *R.E.* suppl. xiii (1973), s.v. "Theseus", 1176f. and 1203—1205.

[6] For the surviving remnants and a discussion of the authorship of the play, whether it is Euripides' or the slightly later Critias', see esp. A. Nauck, *Tragicorum Graecorum Fragmenta,* 546—550, 770; *P. Oxy.* ed. A. S. Hunt 17(1927), 36—45 no. 2078; and D. L. Page, *Greek Literary Papyri,* 120—125. And for the conversation in question see lines 25ff. in Hunt, *op. cit.* 40f. and in Page, *op. cit.* 124, with the correction of line 33 by W.E.H. Cockle, "P. OXY. xvii. 2078", *C.R.* 20(1970), 136f. The release of the two heroes is consonant with the surviving fragments and is, moreover, expressly ascribed to Euripides by Schol. Tzetz. Chil. *ap. Anecd. Oxon.* iii. 359.22, *κατ' Εὐριπίδην σῴζονται καὶ οἱ δύο*; cf. also Diod. 4.26.1 and Hygin. *Fab.* 79, *quo Hercules ad canem triplicem ducendum cum venisset, illi fidem eius implorarunt. qui a Plutone impetravit eosque incolumes eduxit.* This may conceivably be the version followed by Horace, *Carm.* 4.7.27 and it appears to be the intent of the pre-Euripidean scene on the shield-band mentioned in n.1 above.

all, both detained in Tartarus among the eternally damned (601 and 617).[7] Thus Vergil seems to have two incompatible versions of the myth somewhat awkwardly juxtaposed. Why the poet embraced both will perhaps become clearer in the final chapter, when we shall discuss what use Vergil made of these differing versions.

In certain respects, which we shall now consider, the abductions of Helen by Theseus and Peirithous jointly, and of Ariadne by Theseus alone, seem to share a common pattern with this venture into the Underworld. The myths of both these females are likely to date back ultimately to the Mycenaean age,[8] and their original significance will be more readily appreciated if we recognize that they were once goddesses of vegetation.[9] Helen's divinity, seems to be remembered in the assurance given to Menelaus in the Homeric proto-*Nekyia* that he will be transported to the Elysian Fields because his marriage to Helen has made him the son-in law of Zeus.[10] And Helen had in Sparta, where her cult was chiefly preserved, two temples; the Menelaeion at Therapne, where she and Menelaus are said to have been worshipped as gods,[11] and another near the Platanistas, which may have been the centre of a tree-cult.[12] Her original divinity is not

[7] Servius in his commentary on the *Aeneid ad loc.* says that this contradicts the (then) common story, and he seems to imply that this is Vergil's invention: "*frequenter variant fabulas poetae.*" However, Polygnotus' mural at Delphi depicts the heroes as both seated in Hades at the time of Odysseus' visit (Pausanias 10.29.9). The version is perhaps implied in *Odyssey* 11.631. And Diodorus, who is known to have been collecting myths between *c.* 60 and 30 B.C., refers at 4.63.5 to a similar version. Cf. also Hyginus in Aul. Gell. *N.A.* 10.16.

[8] M. P. Nilsson, *The Mycenaean Origin of Gk. Mythology,* 166.

[9] The evidence, archaeological and mythographical, is fully presented in Nilsson's *The Minoan-Mycenaean Religion*², 523—8 (for Ariadne), 528—532 (for Helen).

[10] *Od.* 4.569. Cf. p. 97 above.

[11] Isocr. 10.63; cf. Paus. 3.19.9. Worship of Menelaus as a god seems not to have predated the eighth century B.C. For the date of his cult and alleged Homeric influence upon it see J. M. Cook "The Agamemnoneion", *B.S.A.* 48(1953), 31ff. And for more recent archaeological confirmation of the influence of epic poetry upon hero-cults generally from the eighth century onwards, see J. N. Coldstream, "Hero-cults in the age of Homer", *J.H.S.* 96(1976), 8ff. Cf. T. B. L. Webster, *From Mycenae to Homer*², 137f.

[12] As G. Kaibel, "Theokrits *ΕΛΕΝΗΣ ΕΠΙΘΑΛΑΜΙΟΝ*", *Hermes* 27 (1892), 254ff. argues, citing esp. Theoc. 18.38ff. and Paus. 3.15.3.

of course proved by her worship alone, but added to this her association with trees and her non-Greek name all point to her being in origin a pre-Hellenic goddess of vegetation and fertility. A revealing story of how upon the death of Menelaus she was driven from Sparta and escaped to Rhodes, where she was subsequently hanged from a tree, is told by Pausanias, who adds that there is in Rhodes a sanctuary of Helen *δενδρῖτις*, Helen of the Tree.[13] It is probable that with Helen, as with Dionysus above,[14] the hanging reflects a vegetation rite in which images of the deity were suspended from the boughs of trees. Similarly Ariadne, when she was abandoned by Theseus on the Island of Naxos, met her death by hanging.[15] Her cults in several places are attested by the mythographers,[16] though her connection with the dance performed in Crete[17] indicates that she is probably of Minoan origin.

The hypothesis that Ariadne and Helen were formerly deities of the earth is attractive and, if accepted, at once makes clear that their abductions are akin to that of the goddess Persephone-Kore by the Lord of the Underworld himself and to the attempted abduction of her by Theseus and Peirithous subsequently. The suggestion that Theseus might himself have been a death-figure comparable to Pluto has been noted already above.[18] In this connection it should be emphasized that Pluto's adventure and the catabatic motif in the existing versions of Theseus' descent are but two sides to the same coin. Helen and Ariadne, moreover, are seized from Laconia and Crete respectively, not actually from the Underworld, but the general pattern of these myths resembles the actual descent which Theseus made in the attempt to carry off the underworld Queen herself. It is in no wise impossible that the early transition of these two deities from cult to heroic mythology occurred because the immigrated Greeks did not fully grasp the sacred nature of their myths.[19]

[13] Paus. 3.19.10.
[14] Chap. 4 n. 11 above.
[15] Plut. *Thes.* 20.
[16] See discussion indicated at n. 9 above.
[17] E.g. Hom. *Il.* 18.590.
[18] At chap. 3 n. 49.
[19] M. P. Nilsson, *The Mycenaean Origin of Gk. Mythology,* 74—76, 173.

The tendency towards humanizing may be illustrated further with regard to the goddess Persephone herself, who in the rationalizing forms of Theseus' Descent already outlined in chapter 2 above appears as a mortal queen.[20] Her husband, the Lord of the Underworld in the canonical version, has been rationalized as a king of the Molossians or Thesprotians and given the name Aidoneus. He, as we have seen, offered his daughter to any suitor who could overcome their dog Cerberus and when he realized that Theseus and Peirithous came not to woo, but to steal his daughter or wife, he handed over Peirithous to the dog and held Theseus until Heracles rescued him.

But whereas Persephone-Kore, with the exception of this humanizing myth, has invariably retained her original status, being assuredly too great a goddess to be forgotten, Helen and Ariadne, evidently at some very early stage, have become almost completely humanized as mortal princesses. We may surmise, then, that the Attic myths, in which Ariadne and Helen are captured on separate occasions by Theseus, are closely related variations of the abduction theme of the Queen of the Underworld. As such they may be regarded as thinly disguised catabatic ventures in which the city stronghold appears to have taken the place of the Underworld itself.

Helen, as might be expected from her origin, is not held by Theseus for long. She is shortly afterwards recovered from Theseus' stronghold of Aphidna near the Plain of Marathon by her twin brothers, the Dioscuri. These, known separately as Castor and Polydeuces (Pollux), also abduct Leucippos' daughters or his horses or his cattle in a mythical raid which shows variations of a similar theme.[21] During this raid Castor was killed and allowed to share his twin's immortality. The mythographers are sharply divided over how this happens. Some say that both the twins journey together into the world below on alternate days, others that each spends a day in the Underworld while the other lives on Olympus.[22] The *Odyssey* 11.298—304 does not make clear which arrangement is meant, but this ambiguity is settled for the early classical period by Pindar (*Nemean Ode* 10.55ff. and

[20] On pp. 62—63.

[21] Cf. J. G. Frazer on Apollodorus *Bibl.* 3.11.2.

[22] The authorities for each arrangement are tabulated by E. Bethe, *R.E.* s.v. "Dioskuren", 5.1091.

schol.), who explains that Polydeuces chose to share his immortality by dying on alternate days precisely in order to be with his brother. In either event when the brothers were not among the gods on Olympus, they were supposed to lie buried in the underworld caves of Therapne, the place of Helen's cult in Sparta. And from this myth, too, Vergil is furnished with another prototype for Aeneas' descent, for Pollux is named by Aeneas in company with Orpheus, Theseus, and Heracles as having also anticipated him in returning from the journey to the dead.[23]

The carrying off of Helen took place on three other occasions at least. Hermes took her to Egypt. She was seized by a robber who carried her off to Mount Parnon. And cardinal even to the myth of the Trojan War was her abduction from Laconia to Troy by Paris-Alexandros.[24] On this occasion she was recovered not by the Twin Dioscuri, but by the so-called "Twin" Atreidae. All of these variations suggest that Helen's abduction, which has a marked sacral appearance,[25] was a pre-Greek myth which was grafted on to the myth of the Trojan War. It is likely that the incoming Greeks did not understand the religious significance of the myth of the rape (we have already seen that only the rape of Kore by Pluton retains its sacred character), but thought it to be simply a common tale of the carrying off of a fair woman. Thus Helen, as Nilsson points out, came to be humanized as the queen of the city in which she still was especially venerated, and the double name of her abductor is explained by the amalgamation of the myths which resulted in the identification of the Trojan prince Paris with Alexandros, the typical robber in Greek myth.[26] Insofar, too, as Helen's abduction was the alleged *casus belli* between the Greeks and the Trojans and the entire war was fought for Helen's recovery, the strange Homeric episode of Odysseus' entry into Troy as a disguised and mutilated beggar to meet with Helen,[27] from whom

[23] Verg. *Aen.* 6.121f.

[24] Hom. *Il.* 3.87 etc.

[25] M. P. Nilsson, *Geschichte der Griechischen Religion*, i², 475 has stressed that the myths of her being carried off are appropriate to a goddess of vegetation. Cf. also ch. 4 nn. 78 and 80 above.

[26] *Id. Homer and Mycenae* (London 1933), 251—253.

[27] *Od.* 4.240ff.

he obtained a State-secret[28] leading to his re-entry into Troy (this time within the belly of a horse), likewise resembles the mythical pattern in which a hero descends into the Underworld to bring back the goddess.[29] Again a city stronghold seems to have taken the place of the Underworld. But Helen's recovery in this episode is postponed, presumably as a means of prolonging the war until the sack, and the pattern has been further overlaid with at least three themes: *evocatio*, the folkore of the treacherous queen, and the use of beggar or werewolf motif as spy. It is perhaps at this point worth observing that Helen, when she lost her fertility aspect as an underworld goddess and became humanized instead as a figure of youth and beauty and wealth, acquired political significance as a symbol of sovereignty between two rival camps. Her recovery in the Homeric epic thus implies a vestigial tradition of liberty for Greece and in this sense, and without the necessity for matrilinear interpretations, Helen in the Trojan myth represents the title deeds of the Western Kingdom. We shall see shortly that in another sense, too, Odysseus' entry into Troy to meet with Helen appears to be related to the myth of Theseus' abduction of Ariadne, but this is to anticipate an argument of a different kind to be touched upon presently.[30]

The abduction by Theseus of the Minoan vegetation goddess from Crete, to which we now turn, is closely associated with the myth of the Cretan labyrinth and Theseus' victory over the Minotaur within. According to the most familiar form of this myth, Minos of Knossos kept peace with Athens on condition that every nine years he received from the Athenians a tribute of seven youths and as many maidens, whom he shut up with the Minotaur in the labyrinth built by Dae-

[28] *Ibid.* 258, *κατὰ δὲ φρόνιν ἤγαγε πολλήν*. The significance of Odysseus' quest has been further developed through comparative myths in a fascinating article by H. W. Stubbs, "Troy, Asgard, and Armageddon", *F. L.* 70(1959), 440—449.

[29] The pattern is perhaps recognized in the *Gesta Romanorum* 156, in which the reader, having been told the story of how Ulysses detected Achilles in Scyros and took him to Troy, is informed that Paris represents the devil, Helen the soul, or all mankind, and Troy Hell; Ulysses stands for Christ, and Achilles for the Holy Ghost. Here the pattern has been given a Christianised twist.

[30] See esp. pp. 135ff.

dalus.[31] The details of how Ariadne, the daughter of Minos, saved Theseus from the labyrinth, by providing him with a clue of thread that he might find his way out after killing the Minotaur, are well known. How the goddess and the Minotaur came to be associated with the labyrinth, and even what the labyrinth originally was, are, however, disputed questions. Nilsson was of the opinion that the labyrinth of the Theseus-Ariadne myth was a "recollection" of the Cretan palace in its splendour before its fall in about 1400 B.C. and that the myths of the labyrinth and the Minotaur were "quite naturally attached to the hero who carried off the vegetation goddess, because both myths were of Minoan origin."[32] This, however, suggests a very loose association behind the process of the mythical accretion, and relies upon the view advanced by the excavator Sir Arthur Evans that the Cretan labyrinth was the complex palace itself.[33] In fact the idea of a labyrinth, which is a Cretan symbol *par excellence*, may be older than the palace. Herodotus speaks of an Egyptian labyrinth situated above Lake Moeris in imitation of which Diodorus, Varro and other ancient authorities say the Cretan labyrinth was built.[34] And whereas these same writers record the tradition also that the Egyptian labyrinth was either a king's tomb or palace,[35] subsequent excavation has since identified it at Hawara in the Egyptian Faiyum as a funerary building erected by Amenemhet III of the Twelfth Dynasty (*c.* 1800 B.C.).[36] Predating this, moreover, on an Egyptian schist seal

[31] Plut. *Thes.* 15. Cf. Verg. *Aen.* 6.21f., which mentions an annual tribute of seven youths only. Numerous other references are assembled in Roscher, *Lex. Myth.* s.v. "Labyrinthos", 2.1778ff.

[32] M. P. Nilsson, *The Mycenaean Origin of Gk. Mythology*, 176f.

[33] Sir Arthur Evans, *B.S.A.* 6(1899—1900), 33.

[34] Herod. 2.148—9, cf. Strabo 17.1.37, p. 811: Diod. 1.61 and 66 and 97, Varro and others *ap.* Pliny, *N.H.* 36.84—93.

[35] For this labyrinth as the king's tomb see Diod. 1.61 and Pliny *N.H.* 36.84 (quoting Lyceas Naucratites, and Manetho fr. 34—36 ed. Müller, *Frag. hist. Gr.* ii, 560). Other sepulchres too are mentioned in this passage as having been built in the form of a labyrinth, e.g. Varro *ap.* Pliny 36.91: *Sepultus* (sc. Porsenna) *sub urbe Clusio, in quo loco monumentum reliquit lapide quadrato quadratum, singula latera pedum tricenum, alta quinquagenum, in qua basi quadrata intus labyrinthum inextricabile, quo si quis introierit sine glomere lini, exitum invenire nequeat.*

[36] See H. R. Hall, "The Two Labyrinths", *J.H.S.* 25(1905), 328, A. B. Cook,

of the Sixth Dynasty (*c.* 2300 B.C.) is a figure in the middle of a stylized labyrinth, and two figures are depicted within a labyrinthine fret from Memphis in the Eighth Dynasty (*c.* 2200 B.C.), which have been tentatively interpreted as representing respectively a king-god in his sacred tomb and a king-god with his royal consort at the sacred marriage which formed an essential part of the king's coronation ceremony.[37] An even earlier architectural labyrinthine pattern has been traced in the design of the Egyptian royal tomb of King Perabsen at Abydos in the Second Dynasty (*c.* 3000 B.C.).[38] These pieces of evidence show at least that the Cretan labyrinth was not the earliest known labyrinth, and that earlier Egyptian labyrinths were used in connection with tombs and possibly also with their rites.

Labyrinths were not, of course, restricted to tombs only. Their tactical purpose is commonly applied to the building of fortifications, of which the Iron Age rampart of Maiden Castle in Dorsetshire in Britain is a very good example.[39] Nevertheless the association of labyrinths with tombs is widespread, and when merely found drawn upon them the labyrinthine pattern may have a magical purpose also. The city of Babylon, too, came to be regarded as a labyrinth, since turf mazes are known in Lapland as "Babylons".[40] Whether the recognition of this city as a labyrinth represents a very ancient way of thinking is uncertain, but in the once independent "Hymn of the Soul" incorporated now in the apocryphal *Acts of Thomas* a Journey to Babylon and to the walls of Sarbug is told in such a way that Sarbug almost certainly refers to Babylon; and the Syriac word Sar-

Zeus, 1.472, and other references in H. Kees, s.v. "Labyrinthos" in *R.E.* xii. 324—326.

[37] C. N. Deedes, "The Labyrinth" in *The Labyrinth* ed. S. H. Hooke (London 1935), 7—8 with figs. 7 and 9 = Sir W. M. Flinders Petrie, *Buttons and Design Scarabs* (London 1925), 7, Plate IV nos. 237—238.

[38] *Ibid.* 12, fig. 17 = Sir W. M. Flinders Petrie, *Royal Tombs of the Earliest Dynasties* (London 1901), II, Plate LXI, and p. 11. See also W. F. J. Knight, *Cumaean Gates*, ch. 4 in *Vergil: Epic and Anthropology*, 188ff.

[39] See Knight, *ib.* 190 and Plate II facing p. 135 (after R. E. Mortimer Wheeler, *The Antiquaries Journal* 15 [1935], 265ff. and Plate XXIX).

[40] See e.g. W. H. Matthews, *Mazes and Labyrinths*, 150; A. B. Cook, *Zeus*, 1.488f.

bug is rendered in the Greek version by *Λαβύρινθος*.[41] Moreover the chthonic aspect of Near Eastern cities generally has been investigated by Jackson Knight who gives reasons for thinking that Troy and "seven-gated" Thebes are further instances of labyrinthine cities overlaid with death imagery.[42] The widespread association of labyrinths in northern Europe with the name *Troia* or *Truia*,[43] and in particular the elaborate comparison by Vergil at *Aeneid* 5.545ff. of the movements of the *Troiae lusus* ("Troy game") as performed on horseback both at the funerary games in honour of Anchises and subsequently in the foundation of Alba Longa to the windings of the Cretan labyrinth, all point to Homer's Troy being a labyrinthine city.[44] If, too, we remember Helen's original role as a Kore, Odysseus'

[41] *Acts of Thomas*, 108ff. esp. 109.15, 111.6f. and 4 with *app. crit.* ed. M. Bonnet trans. M. R. James, *The Apocryphal New Testament* (Oxford corr. ed. 1953), 411—415 (vss. 19, 50, 69). A description of Babylon by the monk John Colobus, which is discussed by W. E. Crum. *J. Th. S.* 44 (1943), 123 n.1, strengthens the identification of the city with a labyrinth and accords with the Russian medieval myth telling how a foundling king rebuilt Babylon on seven hills and seven terraces like a ziggurat. For this myth see W. F. J. Knight, *Vergil: Epic and Anthropology*, 240. Further examination of the passage by Colobus I leave to Mr. J. H. Cowell, who first drew my attention to Crum's note and the Hymn by kindly permitting me to read his as yet unpublished article "Labyrinthine Cities, and Hades".

[42] Knight, *ib.* 298ff. for the chthonic aspect generally; 221f. and 298 for Thebes; and 218 and 236 for the mortuary aspect of Troy. The labyrinthine principle at Troy is found by Knight in the city's circular magic and the dances (211ff., 234ff., and cf. Krause, n. 44 below), in its walls and enfiladed gate (191), and in the city's very name (meaning "turning to and fro", 227ff., and cf. Krause again, n.44 below).

[43] The earliest occurrence of the actual word *Truia* is within a maze pattern shown on a seventh century B.C. Etruscan *Oinochoe* from Tragliatella. The maze extends from the tail of the second of two mounted horses. That the Etruscan potter was depicting the "Troy game", to which Vergil refers immediately below, has long been recognized. For details see G. Q. Giglioli in *Studi Etruschi* 3(1929), 111—160 and cf. next note.

[44] For the association of the Troy-names *Troia, Truia, Trojeborg, Trojenborg, Tröborg, Trojin,* "Troy-town" etc. with labyrinths see E. Krause, *Die Trojaburgen Nordeuropas* (Glogau 1893), where on pp. 109ff., 262—300 it is further suggested on the basis of northern folklore that the myths of Troy and Knossos are both memories of the northern "Troy" myths in which a maiden is rescued from the labyrinth. On pp. 10ff. Krause explains the root of the Troy-names as meaning "Umwallung, Umhüllung, Umkreisung'; cf. n. 42 above. Further literature on the

entry into the labyrinthine city of Troy has much in common with the catabatic pattern and Knight has endeavoured on both accounts to point out that Troy is in a way a Death-City.[45]

Labyrinthine patterns, then, assume a variety of forms. And not only architectural buildings (including tombs, forts, and city walls) but also maze-like dances can be called "labyrinths". They may indeed be interconnected if, as seems to be the case, labyrinthine dances were performed around tombs or city walls or at the entrances of caves. That their performance sometimes takes place at cave-entrances is appropriate since the tactical and magical purpose of labyrinths seems to be one of "exclusion and conditional penetration", to keep intruders out and keep the inside inviolate,[46] and from cave rites are said

"Troy game" will be found in E. Miehl, *R.E.* suppl. viii(1956), 888—905 s.v. "Troiaspiel". In Biblical tradition the figure was also known as Jericho or Nineveh and (in Finland) as "St. Peter's game".

[45] See also p. 132 above. Note conversely that, from the Trojan viewpoint, the Greek camp seems to take on a similar aspect when Priam journeys to fetch back Hector's corpse, which lay in Achilles' possession. Homer perhaps modelled this episode on a Journey of the Dead since at *Il.* 24.322ff. he describes how Priam on his journey to the Greek camp is joined near the tomb of Ilus by the psychopompos Hermes, who conducts him over the river Xanthus, which practically acquires the significance of an underworld river, past the guards, who like Cerberus are miraculously sent to sleep by Hermes, until they reach Achilles in his hut, who appears like a Hades-figure in a Land of the Dead. On this episode see F. Robert, *Homère*, 200—4, who asks, "N'aurait-on pas, à l'entour du tombeau d'Hector, raconté en poèmes rituels quelque descente de Priam aux Enfers pour racheter son fils par une négociation avec le roi des ombres?" Cf. also C. H. Whitman, *Homer and the Homeric Tradition* (Camb. Mass. 1958), 217f. Leaping across the centuries we find also a Christianized adaptation of Priam's journey in that part of the apocryphal *Gospel of Nicodemus*, preceding the *Descensus Christi ad Inferos*, known as the *Acta Pilati*. In the second Greek recension ed. C. Tischendorf, *Evangelia Apocrypha*², esp. 311—313 we read, in language that strikingly recalls Homer, how Joseph journeys with Nicodemus to Pilate to beg for the body of Jesus. For an indication that the Christian event has been Homerized see also J. Rendel Harris, *The Homeric Centones and the Acts of Pilate* (London 1898), 51—58. Perhaps the tendency to identify the enemy with the Underworld is as common in antiquity as in modern times. For a particularly good modern instance see Joseph O'Neille, *Land Under England*, published four years before the outbreak of the Second World War, describing a descent (in the classical tradition) to a hostile Underworld whose inhabitants were planning to invade the Upperworld.

[46] W. F. J. Knight, *Vergil: Epic and Anthropology*, 189 and 249. This principle

to come "firstly initiation ceremonies of many degrees, secondly prophecy, since access to the dead might be access to ancestral wisdom, and thirdly the myths of descent to the lower world."[47] Labyrinthine ritual, moreover, is not restricted to Egypt, the Near East, or Northern Europe, but is enacted also, for instance, even by the present day "megalithic" Malekulans in the New Hebrides before cave-entrances to the dead. It is, in this instance, undeniably a mortuary ritual, of which Layard writes: "the motive governing the supposed journey of the dead is not death, but renewed life through the association with dead ancestors living beyond the tomb."[48] It has been thought that Plato's allusion to the winding rituals practiced on earth as a foretaste of the soul's future journey in the next world also refers to a maze-like dance, performed in the mystery rite at Eleusis where the torch-bearers were supposed to represent the wanderings of Demeter in her search for Persephone.[49] It is, of course, unlikely that any full-scale dramatic representation could have taken place inside the Telesterion itself.[50]

From this brief summary of the association of ritual with labyrinths it is hoped that we may try to gain some insight into their significance. In particular it enables us to question whether the labyrinth of the Ariadne myth is adequately explained by the mere existence of the palace at Knossos. The Cretan labyrinth as a building is not, in

seems to be an extension of what had already been concluded by C. N. Deedes in *The Labyrinth*, 42 from Egyptian evidence.

[47] *Ibid.* 252. To the labyrinths mentioned by Knight in connection with caves, add the suggestion of a labyrinth in the form of spikes and railings with gates through them before Trophonios' oracular cave known (p. 56 above) as the *καταβάσιον*; for this see W. K. C. Guthrie, *The Greeks and their Gods* (London 1954), 230.

[48] J. Layard, "Maze-Dances and the Ritual of the Labyrinth in Malekula", *F.L.* 47(1936), 131, cf. *id.* "The Journey of the Dead" in *Essays Presented to C. G. Seligman* (London 1934), 113—42.

[49] Plato, *Phaedo*, 108A and for the maze-like character of the dance at Eleusis, W. F. J. Knight, *Vergil: Epic and Anthropology*, 266—7 and G. Thomson, "Mystical allusions in the *Oresteia*", *J.H.S.* 55(1935), 24f. For the wanderings see L. R. Farnell, *The Cults*, 3.181 and cf. the Homeric *Hymn to Dem.* 40ff.

[50] For various theories see N. J. Richardson, *The Homeric Hymn to Demeter* (Oxford 1974), 24f., 162, 165.

fact, attested by the Greeks before Pherecydes in the fifth century B.C., and the fact that the labyrinth is shown also in art in the latter half of the same century as Minos' palace is, as A. B. Cook long ago suggested, not proof that such was its original character.[51] Indeed much earlier in Homer it seems to have been associated with a dance. And this indication is strengthened if the title "Lady of the Labyrinth", *Λαβυρίνθος ποτνία(ι)*, which has been identified by Palmer on a Knossos tablet,[52] refers, as in all probability it does, to Ariadne, for whom Homer tells us Daedalus made a "dancing-floor" at Knossos.[53] The scholiast on the Homeric passage explains that Theseus, having escaped from the labyrinth with the aid of Ariadne's thread, learned from Daedalus how to weave the circling dance for the gods that resembled his own entrance into and exit from the labyrinth.[54] To this explanation Eustathius adds that a dance intended to recall the windings of the labyrinth was actually performed in his own day by sailors and old-fashioned folk.[55] The "Labyrinth" as the name of a dance is also mentioned by Lucian in a list of Cretan dance-themes.[56] And Plutarch tells of the so called "Crane" dance, said to have been brought by Theseus to Delos, whose motions imitate the windings and exits of the labyrinth from which Theseus escaped.[57]

[51] Pherecydes fr. 148, Jacoby *F. Gr. Hist*. 1. p. 98, apparently refers to the lintel of the labyrinth's door: *τὸν ζυγὸν τῆς ἄνω θύρας*. See also A. B. Cook, *Zeus*, 1.473f. with fig. 329.

[52] Knossos Gg. 702.2 interpreted by L. R. Palmer, "Observations on the Linear 'B' Tablets from Mycenae", *B.I.C.S*.2(1955), 40. See also J. L. Heller, "A Labyrinth from Pylos?", *A.J.A*. 65(1961), 57—62 and Pl.33.

[53] *Il*. 18.591f.

[54] Schol. A.B. *Il*.18.590.

[55] Eustath. *Il*. p. 1166, 17ff.

[56] Lucian, *de Salt*. 49.

[57] Plut. *Thes*. 21, Dicaearchus *ib*. fr. 85 Wehrli, and cf. Pollux 4.101. The François vase shows a dance of the liberated Athenian youths and maidens in Crete, not in Delos as was once thought; see P. E. Arias-Hirmer-Shefton, *A History of Greek Vase Painting* (London 1962), 288 and Pl. 43. The "Crane" or *geranos* is explained by L. B. Lawler, *The Dance in Ancient Greece* (London 1964), 47f. as a gyrating rope-dance. The thread with which Ariadne helped Theseus escape from the labyrinth in the myth may therefore be a mythological elaboration of the cord known to be held in Cretan rope-dances; on this see e.g. A. B. Cook, *J.H.S*. 14 (1894), 101f. and n. 131. For a different interpretation of the thread as part of

If Ariadne, as we have supposed, was originally a goddess in Crete, it is by no means inconceivable that the winding dance belonged in origin to Ariadne's cult and was performed before Theseus' supposed visit to Crete. If the goddess of the dance, also a vegetation goddess, was worshipped in the palace, her identity in myth with Minos' daughter would be readily explained. The canonical story of how Theseus entered the labyrinth and escaped from Crete with Minos' daughter would in that case be a reinterpretation of the original dance, in which Ariadne's divine status has been depressed and her dance rationalized as the place built by Daedalus for Minos in which the Minotaur was kept and into which Theseus was made to go. This outline of the development of the canonical myth from the ritual origin of Ariadne's winding dance also lends credibility to Cook's suggestion, based on the monumental evidence, that the dancing-ground excavated in the Stepped Area of the theatre, and actually identified by Sir Arthur Evans as the material foundation for the Homeric tradition, was probably the labyrinth proper of the palace and that the close relation of this dancing-ground to the palace at Knossos led to the erroneous view that the labyrinth was the complex palace itself.[58]

The role of the Minotaur in the Ariadne-Theseus myth may now be considered. The name has been explained variously as the "bull of Minos" (*Μίνωος ταῦρος*)[59] or as the "bull called Minos" (*τὸν Μίνω καλούμενον ταῦρον*),[60] the semi-rationalized version being preferred by Vergil who made the Minotaur the half-man, half-bull son of Pasiphae and the Bull.[61] Parallels in which a human or divine name is

Ariadne's anatomy see W. F. J. Knight, *Vergil: Epic and Anthropology*, 249ff., cf. 182—5, 231ff.

[58] A. B. Cook, *Zeus*, 1.481 n. 2, referring to Evans' view of the Homeric tradition in *Ann. Brit. Sch. Ath.* 1902—1903, ix. 111. Cook suggests that Evans does not identify this "Area" with the labyrinth because he already regards the whole palace as the labyrinth (p. 133 and n. 33 above).

[59] M. P. Nilsson, *The Mycenaean Origin of Gk. Mythology*, 177 n. 41.

[60] Paus. 3.18.11 and 16. A. B. Cook at first inclined to the view that Minos in his ritual disguise as bull gave rise to the legend of the Minotaur, but he later maintained that the Minotaur was Minos' son, or Pasiphae's, the Crown Prince of Knossos (*Zeus*, 1.491).

[61] *Aen.* 6.25f.: "*Mixtumque genus prolesque biformis/Minotaurus inest.*"

actually combined with that of an animal are few, but on the analogy with Aegipan, who is Pan with Goat's features, the Minotaur could well be Minos with the features of a Bull. And like the Pharaoh who is the perpetual Egyptian king-god, Minos in Crete appears to be the perpetual king-god who wore the mask of a bull. That he kept peace with the Athenians on condition that every one or nine years he received a human tribute, which he shut up with the Minotaur in the labyrinth, is, of course, a central part of the canonical version of the myth already referred to. But alongside this tradition is another in which he is said to have entered a cave himself every ninth year in order to consult with Zeus, whence he returned apparently rejuvenated after receiving new commandments or laws (*προστάγματα* or *νόμους*).[62] He is thus a Frazerish king who sometimes is the deity and sometimes consults with the deity. At first the tradition about him in his cave might seem to be distinct from that of the Minotaur in his labyrinth. Yet the cave into which Minos periodically retired can hardly be separated from the going into the labyrinth every nine years to be slain by the Minotaur.[63] It would appear from this that the periodic withdrawal of the perpetual Cretan ruler into the Dictaean cave to consult with Zeus is respectable history: but respectable history has become entangled with myth. Minos' cave has become amalgamated with the myth of Ariadne, while the bull-king in his cave-tomb has become a bull-monster who in his labyrinthine prison devours all visitors. And once the Knossian palace is itself viewed as the labyrinth, Minos has virtually taken on the aspect of a Hades-figure ruling

[62] Plato, *Min.* 319C, *Laws* 624B, Strabo 476, 482, 726, Dion. 2.61.2, Diod. 5.78.3. Cf. also Homer's allusion to Minos, *ἐννέωρος βασίλευε* at *Od.* 19.179: the sense is elusive, but J. G. Frazer, *The Golden Bough*, 4.59ff., 70ff., refers this, with the other passages, to an octennial, called in Greek a nine-year, tenure of kingship. G. Thomson, "The Greek Calendar", *J.H.S.* 63(1943), 59—65 further suggests that the eight-year tenure of kingship had a Mycenaean origin. Cf. the persistence in Sparta of the ritual eight-year search for omens, discussed by H. W. Parke, "The Deposing of Spartan Kings", *C.Q.* 39(1945), 106—112.

[63] G. Murray, *The Rise of the Greek Epic*, 136f. n. 2. The labyrinth is said to be a cave in *Et. Mag.* 554.26. For other suggestive references see W. F. J. Knight, *Vergil: Epic and Anthropology*, 247, and cf. R. Guénon, "La Caverne et le Labyrinthe", *Études Traditionnelles* 214(1937), 349—354 and 215(1937), 385—390.

over a mythical Land of the Dead,[64] wherein dwells the Minotaur, a death-devouring monster resembling Hades' Cerberus, who permits no visitors to return.

That Theseus entered the Labyrinth, redeemed his own people from the Death-devourer, and married the Devil's daughter may well be a case of history that has been pushed into the procrustean pattern laid down by myth. The victory over the Minotaur, commemorated subsequently by the Athenians in an annual pilgrimmage to Delos where the Crane dance was enacted,[65] conceivably reflects a real historical conquest of prehistoric Athens over Crete,[66] which has been pushed into a catabatic framework. In the process Ariadne was not merely the underworld fertility-queen who has been humanized into a princess; she has also acquired political significance as Minos' daughter. The hero in this Saviour-myth therefore no longer journeys into the Underworld to fetch back a goddess: instead Theseus, the national hero of Athens, whose aspirations are projected back into the Archaic period, marries the Devil's daughter and wins for himself a crown[67] and — because the Athenians now have a King of their own — freedom for his people. Leaping across the centuries we find much the same when a hero kills a dragon and wins the hand of a princess with half the kingdom or, what amounts to the same thing, wins the gold

[64] That is, he is a living ogre ruling over a real land which has acquired the mythical characteristics of an Underworld. An ogre-like character is given to him in the Theseus-myths and as an evil-minded ruler we find him already in Homer, *Od.* 11.322, *Μίνωος ὀλοόφρονος*. The fact that he is portrayed, also in the *Nekyia*, as a just ruler in the Underworld puzzled the scholiasts: schol. Q. *καὶ πῶς* "*Μίνωα εἶδον Διὸς ἀγλαὸν υἱόν*"; schol. T. *πῶς οὖν θεμιστεύει ἐν τοῖς νεκροῖς ὀλοόφρων ὤν*; But there were in fact two opposed traditions handed down about Minos, his underworld role reflecting the alternative tradition in which he was thought to have been a just ruler on earth; cf. Plat. *Min.* 318D—E.

[65] The pilgrimage was despatched on the 6th of Thargelion (Xen. *Mem.* 4.8.2, Plat. *Phaedo* 58A—B, Callim, *Del.* 307—315) and the Crane dance was probably performed on the 7th, G. Thomson, *J.H.S.* 63(1943), 63.

[66] According to H. J. Rose, *Oxford Class. Dict.* s.v. "Minos", the evil character given to Minos in the Attic myths indicates as much.

[67] Ariadne in art is frequently shown holding a crown; see e.g. S. Reinach, *Répertoire des Vases Peints*, 1.509, 2.271 and cf. the late Geometric vase in *J.H.S.* 19(1899), 200 and plate 8. Cf. also the crown given to Theseus by Amphitrite, n. 69 below.

that the dragon has been guarding. That Ariadne, being perhaps originally "not a princess outside, helping Theseus to get away, but a figure corresponding to those maidens of ritual, having her place in the middle",[68] is not inside the labyrinth in the canonical myth matters little. From the Princess in the Middle of the Labyrinth to the Young Man's Accomplice is an easy and natural graduation. Helen held both positions at Troy. In any case it suffices for the Ariadne-myth that the heroine is in the area and helps the hero to overcome his ordeal; and the Underworld, though typified by the labyrinth, is for the purpose of the myth the whole palace, if not Crete itself.

Indication that Theseus' achievement is capable of being cast in a thinly veiled catabatic mould finds further support in a remarkable story of Theseus' descent into the watery domain of Poseidon and Amphitrite, which convinces Minos that his adversary was truly Poseidon's son. In Bacchylides' Ode 12 (xvi) we are told that Minos encounters Theseus on his voyage to Crete with twice seven youths and maidens for the Minotaur and behaves presumptuously towards one of the maidens. When Theseus intervenes to protect her, Minos, angered by the rebuke, calls Theseus' divine parentage into doubt and challenges him to retrieve as proof of his divinity a golden ring, which he straightway flings down into the sea. Theseus, accepting the challenge, leaps overboard and descends into the underwater palace of his father Poseidon. He confounds Minos by returning from the descent crowned with Amphitrite's anadem. Pausanias also tells the story while giving an account of the third mural in the Theseion painted by Micon soon after 475 B.C. ,which makes clear, as Bacchylides did not, that Theseus returns with the ring.[69]

[68] W. F. J. Knight, *Vergil: Epic and Anthropology*, 246, after Krause n. 44 above.

[69] Paus. 1.17.3. Cf. also Hyg. *Astron.* 2.5. Scenes from Theseus' descent are frequently represented in art, the earliest being shown in the inner tondo of a cup of Euphronios *c.* 500—490 B.C. in the Louvre G. 104; *A.R.V.*[2] 318. 1; P. Arias-Hirmer-Shefton, *History of Greek Vase Painting*, plate 134 (with bibliography). The artist Onesimos here depicts Theseus, who is accompanied by Athene, being greeted in her underwater realm by a seated Amphitrite, who holds in her hand a crown resembling a wreath, which she will present to him. For this and other illustrations of the myth with full discussion see P. Jacobsthal, *Theseus auf dem Meeresgrunde* (Leipzig 1911). A recent examination of late archaic and early classical

The success redounding to Theseus' credit from his Cretan exploit is in sharp contrast to his failure to abduct Persephone from the Underworld. Nilsson believes that success would have been the crowning end to the hero's career, and thinks it therefore highly improbable that Theseus' attempt to fetch the vegetation goddess was originally considered a crime. He attributes the failure of the expedition to the fact that Persephone in this myth appears as the Queen of the Dead as well as the Vegetation Goddess, and supposes that the attempt to vanquish the Empire of Death was bound to fail according to the Greek ideas concerning the irresistible power of Death.[70] He surmises accordingly that Theseus' underworld journey to fetch the Vegetation Goddess and Peirithous' descent to fetch the Queen of the Netherworld were originally separate, incompatible myths, and that the two heroes were joined in friendship so as to harmonize them. He explains the puzzle of how the Thessalian hero and king of the Lapiths was brought to Attica by suggesting that a certain Peirithous, the eponymous hero of the Attic family called the Peirithoidae, was joined in friendship to Theseus and only later was identified with the better known Thessalian hero of the same name.[71] The conjecture is not without merit, but overlooks the possibility that the Peirithoidae might have been an immigrant population. In this case the fusion of the two myths, especially if we could be sure that the earliest mention of the heroes in *Odyssey* 11.631 were an interpolation,[72] might conceivably be taken to reflect Cimon's Athenian-Thessalian alliance in the fifth century B.C. However, one cannot lightly rule out a third possibility, that this is a hostile myth. For the implication is that the whole

representations by J. P. Barron, *J.H.S.* 92(1972), 40—41, where is given a more recent bibliography of the paintings of this period, reaffirms that no trace of a copy of Micon's painting on the third wall of the Theseion has been found. The probable influence of Theseus' underwater descent upon Vergil has been referred to already in ch. 4 at nn. 2—3 above.

[70] *The Mycenaean Origin of Greek Mythology*, 173f.

[71] *Ibid.* 174f.

[72] One cannot help but sympathize with the view that this inorganic line has been interpolated, as might also have been the inorganic line at *Il.* 1.265 which introduced Theseus among the Lapiths. The appearance in art of the two heroes together is comparatively late also.

undertaking has gone wrong. Yet *cui bono?* Who would be responsible for circulating a hostile version about Theseus?

We know of at least one anti-Theseus myth casting Theseus, who flung the honest, respectable Megarian prince Sciron headlong into the sea, in the role of a briggand, but this is a Megarian legend which stands the conventional story on its head.[73] And whereas Theseus is not exactly flattered in the myths which tell of his desertion of Ariadne,[74] there is no reason why Athenian mythographers should have sought to denigrate their own king.[75] And with the notable exception of the Persephone-myth this is never done. However, given the context and the environment of the myth, can it be that the Persephone-myth is an Eleusinian story suggesting that even kings should treat the Eleusinian cult with respect? The implication would be that what Theseus did with Helen is not permissible with Eleusinian Persephone. Eleusis is known to have been frank with crowned heads on occasion.[76] And in any case the blame for this sacrilegious descent attaches more to Peirithous, who conceived a desire for the underworld queen, than to Theseus, who was obliged to join in the venture to discharge his debt to Peirithous in connection with Helen. This seems to be remembered

[73] See Plut. *Thes.* 10.2 and 25.4 for the Megarian legend. In the Attic legend found in Simonides *ap.* Plut. *ib.* 10.2 and Bacchylides 13 (xvii), 24f. Theseus heroically destroys Sciron, who is depicted as the wicked robber.

[74] Cf. above p. 129 at n.15, and Theocr. 2.45f. The strange myth told at *Od.* 11.321—325, in which Ariadne was killed by Artemis on evidence from Dionysus, has sometimes been regarded as an Athenian alteration designed to save the fame of Theseus, but is better taken to represent a conflict between the Nature god Dionysus and the old Nature goddess Ariadne in which the former was victorious and the latter's cult was suppressed; see M. P. Nilsson, *The Minoan-Mycenaean Religion*^{2}, 525 n. 63 and T. B. L. Webster, *From Mycenae to Homer*, 49f., 62; though the natural deduction is not that Ariadne deserted Dionysus for Theseus (Nilsson, Webster), but that Ariadne, like Callisto, was Artemis' votary and was reported by Dionysus to be with Theseus on his own island.

[75] Theseus, unlike the Tarquins of Rome, for example, was not associated with the Bad Old Days, though he does have trouble with Menestheus, a kind of democratic opposition leader; Plut. *Thes.* 32.

[76] Even Nero, for fear of rebuke, refrained from taking part in the Eleusinian mysteries according to Suetonius, *Nero* 34. There are, in fact, a surprising number of myths in which kings fall foul of religious centres, e.g. Oedipus, Pentheus, Salmoneus of Elis etc.

in the myths which relate how Heracles rescued Theseus but left Peirithous to his fate in Hades.

In sum, the abductions of Ariadne and Helen and the attempted abduction of Persephone-Kore appear to be three variants of a catabatic theme. The successful abductions of the princesses from Sparta and Crete have political significance. In the third myth the Underworld appears in its own right — though in one tradition it is converted into a well-known Land of the Dead in Epirus — and the failure to abduct the Queen perhaps registers a protest by the Eleusinian cult.

CHAPTER VI

AENEAS' APOCALYPTIC VISION AND THE REFORGING OF TRADITION

For the purpose of illustrating Vergil's art in reforging a complex tradition, the foregoing chapters may have helped sufficiently, it is hoped, to outline the chief mythological patterns associated with the pre-Vergilian catabatic heroes Odysseus, Heracles, Orpheus, Pollux, and Theseus. From these Vergil creates a catabatic hero of destiny, who obtained from the World of Shades a glorious apocalyptic vision of Rome's future greatness under Augustus. Aeneas' search for the new land promised by the gods was actually contemporaneous with the Return of the Greeks to their own Kingdoms after the Sack of Troy. Having come with his band of Trojan refugees to the Italian shore of Cumae, Aeneas passes through the gates of Avernus into the Lower World at about the same time as Odysseus makes his Visit to the Land of the Dead on the far shores of Ocean. Perhaps for this reason Odysseus alone of the above mortal visitors is not mentioned by Aeneas in his appeal to the Sibyl to be allowed into the regions below. Nevertheless, as we shall now see, Odysseus' omission has not diminished the indebtedness of Vergil to Homer's *Nekyia.*

Faced with the necessity of inventing an Approach to Avernus Vergil did what he had already done in the *Georgics.* He drew on earlier themes, some of them associated with descents, and cunningly wove them together. No sooner had Vergil brought Aeneas to Cumae's shore than he directs his steps to the Cumaean acropolis crowned by Apollo's temple in search of the far-famed Sibyl.[1] And there on the

[1] *Aen.* 6.1ff. For an examination of the testimonia, text, and topography as it relates to the Sibyl's cave and the cave's proximity to Apollo's temple, see my "Vergil, *Aeneid,* 6,40ff. and the Cumaean Sibyl's Cave", *Latomus* 36 (1977), 482—495. In local tradition the cave of the Sibyl at Cumae has been and still is sometimes conflated with the underworld cave at Avernus. For the two caves see the following chapter p. 204 below.

temple-gates carved by Daedalus, Aeneas beholds a series of scenes laid in Attica and Crete evoking the figure of Theseus and depicting the Cretan labyrinth at Knossos.[2] It is an unexpected beginning to Aeneas' mission, and one which is said to have delayed the action of the poem, either with "disturbing effect,"[3] or for good purpose because the labyrinth, like Temes-Savsap's delaying maze in the Malekulan mortuary ritual described on p. 87 above, has apotropaic force.[4]

The comparison is suggestive and accords well with Vergil's anthropological interest, but Vergil's Sibyl cannot properly be compared to the Malekulan guardian of the Underworld, who draws part of the labyrinth in order to baffle the uninitiated dead, since far from encouraging Aeneas to gaze at such sights, the Sibyl reprimands him for doing so:

> "non hoc ista sibi tempus spectacula poscit." (*Aen.* 6.37)
>
> ("This is no time for such sight-seeing.")

It has, moreover, been argued[5] that the apotropaic interpretation of Vergil's labyrinth is misleading, since Vergil emphasises the difficulty not of entering, but of leaving the labyrinth:

> hic labor ille domus et inextricabilis error;
> magnum reginae sed enim miseratus amorem
> Daedalus ipse dolos tecti ambagesque resolvit,
> caeca regens filo vestigia. (6.27—30)

(Here was the Cretan building in all its elaboration, with the wandering track which might not be unravelled. But Daedalus himself, who because her love was strong had taken pity on the Princess Ariadne, guided the sightless footsteps by means of a thread.)

[2] It can be rightly argued that the carvings do not *pace* Karl Kerényi, *Labyrinth-Studien* (Zürich 1950), 32, depict a single labyrinth-pattern (see the criticism of Kerényi by H. J. Rose, *C. R.* 2[1953], 113), but the labyrinth does undoubtedly predominate.

[3] E. Norden, *Aeneis Buch VI*³, 120f. on *Aen.* 6.14ff.

[4] W. F. J. Knight, *Vergil: Epic and Anthropology*, 155f.

[5] See P. J. Enk, "De Labyrinthi Imagine in Foribus Templi Cumani Insculpta", *Mnemosyne* 11(1958), 324.

Even so, some apotropaic force remains. For in the Sibyl's famous warning at *Aeneid* 6.126—129 —

> "facilis descensus Averno:
> noctes atque dies patet atri ianua Ditis;
> sed revocare gradum superasque evadere ad auras,
> hoc opus, hic labor est."

> ("Easy is the descent to Avernus. Throughout every night and every day the door of black Pluto [Dis] stands wide open. But to retrace the steps and escape back to upper airs, that is the task and that is the toil.") —

the words *hoc opus, hic labor est* describing the difficulty of returning from the world below appear almost as a flashback to the words *hic labor ille domus*, which describe the complications of the Cretan labyrinth.[6] It seems therefore as though the Entry of Theseus into the Labyrinth, with the aid of the clue provided by Ariadne, foreshadows Aeneas' Descent into the Kingdom of the Dead with the Sibyl's guidance and the Golden Bough.[7] This impression is strengthened further if Varro's words *labyrinthum inextricabile* describing the labyrinthine royal sepulchre of the Etruscan king Porsenna[8] lie behind Vergil's description of the labyrinth as the *inextricabilis error* in the above passage. And since Varro and Vergil are alone known in the pre-Christian era to have used the word *inextricabilis* in the sense of *ambages,* "windings", Vergil's acquaintance with the Varronian passage is likely.[9] It is conceivable also, since we find a reference by Pliny to the Egyptian labyrinth in the words *ad viarum illum inexplicabilem errorem*, that Vergil may have read Pliny's source.[10]

From these indications we might infer, then, that the labyrinth on the

[6] As noticed by Margaret de G. Verrall, "Two instances of symbolism in the Sixth *Aeneid*", *C.R.* 24(1910), 43f.

[7] Probably for these reasons Michael Ayrton in his imaginative novel *The Maze Maker* (London 1967), ch. 39, actually locates the Cumaean labyrinth in the Underworld, where he has Daedalus consult the Sibyl.

[8] The passage is quoted fully in ch. 5 n. 35 above.

[9] As P. J. Enk, *Mnemosyne* 11(1958), 325 points out.

[10] *Ibid.* Enk here finds six similarities in *Aeneid* 6 to the passage in Pliny *N.H.* 36.84—88 which describes Daedalus' Cretan labyrinth.

Cumaean Gates was closely connected in Vergil's thought and poetry with both tombs and the Underworld as places of No Return.[11] The association at any rate makes it appropriate that the labyrinth appears as a kind of prelude to the Underworld Journey on the very approaches to the World of the Dead.

Another person of vital interest besides Theseus is evoked by the scenes of the Cretan labyrinth at Cumae. Eichholz[12] has suggested that Daedalus, the exile who came with less felicitous results to the West, is pictured here in order to be contrasted to Aeneas, who was guided to Cumae with the mission of founding a new city. This contrast is taken to be the focal point of the carvings, providing the clue to the Sibyl's reprimand: Aeneas must be unlike Daedalus, the genius who failed. For whereas Daedalus escaped, with the loss of his son Icarus, from the Cretan labyrinth, of his own making, to recreate the past on the gates of Apollo's temple at Cumae, Aeneas escaped from a god-sent disaster at Troy with rising expectation in his son — *spes surgentis Iuli* — and a future to look forward to. But in spite of the contrast, which is too well balanced to be fortuitous, the pictured maze is not Daedalus-centred. It is true that Theseus is not mentioned by name. However, he is here conspicuous by his absence, and one cannot follow the description of the Maiden, the Minotaur, and the Athenian hostages without thinking of him primarily in his liberating role.

The paradigm is appropriate and suggestive. For liberation legends whether in Roman history or pseudo-history or mythology are few,

[11] The labyrinthine symbolism was later Christianized. A stone inscription at Lyons reads: "Observe by scanning this sight that you will die... Pray to Christ... He rescued me from this Labyrinth":

HOC SPECVLO · SPECVLARE LEGENS · QUOD SIS MORITVRVS : ...
XPM QVESO ROGA · SIT VT IN XPO MEA VITA :
ME CAPVT APRIL' · EX HOC RAPVIT LABERINTO : ...

(For the complete inscription see W. H. Matthews, *Mazes and Labyrinths,* 68).

[12] D. E. Eichholz's conclusions in "Symbol and Contrast in the *Aeneid*", *G. & R.* 15(1968), 105—112 are developed from the symbolistic views of V. Pöschl, *The Art of Vergil* (Ann Arbor 1962), 150: "The pictures symbolically mirror Aeneas' destiny"; and Brooks Otis, *Virgil: A Study in Civilised Poetry*, 284: "Aeneas here... gazes at his own past, though this time at his past symbolically disguised".

and Vergil is clearly conscious of the liberating mission of the Trojans in Italy. In the climax of Aeneas' descent, which is the Show of Heroes, Aeneas' father alludes to the popular legend celebrating the liberation of the people from the harsh rule of the Tarquins and the failure of the Etruscan king Porsenna to restore it.[13] The same legend is pictured proleptically on Aeneas' Shield, and the liberators are there identified as "the descendants of Aeneas" who were seen "dashing to death for freedom's sake", *Aeneadae in ferrum pro libertate ruebant* (8. 648). This is even foreshadowed by Aeneas' own liberating mission to prevent Mezentius from getting back into power — like the exiled Tarquinius Superbus, Mezentius himself was a cruel Etruscan despot, who was overthrown and tried unsuccessfully to come back with a foreign force.[14] And so Vergil naturally thinks of Minos too, who like Porsenna was a foreign oppressor in a deliverance myth.

But in Roman tradition there are no exact parallels to the liberation myths of other countries which celebrate the termination of occupied country. Aeneas, therefore, represents more of a civilizing than a liberating mission. Thus Lavinia might correspond to Ariadne, but — except in the sense in which the Etruscans are to be liberated from their own Mezentius — no victims require liberating and the Cretan story is therefore not developed.

Aeneas is still on the Approach to Avernus. The first third of the Book is taken up with the different incidents that lead to the Descent. After the reprimand outside the temple doors, the Sibyl bids Aeneas perform sacrifices. He then enters into the Sibyl's oracular cave. There follows the magnificent and totally convincing description of the

[13] Diodorus 4.77 and Pausanias 7.4.6 record the tradition that Daedalus escaped to Sicily, and Diodorus at 4.30 adds that he went on to Sardinia. Vergil alone seems to have made him come to Cumae and build the temple with the labyrinth. For more details see G. Verrall, *C.R.* 24(1910), 44 and P. J. Enk, *Mnemosyne* 11 (1958), 330.

[14] *Aen.* 7.647ff., 8.478ff., and 10.689—908. There are no comparable Roman legends. That which grew up around the *decemvir* Appius Claudius, for instance, whose shameful conspiracy against Verginia for his own ends led to the resignation of the whole board of the *decemviri* (Livy, 3.44—48 and H. Gundel, *R.E.* 2nd. ser. 8A, 1530—1535 s.v. "24. Verginia"), is a liberation legend of sorts but is better thought of as a patrician scandal *par excellence*.

Sibyl's prophetic frenzy, Aeneas' plea to visit his father in the world below, and her foreboding reply, that before he can enter upon his quest he must obtain the Golden Bough, the only passport into the "covered-up places of earth" (*telluris operta*, 140), and bury the body of one of his companions who has just met his death. This last sad announcement is soon explained when Aeneas returns to the beach and comes across the body of Misenus. His first duty, therefore, is to build a pyre and bury his dead companion.

Vergil introduces the death of Misenus at this point from earlier traditions associated with both Odysseus and Aeneas. But in pre-Vergilian legend it is not connected with any *κατάβασις εἰς αἵδου*. Why then does Vergil bring in the incident of the death of Misenus just before Aeneas prepares to enter into the World of the Dead? The question takes us back to books 10 and 11 of Homer's *Odyssey*. Elpenor, we recall, one of the companions of Odysseus, had forgotten, after a drunken sleep, to use the stair-case down from the roof of Circe's palace just at the hour when Odysseus was setting out for the Halls of Hades. And having fallen and broken his neck he was still unburied when his ghost besought Odysseus at the threshold of the Underworld to bury his body upon his return, and to plant upon his funeral mound the oar with which he had rowed during his lifetime.

Vergil has evidently shaped his design upon the Homeric incident, but has, even so, wonderfully refashioned it. Misenus had met an equally undignified death — *indigna morte peremptum* (6.163) — having fallen among the rocks near Cumae[15] while challenging the gods to a contest with his hollow shell. And he perished, too, just prior to the Underworld Journey. But, unlike Elpenor, he is to be buried first. Thus Vergil transforms the burial into an essential condition of the descent, having read, perhaps, some ancient criti-

[15] E. Norden, *Aeneis Buch VI*^{3}, 185 on *Aen.* 6.174 assumed that Vergil set the scene of Misenus' drowning among the rocks *(inter saxa)* of Porto di Miseno in the waters of Baiae, where tradition also placed his death (Dion. Hal. *Ant. Rom.* 1.53.2), but this creates topographical awkwardness with Aeneas' Cumaean landing. For the likelihood that Vergil has transferred the drowning from the Baiaean to the Cumaean coast together with other innovations connected with the Cumaean landfall, see my "Misenus and the Cumaean Landfall: Originality in Vergil's use of Topography and Tradition", *T.A.P.A.* 107 (1977), 63—71.

cism condemning Odysseus for leaving his comrade unburied, "since another task was pressing" (ἐπεὶ πόνος ἄλλος ἔπειγε, *Od.* 11.54).[16]

At all events Vergil's hero of destiny cannot be faulted. Nor does he leave out the detail of the oar. Aeneas, unasked, plants the oar upon Misenus' burial mound. It is probable that at this point Vergil was also intentionally invoking local legends in which Misenus was a rower.[17] The episode of the oar may be compared also to the broken blade, from the ship Argo, set over the tomb of Mopsus, "for a possession of the dead" (Lycophron, 881—884). Perhaps originally connected with the same idea is the planting of the branch of the fig tree upon the tomb of the dead man Prosymnus, by Dionysus after he returns from the Underworld to find Prosymnus dead (see p. 105 above). It has also been compared to the planting of the oar in the earth by Odysseus on his last journey (*Od.* 11.128; 23.275; cf. p. 41 above), and has been thought to be for the dead man to cross the river or ocean of death, and to be part of the Golden Bough.[18] The evidence is certainly suggestive of this.

Apart from some topographical difficulties,[19] the arrangement with Misenus and the quest for the Golden Bough works well. We shall consider the Bough more fully in the next chapter. But it is worth emphasising here the stroke of genius involved in making Misenus' burial, as well as the fetching of the Golden Bough, a prerequisite for Aeneas' descent. Vergil has not only safeguarded the *pietas* of his hero. He has dovetailed with the Descent of Aeneas the aetiological legend about Cape Misenum, at whose foot Misenus is buried.[20] And since Misenus is now buried with honour, Vergil must assign to another of Aeneas' companions the other part of the role of Elpenor,

[16] That Vergil for other passages took notice of the Homeric scholia is shown by R. R. Schlunk, "Vergil and the Homeric Scholia", *A.J.P.* 88(1967), 33—44; and *id. The Homeric Scholia and the Aeneid: A Study of Influence of Ancient Homeric Literary Criticism on Vergil* (Michigan 1974).

[17] See further J. Hubaux, "Misène", *A.C.* 2(1933), 146.

[18] See W. F. Jackson Knight, *Vergil: Epic and Anthropology*, 171. Miss Theo Brown, "St. Joseph of Arimathea at Glastonbury", *F.L.* 57(1946), 75—79 has found striking resemblance to this idea also in the staff carried and planted by Joseph of Arimathea.

[19] See my article at n. 15 above.

[20] *Aen.* 6.234f.

namely that of the Unburied Dead Companion who converses with the mortal visitor at the threshold of the Underworld.

As soon as the funeral rites are over and Aeneas arrives with the Golden Bough, the Sibyl invokes the goddess Hecate at the lakeside of Avernus; Aeneas sacrifices to Night, Earth, Proserpine, and Pluto; and the two plunge into the world below past the frightful shapes at the Entrance, past the Tree of Dreams, past the monsters of the Shadow-land, and on until they come to Charon's boat, which is to be envisaged as somehow crossing the Stygian marsh at the confluence of the rivers Acheron and Cocytus.[21]

Aeneas sees here a throng of ghosts anxious to be taken across the infernal water. These are likened to the thickly falling leaves in the woods at the first frost of autumn:

> Quam multa in silvis autumni frigore primo
> Lapsa cadunt folia. (6. 309—310)

(As numerous were they as the leaves of the forest which fall at the first chill of autumn and float down.)

And on a happier note they are compared in a second simile to birds migrating to sunny lands (6. 310—312). The transmission of the second simile must remain largely controversial, but the leaf-simile has assuredly enjoyed a remarkable history in catabatic literature before Vergil took it over. It may perhaps have been inspired by a simile in Homer's *Iliad* (6. 146—149), in which the generations of mankind are compared to leaves that flourish and decay. But the truly evocative quality of the simile springs especially from the memory it conjures up of another simile, which survives in one or more versions of the Greek *catabasis* featuring Heracles. In the version of Heracles' descent recorded by Bacchylides the descending hero sees the spirits of the dead located, appropriately enough, on Cocytus' bank. Here they are compared to the leaves tossed by the wind on Mount Ida:

[21] Charon crosses the Stygian marsh (*Stygiam paludem*, 323, 369, cf. 374, 385, 414), or lake (*Stygios lacus*, 134) and yet he is also guardian of *(servat)* Acheron and Cocytus (295ff.). The souls waiting to cross in his barque are associated with Cocytus at 318, 323, 327, 330 and 384.

> *ἔνθα δυστάνων βροτῶν*
> *ψυχὰς ἐδάη παρὰ Κωκυτοῦ ῥεέθροις,*
> *οἷά τε φύλλ' ἄνεμος*
> *Ἴδας ἀνὰ μηλοβότους*
> *πρῶνας ἀργηστὰς δονεῖ.*
>
> (*Epinician* 5. 63—67)

(There beside the waters of Cocytus he perceived the souls of hapless mortals like leaves aquiver in the wind upon Ida's gleaming headlands grazed by sheep.)

Pindar, too, in *P. Oxy.* 2622, as has been said in chapter 3 above, describes Heracles' Descent; and the leaf-simile may have occurred in the lost clause preceding the fragmented phrase *καὶ ὅσ' ἐν πόντωι...*, which suggests a second simile. Just enough of the scene has survived to make credible the suggestion that here, as in Bacchylides, Heracles saw Meleager (*Με]λέαγρον* is mentioned a few lines after the passage quoted below) and the countless ghosts in Hades:

> *αὐ]τίκα νιν φθιμένων[*
> *]τρέφεται καὶ ὅσ' ἐν πόντωι[*
> *]μενοσ[ ]*
> *]α μ[έγα]ν Διὸς υἱὸν [*
> ...
>
> (a: 12—15)[22]

Equally remarkable is the subsequent history of the simile in catabatic literature after Vergil. It is taken up and enlarged with comparisons to flowers, waves, and birds by Seneca *Oedipus* 600ff. True to the geographical location of the simile in Bacchylides, possibly Pindar

[22] For a more thoroughgoing examination of these and other passages in connection with both the leaf- and the bird-simile in their catabatic contexts, see my article mentioned in ch. 3 n. 39, where I take the Pindaric passage to strengthen Norden's suggestion that there must once have existed an early poem of the *Descent of Heracles* which exercised considerable influence on Bacchylides etc. I have not, however, convinced G. Thaniel, "Vergil's Leaf- and Bird-Similes of Ghosts", *Phoenix* 25(1971), 237—245, who in rejecting my argument pays little heed to the underworld contexts of the similes and, for unstated reasons, supposes (p. 241) that Lobel, Lloyd-Jones, and myself have all been too hasty in attributing *P. Oxy.* 2622 to Pindar, for which cf. my pp. 89—90 above.

(see p. 212), and Vergil, Dante applies the comparison, with a remnant of the bird-simile, too, to the souls of the Godless on the banks of the underworld river, called in the *Inferno* the Acheron:

> Come d'autunno si levan le foglie
>   l'una appresso dell' altra, infin che il ramo
>   vede alla terra tutte le sue spoglie:
> similemente il mal seme d'Adamo
>   gittansi di quel lito ad una ad una,
>   per cenni, come augel per suo richiamo.
> Così sen vanno su per l'onda bruna,
>   ed avanti che sian di là discese,
>   anche di qua nova schiera s'aduna.
>
> (Canto 3. 112—120)

And the Vergilian associations are further adapted by Milton to suggest the wanness and dejection of Satan's fallen spirits as on the infernal beach — observe the location — they assemble

> Thick as autumnal leaves that strew the brooks
> In Vallombrosa, where the Etrurian shades
> High over-arched imbower.
>
> (*Paradise Lost* 1.302—304)[23]

Aeneas is struck by the disorder among the ghosts and learns from the Sibyl that only the buried are privileged to cross immediately in Charon's barque. The others must wait about the shores for a hundred years. As Aeneas ponders on the hard lot of all these souls, he

[23] Could it be that Milton's description of Hell was inspired not only by his reading of classical and mediaeval literature but also by his knowledge of the very region that stimulated Vergil's imagination in the Sixth Book of the *Aeneid?* Marjorie Nicolson gives good reason for thinking that it was, in "Milton's Hell and the Phlegraean Fields", *University of Toronto Quarterly* 7(1938), 500—513. Other passages in English literature independently of the underworld locale recall Vergil's leaf-simile. Shelley inverts the comparison in *Ode to the West Wind* and describes the "leaves dead" as being driven from the west wind of autumn "like ghosts from an enchanter fleeing." Compare also, for a reminiscence of Bacchylides, Marlowe, *Tamburlaine* Part 2.III. 5.3: "In number more than are the quivering leaves/Of Ida's forest".

recognizes and speaks to the shade of his unburied helmsman Palinurus, who just before the end of the voyage to Italy when touched by the wand of the god of sleep had fallen overboard from his ship taking with him the rudder and a section of the stern.[24] Vergil has so arranged matters that Aeneas knows nothing of Palinurus' death before this encounter with his ghost, so that no blame attaches to him for not having already buried his dead companion. Palinurus' ghost now tells Aeneas that having fallen overboard he had made it to shore only to be killed by savages, and he begs Aeneas to give him a burial. Several Homeric threads are interwoven into this episode. In particular the manner of Palinurus' death seems to have been suggested by the death of Phrontis, Menelaus' helmsman, slain off Cape Sunium by the gentle arrows of Apollo (*Odyssey* 3.278—283). And his long swim recalls Odysseus' own marathon swim after leaving Calypso's island at *Odyssey* 5.313ff., except that Odysseus let the steering-oar go from his hand as he fell from his raft, whereas Palinurus hung on. But most important for our purpose here is that the role of Elpenor as the unburied Dead Companion in the Underworld has been transferred to Palinurus.[25]

Elpenor's five lines at *Odyssey* 11.74—78 have thus been skilfully expanded by Vergil into two quite separate episodes involving both Misenus and Palinurus. Although it is a still widely held view among Vergil's readers that Misenus is an inferior doublet to Palinurus, this view is scarcely justified. For if Misenus had been omitted altogether, there would have been no burial; and if Misenus had been omitted and Palinurus buried instead, requiring a voyage of more than ninety miles, there would have been no hero to meet Aeneas at the threshold.[26]

Moreover by assigning to Palinurus this part of Elpenor's role, Vergil manages to incorporate one more figure from the pre-Vergilian Aeneas-legend, even though the traditional landing at Cape Palinurus, which bears his name, is omitted. For when Aeneas hearing of his helmsman's misfortune is about to reply to the ghost, the Sibyl interjects to assure him that Palinurus will be buried in a tomb in a land

[24] *Aen.* 5.858ff. Cf. also 6.349ff.

[25] See for a specific comparison of the Homeric and Vergilian treatments T. A. Dorey, "Homer and Vergil: the World of the Dead", *Orpheus* 3(1956), 119—122.

[26] R. S. Conway, *New Studies of a Great Inheritance* (London 1921), 130.

which will bear his name forever. Vergil loves, it seems, to bring in people who left marks on toponomy.

There is also a hint from Horace and Varro that by Vergil's day the conversation between the unburied shade and the mortal visitor to the Underworld had already become a stock ingredient in catabatic journeys. But in these authors it is put to mock-heroic use. For having parodied the theme of Odysseus' *Nekyia* for a contemporary purpose in *Satires* 2.5 and introduced an imaginary *catabasis* in *Odes* 2.13, Horace appears to have put the ghost of the renowned Pythagorean philosopher Archytas of Tarentum in Elpenor's predicament in *Odes* 1.28 (published in 23 B.C.). It seems that Archytas has suffered shipwreck, and while his body is lying unburied by the Matine shore in southern Italy a mariner addresses his ghost (lines 1—20). The ghost then asks him to provide a burial for its corpse (lines 21—36). The conversation takes place presumably at the threshold of the Underworld.[27] If this interpretation of this puzzling Ode is accepted, the irony will consist in the fact that the eminent philosopher, for all his Pythagorean learning, shares the same need as any commoner to be sprinkled after death with three handfuls of earth. Similarly Varro (116—27 B.C.) tells in the Menippean Satire *Sesquiulixes* of how his "Ulysses-and-a-half" or "Super-Ulysses" wanders far in search of the views of different schools of philosophy.[28] Horace leaves his mariner (*nauta* at line 23) unidentified. But the idea for a conversation between a wandering mariner and an unburied Pythagorean is so closely related to this theme as to suggest that Varro's Satire, with which Horace was familiar,[29] may in fact have been Horace's model for this Ode. A comparable underworld episode may even have appeared in the lost fragments of the *Sesquiulixes*, since the Greek

[27] Ross S. Kilpatrick, "Archytas at the Styx (Horace *Carm.* 1.28)", *C.P.* 63(1968), 201—206 and "Two Notes on Horace *Carm.* 1.28. 21—23", *C.P.* 64(1969), 237. The interpretation depends upon taking the opening lines "*Te.../...cohibent, Archyta,/pulveris exigui prope litus parva Matinum/munera* (sc. *danda*)" to mean, "the (lack of a) small gift of a little dust confines you, Archytas,...".

[28] For text see e.g. A. Riese, *M. Terenti Varronis Saturarum Menippearum reliquiae* (Leipzig 1865), 209—214.

[29] As noted by Kilpatrick, *C.P.* 63(1968), 204 referring to E. C. Witke, "Varro and Horace *Carm.* 1.9", *C.P.* 58(1963), 112—115.

Cynic and Satirist Menippus of Gadara in the third century B.C. himself wrote a *Nekyia*[30] (imitating Crates'), which numbered among the Satires from which Varro's *Saturae Menippeae* were adapted. And Lucian in the second century A.D. wrote a work entitled *Menippus* depicting a Descent into the Underworld by Menippus, whom he also represents in his *Dialogues of the Dead* at 414.3 as interviewing the dead Pythagoras and other philosophers in a most scurrilous manner.

Vergil's successors further illustrate the motif. In Lucan's epic poem *Pharsalia* at 6.588ff., Sextus Pompeius, the unworthy son of Pompey the Great, speaks through the agency of the wicked Thessalian witch Erichtho to the unburied corpse of one recently slain in battle. The ghost is summoned back before it has fully entered the Underworld and is made reluctantly to enter a second time into its as yet undecayed body, to tell what it has learnt below of the disasters in store at the forthcoming battle at Pharsalia. The ghost hovers on the threshold of Orcus — *primo pallentis hiatu/haeret adhuc Orci*, 6.714f. cf. 777–779 — not, I think, in this instance because it is one of the untimely dead, *φθίμενος ἄωρος*,[31] but because, true to the catabatic tradition, which Lucan has here adapted, it is numbered among the unburied, *ἄταφοι*, which are excluded from crossing the Styx. It then describes a pageant of Roman Heroes reminiscent of the Show of Heroes viewed by Aeneas during his descent. But it is a severely partisan Underworld that the Heroes now occupy in Lucan's epic, of the kind we will not find again until Dante.

Silius Italicus in his *Punica* 13.445—487 similarly casts Scipio and Appius Claudius in the roles of the epic hero and unburied shade. Here as in Lucan there is no actual descent, for Scipio summons the unburied shade upwards. Vergil's great imitator Silius, while retaining for the scene the Cumaean and Avernian setting of Vergil, reverts, then, to the Homeric nucleus of necromancy.

No less remarkable is what seems to be the extreme tenacity to tradition of Palinurus' fall overboard with the ship's rudder and a

[30] Diog. Laert. 6.99, *τὰ δ' οὖν τοῦ κυνικοῦ βιβλία ἐστὶ δεκατρία, Νέκυια, κ.τ.λ.*

[31] M. P. O. Morford, *The Poet Lucan* (Oxford 1967), 71. For the notion that the "untimely dead" were forbidden to enter fully into the Underworld see further p. 163 with n. 43 below.

part of the stern. An arresting explanation[32] has already been suggested that the episode is an echo from the *Epic of Gilgamesh*, in which Gilgamesh before crossing over the Waters of Death destroys some essential part of Urshanabi's boat, perhaps the "paddles".[33] The conjecture that the paddles had been damaged by Gilgamesh is a solution to a philological crux that is appropriate, since Gilgamesh overcomes the defect of the boat by cutting down a quantity of punt-poles. Gilgamesh, we may add, had already passed between Twin Rocks (the "Mashu") before approaching the ship, the vital part of which he damaged in a fit of violence. No solution has been offered regarding any line of transmission from the Near Eastern Epic, but the pre-Homeric saga which tells how the ship called Argo lost the extreme end of the poop, as it passed between Twin Rocks known as the "Symplegades" or "Clashing Rocks"[34] into an Otherworld beyond,[35] opens interesting possibilities. We may note that whereas the author of the Gilgamesh Epic seems to have been in a quandary as to how to get the boat damaged (which the Near Eastern tradition perhaps required) and hence made Gilgamesh wreck it, the Greek story puts the Rocks in the sea and makes them collide to catch the stern of the Argo. The conflation effects a tremendous improvement.

Vergil appears to have recognized as an essential ingredient that a part of the boat associated with the helm or steering should be missing in Otherworldly Journeys, and to have transferred it to the boat crossing to Cumae's shore. Aeneas' helmsman, who like Tiphys,[36] the helmsman of the Argo, died before the journey's end, is made to take with him the corresponding part of the boat. Seneca, in a passage that is unlikely to be his own invention, tells of Orpheus' descent into the infernal

[32] W. F. Jackson Knight, *Vergil: Epic and Anthropology*, 159f. and 171.

[33] R. Campbell Thompson, *The Epic of Gilgamish*, 46 n.3.

[34] Ap. Rhod. *Argon.* 2.601f. Homer, who refers to the passage of the Argo through the rocks, and says that Zeus' doves regularly pass through to fetch for himself ambrosia (*Od.* 12.59—72), seems to have transferred the tale to the "Planc tae" or "Wandering Rocks" and to suggest that these rocks move only in the indirect phrase, "the smooth rock is for ever catching the odd dove and the Father sends in another to make up their number" (12.64f.). The theme is widely dispersed in folktale, see J. G. Frazer, *Apollodorus*, vol. 2, pp. 355—358.

[35] See pp. 34—35 above.

[36] Ap. Rhod. *Argon.* 2.850ff.

regions, and there Charon's boat approaches "oarless", *nullo remigio*.[37] Here the motif is attached more properly to the boat of the dead itself.

Since, moreover, Gilgamesh's boat, Jason's boat, and Aeneas' boat are alike damaged, and the boat in which Odysseus sailed to Persephone's groves and the Halls of Hades is said by Circe to need no pilot,[38] the further question arises whether this boat, too, is part of the same tradition. Professor Page suggests that Elpenor was introduced in order to forge a link between the *Nekyia* and events on Circe's isle.[39] But if Homer knew the story that the boat to the Land of Shades had a part missing and was unpiloted, could Elpenor's fall from Circe's roof and his concern for his oar be a displaced part of this tradition told in this manner because Homer, who already has one helmsman killed (see p. 157 above), perhaps wished to avoid repetition? The change leads to some confusion over whether or not Odysseus knew when he set off from Circe's island that Elpenor had died.[40] But it is not without psychological effect. For the account of Elpenor's death adds a touch of humour and humanity to this incompetent and exasperating bungler. And this is precisely what gives the passage some literary merit. Whether Circe's suggestion that Odysseus' boat to the Shades will be unpiloted is responsible for the fact that Charon's boat also is without oarage, as has been seen in Seneca (Charon does not appear in Homer), we cannot tell. But the Homeric tradition may well be remembered by the author of the fourteenth century romance *Huon d'Auvergne* (a long poem surviving in what is virtually an Italianised form of French), in which Huon, a count who has been sent on an ambassadorial mission to

[37] *Hercules Oetaeus* 1072. For the oarless attribute of an underworld boat in a modern descent story see John Cowper Powys, *Morwyn* (London 1937), 148. In Joseph Conrad's *Heart of Darkness* Marlow experiences a "Descent into Hell" modelled on both Vergil's Sixth Book and Dante's *Inferno* and is made to lose his helmsman as he approaches the "Underworld" in the heart of Africa.

[38] *μή τί τοι ἡγεμόνος γε ποθὴ παρὰ νηΐ μελέσθω,*
ἱστὸν δὲ στήσας ἀνά θ' ἱστία λευκὰ πετάσσας
ἧσθαι· τὴν δέ κέ τοι πνοιὴ Βορέαο φέρῃσιν.
(*Od.* 10.505—507, cf. however 11.10)

[39] *The Homeric Odyssey*, 44—46.

[40] *Ibid.* Cf. also W. B. Stanford, *C.R.* 59(1945), 38, and my p. 153 with 75 above.

Lucifer in Hell, is met near the sea after a long journey by the Shades of both Aeneas and Guillaume d'Orange; they all three cross over the sea in an unpiloted boat that takes them to the abyss of Hell;[41] and they later cross over the infernal river of Acheron in Charon's bark.

As we follow Aeneas through the World of the Dead we find that many other scenes, too, balance Homer's. But Homer's Hades is not divided into regions, as is Vergil's more developed Underworld, and consequently Aeneas' Journey through the infernal world is on a far grander scale than Odysseus'. Vergil has not only extended the underworld geography beyond Homer's, but he has also most skilfully arranged Aeneas' passage through the World of Shades so that, as was observed by one of Vergil's most sensitive critics, he encounters his past represented by the three ghosts of Palinurus, Dido, and Deiphobus in a definite order — "the inverse order to that in which they have formerly met us in the narrative".[42] This observation should be carried still further, for in fact all of Aeneas' encounters in the *catabasis*, both past and future, seem to be arranged on a grand chiastic plan. Such an elaborate arrangement suggests that the various stages of Aeneas' journey through the kingdom of darkness are represented as having a definite purpose. We shall try now to indicate this purpose and to observe at the same time how Vergil rehandles the corresponding Homeric scenes.

Viewed in this light the burial, not far from Cumae, of the Trojan hero Misenus, just prior to the descent, cements in Italian soil the most recent link with Troy. The death of Palinurus, whose ghost Aeneas meets wandering despondently by the Styx, takes us back towards the end of his travels and provides a convincing link between the events of this Book and the last. We feel after all as though we meet again a man whom we knew alive but yesterday. Aeneas is next ferried

[41] D. D. R. Owen, *The Vision of Hell*, 189 regards this as a reminiscence of Celtic romance. For examples of unpiloted or rudderless boats in Celtic literature see H. R. Patch, *The Other World* (Camb. Mass. 1950), 243f., 252—257, 272f. and 283. But since the author of *Huon d'Auvergne* seems to have drawn on Homer, especially from the *Nekyia* in which Odysseus saw Heracles' wraith frightening with his bow the souls around him, it is possible that this feature too was adapted from there.

[42] R. S. Conway, *New Studies of a Great Inheritance*, 129.

over the Styx, and is taken past the hell-hound Cerberus drugged by the Sibyl. And in succession he passes through the "Bourne of the Infants", the "Bourne of the Unjustly Condemned", and the "Bourne of Guiltless Suicides". The proximity of these regions to the threshold of Orcus perhaps reflects Vergil's awareness of the notion that those who had died untimely were not allowed to enter fully into the Underworld,[43] even though he allowed the Infants to cross the Styx. The poet no doubt located them early as well to increase the sorrow preparatory to Dido's appearance. The three classes of souls inhabiting these regions are at any rate described briefly, and no individuals are named. But this changes when Aeneas comes to the "Mourning Fields", the *Lugentes Campi.* Here the ghost of Dido appears, the symbol of his remoter past. Her silence, as she drags herself away to rejoin her former husband Sychaeus, in response to Aeneas' tender entreaty — *funeris heu tibi causa fui*? (6.458) — is reminiscent of Ajax's angry silence towards Odysseus (see pp. 76f. above), and makes clear that she is still implacably hostile towards him. But whereas Odysseus indicates at *Odyssey* 11.565—567 that Ajax might eventually have been brought to speak to him if he had not been in such a hurry himself, Vergil elaborates in making Dido's silence absolute.

Aeneas' encounter later with Deiphobus' ghost in the *Arva Ultima*, the "Haunts of Warriors", symbolises a still remoter past which recalls disaster at Troy and the memory of friends. In this region we might have expected Aeneas to meet and converse also with the ghosts of Hector and of his late wife Creusa. But Deiphobus alone occupies

[43] For this notion compare the remark by the ghost of one of the untimely dead in Plautus, *Mostellaria*, 499f.; "*Nam me Acheruntem recipere Orcus noluit,/Quia praemature vita careo.*" And see further H. Nettleship's note on *Aen.* 6.427 in J. Conington, *P. Vergili Maronis Opera*[3], 3.521. The more complex deductions concerning the theology, familiar from Norden's *Aeneis Buch VI*[3], 11f., that the untimely dead in Vergil had to wait in their limbo until the completion of their full life, are, however, to be rejected. This argument is based on Lucian, *Cataplus* 5f., Macrobius, *Somn. Scip.* 1.13.10f., and particularly on information given by Tertullian, *De Anima* 56 *(Aiunt et immatura morte praeventas eo usque vagari istic, donec reliquatio compleatur aetatum, quas tum pervixissent, si non intempestive obiissent).* But whereas such souls are entirely banished from the nether world by Tertullian, in Vergil they are said to be in it. See also A. Dieterich, *Nekyia*[2], 152n., and J. ter Vrugt-Lentz, *Mors Immatura* (Groningen 1960), 69.

Aeneas' attention, and for more than forty lines. The reason begins to suggest itself as soon as we realize how Homeric have been Aeneas' experiences so far. Not only do Misenus and Palinurus balance Elpenor, and Dido Ajax, but the Heroines appearing to Aeneas in the Mourning Fields correspond to Homer's Catalogue of Fair Women in the *Nekyia.* Yet while in the Vergilian Catalogue Eriphyle echoes her Homeric appearance, the sympathies are altered,[44] which suggests that the Vergilian Catalogue is not exclusively Homeric in approach. For this heroine the Latin poet seems, for instance, to have made use of post-Theban drama dealing with her treatment from Alcmaeon's viewpoint. Moreover, the mention of Sychaeus, who does not actually appear to Aeneas, and the masculine relative *quos* at line 442 show that men also inhabit this region.

This now leaves only Achilles and Agamemnon from the ghosts in Homer's *Nekyia* to balance Deiphobus. And of these Achilles, happy in the knowledge that his son Neoptolemus is enhancing his glorious reputation,[45] could scarcely have been made to match Deiphobus, who dies ignobly and childless.[46] Perhaps the only proper analogy to Achilles would have been Hector, but this Trojan warrior had another role to play. He had already appeared in a vision soon after his death at Troy, to announce that his city's Fall was beyond human control, and to lay upon Aeneas the mission to continue the Trojan settlement overseas (2.268—295). Aeneas was thereby made Hector's chosen successor. The poet had, of course, to ensure that the Trojans, though losers at Troy, were fit ancestors for Rome, and that Aeneas, though not among the first rank of Homer's heroes, was of sufficient heroic stature for his Epic. The appearance of Creusa's ghost, too, in

[44] *Cf.* his Phaedram Procrinque locis maestamque Eriphylen
crudelis nati monstrantem vulnera cernit. (*Aen.* 6.445f.)

with

Μαῖράν τε Κλυμένην τε ἴδον στυγερήν τ' Ἐριφύλην,
ἣ χρυσὸν φίλου ἀνδρὸς ἐδέξατο τιμήεντα. (*Od.* 11.326f.).

And for Eriphyle's death see e.g. Thuc. 2.102.

[45] *Od.* 11.477—540. Cf. Vergil's adaption of the scene, reflecting pro-Trojan sympathies, at *Aen.* 2.547—549.

[46] *Aen.* 6.494ff.

a vision foretelling kingship, happiness, and a royal wife for Aeneas (2.776—789) furthered this same purpose. Hence Vergil chose Deiphobus alone as the sign of a sad past which is over.

For the meeting of Aeneas and Deiphobus, Vergil has, in fact, kept the conversation between Odysseus and Agamemnon's ghost closely in view. The two scenes correspond in a number of ways. In each case the man who failed on account of his marriage encourages the man who will succeed on account of his. Aeneas first explains how, as soon as he had heard that Deiphobus had perished at Troy, he had set up for him an empty tomb upon the nearby Rhoetean shore. This is the third burial with which Aeneas concerned himself in the Sixth Book. And this time he is thanked from the dead man's lips for fulfilling his duty:

"nihil o tibi, amice, relictum;
omnia Deiphobo soluisti et funeris umbris." (6.509—510)

("You, Friend, have left nothing undone; you have paid every due owed to Deiphobus himself and even to his dead body's shade.")

He also learns that Deiphobus had received his mangled and disfigured form through the deceit of his wife Helen:

"sed me fata mea et scelus exitiale Lacaenae
his mersere malis; illa haec monimenta reliquit."
(6.511—512)

("It was my own destiny and the murderous wickedness of Spartan Helen which have sunk me in this depth of affliction; it was she who left upon me these remembrances of her.")

But Deiphobus prophecies a "better fate" for Aeneas:

"melioribus utere fatis." (6.546)

The meeting with Deiphobus thus takes Aeneas back to the cause of his wanderings. It recalls at the same time the Sibyl's prophecy that there will be another Trojan War and another Helen of Troy:

"bella, horrida bella
et Thybrim multo spumantem sanguine cerno.

non Simois tibi nec Xanthus nec Dorica castra
defuerint; ...
causa mali tanti coniunx iterum hospita Teucris
externique iterum thalami." (6. 86—94)

("I see war and all the horrors of war. I see the Tiber streaming and foaming with blood. You will find there a Simois and a Xanthus and a camp of Greeks;... Again, as before, the cause of dire calamity for Trojans will be a wedding with a foreign bride from the family of a host.")

If Aeneas has learnt anything from his underworld visit so far, it is the realisation that the past is unalterable and the assurance, given especially in lines 509—510 quoted above, that nothing more could have been done by Aeneas for Deiphobus, who symbolizes all dead Trojans.

Vergil through the three burials of Misenus, Palinurus, and Deiphobus and the earlier visions of Hector and Creusa has taken every opportunity to obliterate the unfavourable tradition in which Aeneas appeared as a deserter and traitor to his homeland.[47] And when Aeneas leaves Deiphobus, he passes out once and for all from the Bronze Age of Troy. He hears from the Sibyl the terrible punishments of the eternally damned in Tartarus,[48] and moves into the sunlit plains of Elysium to meet his father Anchises, at whose command the descent was undertaken, that he may learn of his future race and city walls:

"tum genus omne tuum et quae dentur moenia disces."
(*Aen.* 5.737)

("And you shall learn then all your future descendants and what manner of walled city is granted to you.")

Here in the meeting with Anchises, Aeneas, having journeyed backwards from the end of his wanderings to the very source of his being, is to take a glimpse of the future that looks forward to Rome. First

[47] For the tradition hostile to Aeneas, see G.K. Galinsky, *Aeneas, Sicily and Rome* (Princeton 1969), 46—50.

[48] *Aen.* 6.548—627.

Anchises explains the doctrine of how the souls of the dead progress through purgatory and reincarnation (we shall return to this later), and then points to a vision of souls awaiting rebirth in the secluded Grove through which flows the River of Lethe (703—892). Here Aeneas sees rulers like Silvius and Procas, who will establish the settlement at Alba Longa in the near future (760ff.), Romulus, who will found Rome in the remoter future (777ff.), and Augustus Caesar, who will inaugurate the Golden Age in the very remote future (791ff.). After describing more scenes from Roman history Anchises, like Teiresias, focuses attention on the immediate future: Aeneas must first found Lavinium.[49] Aeneas is then dismissed somewhat paradoxically through the Ivory Gates (whence issue false dreams), with the immediacy of the future fresh in his mind. The task before him occupies the remainder of the *Aeneid.*

The futuristic Show of Heroes has no equivalent in Homer, whose *Nekyia* was not part of a Foundation Legend. Nor was Homer writing to flatter Crowned Heads. For this reason the mystic vision is brilliantly appropriate only to the *Aeneid.* By means of it, Vergil has managed to blend the imperial aspirations of the nation with the experiences of his hero.

Norden has remarked upon the paired arrangement of the Heroes (Decii—Drusi, Torquatus—Camillus, Caesar—Pompeius, Mummius—Paulus, Cato—Cossus, Gracchi—Scipiones, Fabricius—Serranus) and suggested that Vergil's "Heldengalerie" resembled the arrangement of the Statues of prominent Romans around Augustus' Forum.[50] The portraits of the Alban Kings, Roman Kings, and Republicans were grouped together to the west and east in the forecourt of the Temple of Mars Ultor. But whether he thought Vergil had put the idea into Augustus' head, or Maecenas or Augustus had spoken to Vergil about their intentions for the proposed new Forum, Norden does not say. The question, however, is an interesting one. And although the temple was not formally dedicated until the completion of the *Forum Augustum* in 2 B.C., the fact that it was vowed by Augustus, even before the Battle of Philippi in 42 B.C., to the god who could

[49] *Aen.* 6.890ff.

[50] E. Norden, *Aeneis Buch VI*³, 315 on *Aen.* 6.752ff.

avenge the death of Julius Caesar has led Drew to assume, I think rightly, that the masterpieces were already being collected in 23 B.C., when Vergil read the Sixth Book to Augustus and Octavia. It appears that Horace and Vergil both made use of the portrait galleries, but in different ways for different purposes.[51] Perhaps we should look to see how Vergil has transferred to the mystic vision some details of the sculpture. The lines referring to the double plumed helmet worn by Mars, the father of Romulus —

> "viden ut geminae stant vertice cristae
> et pater ipse suo superum iam signat honore?" (6. 779–780)

("Do you see how on his head the twin crests stand, and how his Father already marks him for the exalted life above with his own emblem?") —

were certainly full of contemporary significance if understood to have been inspired by Romulus in front of Mars Ultor. And the description of the unborn Silvius at line 760 as a "youth leaning upon a headless spear" *(pura iuvenis qui nititur hasta)* is statuesque enough.[52]

But the idea for a Show of Heroes, even so, may have come to Vergil in a variety of ways. One suggestion is that it occurred to him when reading of the statues of the kings to be found inside the Egyptian labyrinth.[53] Another possibility is that Vergil envisaged Anchises as taking Aeneas on a kind of expanded conducted tour of a Roman *atrium*-type house in which the effigies of Rome's national figures, and not merely those of an ordinary family, were on show.[54] Or the idea suggested itself to Vergil from the *Eleusinia* where, according to Themistius, the statues of gods and heroes were exhibited to the view of the initiated.[55] The description at *Aeneid* 7.177—191 of Latinus' temple

[51] D. L. Drew, "Horace, *Odes* I. xii. and the *Forum Augustum*", *C.Q.* 19(1925), 159—164, esp. 161. Cf. also Ovid, *Fasti* 5. 563—566.

[52] *Ibid.* 161. At *Aen.* 6.847f. Vergil is thought to be giving his opinion *(credo equidem)* on the superior merits of the Hellenic sculptors over those at Augustus' command.

[53] Cf. Pliny *N.H.* 36.88: *intus columnae porphyrite lapide, deorum simulacra, regum statuae, monstrificae effigies*, with discussion to n.10 above (cf. P. J. Enk, *Mnemosyne* 11[1958], 329).

[54] J. G. Griffith, "Again the Shield of Aeneas", *P.V.S.* 7(1967/68), 60f.

[55] See Themistius *Or.* 20.235B quoted in C. A. Lobeck, *Aglaophamus*, 52f.

adorned with the figures of his divine and human ancestors, though admittedly a vista of the past, is also a counterpart to this underworld scene, and, as Conington remarks, this picture of national and patriotic pride under a monarchical rule is probably not without reference to the feelings of Augustus.

Shakespeare's Macbeth too has a futuristic vision, ending with a show of eight kings and a graceful compliment to James I. Here, however, there is no actual *catabasis* except for the hint in Hecate's verses, believed by many to be interpolated, where she bids the Witches meet her "at the pit of Acheron" (IV. v. 15). And whereas Aeneas consults a genuine deity in authorized manner and receives a message for the good, Macbeth consults an anti-deity in unauthorized manner, and the ambiguity of the messages induces in him a false optimism which is not ratified by the event.[56] Shakespeare's Show of Kings is thus closer to the Pageant of Heroes in Lucan's *Pharsalia*,[57] which as remarked above (p. 159) owes much to Vergil, yet insofar as Sextus Pompey obtains his vision through a witch and learns of catastrophe for the Republic and failure for himself, it is the very antithesis of Vergil's theme. Aeneas, on the contrary, having reached Italy with the assurance that in Latium "Troy's realms are fated to rise again" (1.206), glimpses at the future stages by which this glorious destiny will be fulfilled. The underworld journey is thus a fitting expression of the death of the Trojan past and the hope for the future yet to be born.

Let us consider now the fate of the souls in Tartarus and Elysium. The judgement (viewed proleptically) which sends the departed to these regions is in fact no less a historical commentary than is the Show of Heroes itself. Thus Tartarus holds a number of mythical figures, among them the Titans, whom Zeus overthrew; the Aloids, who rebelled against the Olympian gods; and Salmoneus, who like Mezentius

[56] For elucidation of the symbolism of Macbeth's futuristic vision see G. Wilson Knight, *The Shakespearian Tempest* (Oxford 1932), 191—4 and *Shakespearian Production* (London 1964), 137—39.

[57] J. A. K. Thomson, *Shakespeare and the Classics* (London 1952) passes over this scene without comment, but on p. 123 suggests a Shakespearian reminiscence (at *Macbeth* III. v. 23f.) of Lucan *(Phars.* 6.669, *virus lunare)*, who was certainly known to the Elizabethan dramatists.

was not so much a rebel as a king with ideas above his station.[58] But soon the list continues with those who hated their brothers, or beat their fathers, defrauded their clients, or were avaricious, or set no part of their wealth for their family (we are told that these are many), or were slain for adultery (presumably these had no opportunity to make amends), or followed unholy war (*impia arma* not further defined, but suggesting subversive or civil wars), or fearlessly broke faith with their masters.[59] One sold his country for gold and imposed upon it a tyrant lord, another forced his daughters to bed,[60] and so on. This list of the damned classed according to the crimes committed takes us right out of the mythical framework and makes Tartarus much more personal. It is a far cry from the amorphous Hades of Homer, whose "Sinners" are named mythical figures, and whose ordinary dead are not given good or evil deserts, despite the presence of Minos, according to their deeds done in this life.

Vergil is not, of course, the first to have introduced punishments and rewards for certain categories of ordinary mortals after death. Pausanias, for example, describes Polygnotus' fifth century *Nekyia* as showing beneath a number of mythical sufferers in Hades a man being punished for maltreating his father, another for committing sacrilege (10.28.4f.). More extensive are the classifications of the sinners and righteous described or implied in Plato's *Gorgias*, *Phaedo*, *Republic*, *Phaedrus*, and *Laws*. The initiated in the Eleusinian Mysteries were, moreover, promised a future life of Blessedness, while a different fate awaited the others. Aristophanes' caricature of the plight of evildoers in the *Frogs*, including those who wronged a stranger, or had intercourse with a boy, or struck a mother or father, or committed perjury (145—151), suggests that various categories of sinners were assumed by the Mysteries. A detailed study of all the sources in both literature and art that might have contributed to Vergil's eschatology at this point is impossible here, for they are too many and too varied.[61]

[58] *Aen.* 6.580—594.

[59] *Aen.* 6.608—613.

[60] *Aen.* 6.621—623.

[61] The chief references are assembled and discussed by F. Solmsen, "Greek ideas of the Hereafter in Virgil's Roman Epic", *Amer. Philos. Soc.* 112(1968), 8—14, and for the eschatological development of the Greek Underworld as reveal-

Special mention, however, may be made of an Orphic descent preserved on an Egyptian papyrus, now at Bologna, in which are listed several categories of human beings, who are assigned, for specific achievements or offences, to either Elysium or Tartarus. The first editor of the papyrus duly recognizing the remarkably close correspondence between the groups of the elect and damned in this Descent and that of Aeneas — compare, for instance, the line *inventas aut qui vitam excoluere per artes* (*Aen.* 6.663) with *αἳ δὲ βίον σοφίῃσιν ἐκόσμεον* (fol. III recto 7) — attributed the poem to the Christian era.[62] However the differences between this epic poem and the *Aeneid*, Vergil's setting being peculiarly Roman, suggests a Vergilian borrowing, rather than viceversa, and a Hellenistic date for the poem.[63] If so, it is likely that this poem too, or that from which it is derived,[64] must be counted among the Greek sources used for the *Aeneid.* And what, above all, distinguishes the Vergilian classification from its predecessor is the subtle manner in which it lends topicality to Tartarus, and leaves us at the end to imagine which particular cap fits which particular individual.

Vergil's consummate art in making Tartarus topical and personal is of special interest in showing how the poet has reforged tradition to make it relevant to the aspirations of Rome in his own day. He thus alludes to the Civil Wars, first, at *Aeneid* 6.280, by personifying "Strife the insane" *(Discordia demens)* among the denizens at the Entrance of the Underworld; then, at 6.612f., in the phrase *quique arma secuti/impia* ("those who followed unholy war") referring to the damned in Tartarus; and again, in the Show of Heroes, where Anchises points out Caesar and Pompey with the lament:

> "heu! quantum inter se bellum, si lumina vitae
> attigerint; quantas acies stragemque ciebunt" (*Aen.* 6.828f.)

ed through various *Descents* see an admirable article by J. Mavrogordato, "Modern Greek Folk-Songs of the Dead", *J.H.S.* 75(1955), 42—53.

[62] See the article by R. Merkelbach already cited at chap.4 n. 62.

[63] Advocated by M. Treu, "Die neue 'Orphische' Unterweltsbeschreibung und Vergil", *Hermes* 82(1954), 24—51, esp. p. 39.

[64] See the article by R. Turcan already cited at chap.4 n. 62 and *cf.* further C. A. Disandro, "Una nueva fuente para el libro VI de la Eneida", *Humanitas* 3(1957), 117—125, and F. Solmsen, *Amer. Philos. Soc.* 112(1968), 9—11.

("Oh, the dreadful war, and the bitterness of battle and carnage which in mutual conflict they will begin!").

The civil wars are a theme to which Vergil often refers. In the First *Georgics* an "unholy generation", *impia saecula* (468), witnesses in 44 B.C. the assassination of Julius Caesar, at which all nature went dark in sympathy. This act of civil disobedience led to civil strife in 42 B.C. at Philippi, to which Vergil refers in lines 489f., and a plea is made at lines 498—511 that Octavius Caesar put an end to *Mars impius*, the God of unholy war. Thus, as Conington remarks in his Commentary on *Aeneid* 6.612f., Augustus would not be likely to regard himself as glanced at in the phrase *quique arma secuti/impia*, as some commentators have feared that he might, since he doubtless considered his mission, like that of Aeneas himself, to be that of putting an end to such impious conflicts.[65]

Later, in the Third *Georgics*, having undertaken to fashion a poem designed like temple-doors on which Caesar's achievements will be highlighted, Vergil seems to express his reprobation of the enemies of Caesar by placing them in the infernal world:

Invidia infelix furias amnemque severum
Cocyti metuet tortosque Ixionis anguis
immanemque rotam et non exsuperabile saxum.
(*Georg.* 3.37—39)

(Luckless Envy shall be portrayed in fear of the Furies and the dismal stream of Cocytus, in fear too of Ixion's coiling snakes and the huge wheel, and of the unconquerable stone.)

"Envy" here, as Conington again points out,[66] must refer to "political malcontents". The same technique of relegating harmful individuals to Tartarus is found in the Eighth Book of the *Aeneid*, where Aeneas' Shield is described. Catiline is depicted on the Shield in Tartarus:[67] Cato is his counterpart among the righteous, presumably in Elysium.[68] Vergil does not specify which Cato is meant, but it is

[65] Compare what Augustus says of his own achievements in the *Res Gestae* at 1.1.
[66] *Ad. loc.* and on *Aen.* 8.667.
[67] *Aen.* 8.666—9.
[68] *Aen.* 8.670.

probably the younger Cato of Utica as providing a contemporary contrast with Catiline. There is a value in the ambiguity, nonetheless, in that it reflects glory on the whole family. Neither Catiline nor Cato is mentioned in the Sixth Book of the *Aeneid*, because the Sibyl knows from Hecate only the present inmates of Tartarus and Anchises gives Aeneas a futuristic vision of Roman history: but the scene on the Shield suggests that for the description of Tartarus and Elysium also, Vergil had the contemporary historical period in mind.

With the exception of Catiline, who is named in the Eighth Book of the *Aeneid* as an inmate of Tartarus, Vergil has not savagely maligned any particular individual. Indeed he could hardly have referred by name in the Sixth Book to his own contemporaries in Tartarus, since at the time of Aeneas' Descent Rome was not yet fulfilled. And even supposing Servius' oft reiterated view were true that the younger Curio fits the bill for the one who sold his country,[69] Vergil has with good reason refrained from being specific. An unequivocal reference to Curio would also have reflected on Caesar, the buyer, whose "crime", since he betrayed no trust, might be considered to be merely *superbia* rather than corruption. This particular aristocratic misdeed is a cap that could no doubt have fitted many heads. And it is unlikely that Vergil would have wished to malign Caesar, whose very name "Iulius" he associates with Aeneas' son "Iulus", to support the claim of the first two Caesars that they were of Trojan descent.[70] Hence Curio is not singled out among the damned.

Nor has Vergil been malicious towards Caesar's assassin Brutus. For despite Augustus' bitter reference in the *Res Gestae* at 1.2 to "the people who murdered my father", Brutus had not become a dirty word, and by the late twenties one could afford to be magnanimous to

[69] *Aen.* 6.621f. (see the list at n. 60 above). Macrobius *Sat.* 6.1 states that these lines are adapted from Varius' "*vendidit hic Latium populis, agrosque Quiritum/eripuit*"..., which shows that they did not originate with Vergil to single out Curio in particular. For Varius' poem see A.S. Hollis, *C.Q.* 27 (1977), 187ff.

[70] Esp. at *Aen.* 6.789f.: *hic Caesar et omnis Iuli/progenies* (cf. 1.267ff. and 288). Note too that in the *Forum Augustum* the statues of Aeneas and Romulus were juxtaposed with those of Julius Caesar and Augustus to suggest subtly the latter's claim to Trojan descent, see J. Gagé, "Romulus-Augustus", *M.E.F.R.* 47(1930), esp. 138—156.

the real Republicans.[71] The Bruti family, after all, were part of the foundation legend of the Roman Republic, and Augustus had no wish to rewrite royal tradition. Insofar as we are perhaps given a personal glance at Brutus the Assassin, we might find it in these lines addressed to Aeneas by Anchises:

> "vis et Tarquinios reges, animamque superbam
> ultoris Bruti fascisque videre receptos?"
>
> (*Aen.* 6. 817f.)

("Do you wish also to see Tarquin's dynasty and the arrogant soul of Brutus the avenger, and see the rods of office won back again?")

The Brutus who assassinated Caesar is not of course this Brutus, who delivered Rome from Tarquin oppression. But the transferred epithet *superbus* implies that the old Brutus had a touch of Tarquin about him. And this quality might be expected to have sped through the centuries.[72] Vergil in any case doubtless thinks not so much of individual crimes as of honest people making mistakes. He has no category in Tartarus, therefore, into which Brutus in particular fits, even though he does have contemporary history in mind when writing the Tartarus passage. In this more general sense Tartarus contains the whole misrule that is over.

It is thus evident that throughout Aeneas' Underworld Journey Vergil is writing strongly in the apocalyptic idiom. By this I mean that the message which Aeneas receives in the infernal regions is largely in the form of a revelation of the future, comparable in many ways, as we shall see, to that of the later Christian Apocalypse in the Book of the *Revelation.* It is a new idea in Greek or Latin literature, for which Vergil may have owed to Hesiodic myth a hint of the kind he was adept at exploiting. For by analogy with the Cosmic Battle in Hesiod between the Old and the New Régime of the Gods, telling how Zeus in victory consigned the Saturnian Titans to Tartarus,[73]

[71] Cf. Augustus' own attitude in the *Res Gestae* at 1.3, and Horace's careful joking about the past in *Odes* 2.7.

[72] This conclusion is worked out in a series of articles by W. F. Jackson Knight referred to in his *Roman Vergil*, 367f. For the liberation from Tarquinius Superbus, see p. 151 above.

[73] Hesiod, *Theog.* 72—74 and 664ff.

Augustus heralds in a New Golden Age, puts an end to the Civil Wars, and relegates the whole of the preceding political Régime to Tartarus.

Vergil further extended Hesiodic myth to fit the future of Rome by suggesting, in Messianic language, that the times of Saturn are coming once more: Anchises at 6.791—794 prophesies that Augustus will actually bring back to Latium the Saturnian Age of Gold. Like the Child in the Fourth *Eclogue*, at whose coming the Golden race will arise and the Iron race will cease (6—9), Augustus and perhaps Aeneas too are portrayed as Saturnian culture heroes. Here Vergil has not solved the difficulty that Saturn was both the Bad Ruler exiled by Zeus in the Battle of the Gods and the King of a bygone Golden Race,[74] who after his release from Tartarus presided over a distant Wonderland of departed heroes.[75] For as the defeated leader of the Old Régime in Hesiod's myth, Saturn remains an inmate in Vergil's Tartarus (p. 169 above). But in the Messianic context associated with Augustus, Vergil projects him from Tartarus to the West in prehistoric Italy, apparently synchronizing the two separate periods of his good rule so as to make Saturn the first King in Latium, who also introduced to it the many benefits of civilization.[76] Similarly Aeneas will save Etruria from Mezentius, quell the forces of anarchy, and go on to found Lavinium in Latium. And Augustus will quell Republican disorder and begin Rome's mission to establish a civilized, peaceful existence on earth. Clearly the return under Augustus of Saturn's Golden Age and the quelling of the preceding Age of Iron implies a cataclysm. But because of the superior culture throughout, and because Vergil presumably had no severe grievances of the kind endured by the author

[74] Hesiod, *Works and Days*, 109ff. H. C. Baldry in "Who invented the Golden Age?" *C.Q.* 2(1952), 87f. points out that Hesiod speaks of a golden "race" of men, not a golden "age". Latin poetry seems responsible for the transition from a golden race to a golden age, facilitated in the main by the ambiguity in the words *aetas* and *saecula.*

[75] *Ibid.* 167ff. and Pindar *Ol.* 2.68ff. with *Pyth.* 4.251. No other Primeval Being is said in Classical antiquity to have broken out or to have been released from the world below.

[76] *Aen.* 6.791—794 and cf. 8.319ff. and *Georg.* 2.538. According to another, euhemerising story told by Plutarch, *De facie* 941ff. and *De def. orac.* 419E—F Saturn is projected also to one of the islands off the coast of Britain.

of the Christian Apocalypse, the poet does not envisage at Rome such an explosive cataclysm as is depicted in the later work, where the Saints rejoice over the Overthrow of Babylon, represented as being inhabited by Devils.[77] Thus although Vergil's Tartarus and Show of Heroes is written in the same idiom as the Christian Apocalypse, the cataclysm it foretells is less pronounced.

When we reach Elysium we find that it is reserved for protective heroes, holy priests, inspired poets, inventors who have ennobled life, distinguished benefactors, and all the eponymous heroes of Troy,[78] but not, it appears, the Heroes of the War. Hector, for example, does not appear in Elysium. But he could scarcely have been included and Achilles not. And if Hector were included, why not also Deiphobus? Vergil wisely, therefore, has refrained from mentioning any of his former companions. The list of those who dwell in Elysium is, in fact, almost conspicuous for the paucity of names — six are given in all including Orpheus, who is alluded to by a sobriquet.[79] And surely this silence is eloquent. For unlike Tartarus, which was crammed full, the emphasis is on the natural features and spaciousness of the Elysian Fields. The gloom of Tartarus is dispelled and Elysium is lit by a "purple" light, which shines through an ampler aether from its own sun and stars. Here the blessed listen to music, sing, dance, take part in athletics, and are free to wander over lush meadows broken by shady groves, streams, and mountains (6.637ff.). This conception of Elysium as a land of light where the blessed pursue various sensual activities is borrowed from Greek popular and religious belief. Taking a hint from Pindar, whose underworld Elysium includes horses too,[80] Vergil also depicts the unmanned chariots of Teucer's line, their scattered arms, and steeds turned loose, marking the extreme security of the place where heroes are at rest from war. Such is the contrast between Tartarus and Elysium which will give to Romans a pride in their past.

[77] *Revelation* 18.2ff. The picture of Babylon in the Apocalypse inhabited by devils (*καὶ ἐγένετο κατοικητήριον δαιμόνων*) shows again the tendency to regard the enemy stronghold as an Underworld. See, e.g., at chapter 5 n. 45 above.

[78] *Aen.* 6.648—650 and 660—665.

[79] Quoted in chapter 4 n. 55 above.

[80] Fr. 114 (ed. Bowra).

So far I have sought to show the ways in which Vergil has made topical to Rome the various parts of the Underworld Journey. But I have left still unasked an important question, namely: does the whole divine scheme of Creation, which Anchises unfolds just before explaining the Show of Heroes, serve any purpose for Rome? The question arises from the long speech which Anchises delivers as he points into the secluded Grove inhabited by souls, including the great figures of later Roman history (p. 167 above), who are to return to this life in different bodies. In this speech Anchises outlines a doctrine of purgation and reincarnation, which beneath its Stoic guise resembles ideas to be found also in Pindar, Empedocles, the Gold Leaves, and in Plato. The essentials of this doctrine are that the souls of the dead undergo prolonged purification by wind, water or fire (735—742), and when through cleansing these become the spark of elemental fire, *πνεῦμα πυρωδές*, they once were, they eventually after turning the wheel through a thousand years return to the upperworld in other bodies as different personages (745—751).

The seemingly clear outlines of this doctrine are made less certain by the awkward appearance of two lines, in which Anchises refers in the first person to himself and the community in Elysium:

> quisque suos patimur manis; exinde per amplum
> mittimur Elysium et pauci laeta arva tenemus.
> (*Aen.* 6.743—744)

"Each of us endures his own afterlife." So down to *exinde*. But from *exinde* onwards the sense of these lines is disputed. The best manuscripts of Vergil are wanting in authentic punctuation, so that we cannot be sure either of the run of the words within the lines, or of the run of these lines within the context explaining the system of purgation. If we take *pauci* with both halves of the sentence, Anchises means, "we Few reach wide Elysium and possess its Happy Fields." But gramatically and with the aid of a comma after *Elysium* in 744, which may be expressed or just understood, he could mean "a lot of us reach wide Elysium, but only a few of us stay here." So saying, he sets up the idea, not only that the dead are individuals, but that there are two categories of souls. But have the "Few" who abide in the Happy Fields gone through purgation, and will they too drink of

Lethe? Do all souls pass alike through Elysium, and are all involved in the Wheel? And are there two purgations, one prior to and one within Elysium? For according to the second rendering, in which *pauci* goes closely with *tenemus*, and *mittimur* refers to the whole number of the departed, Elysium is not exclusively the permanent abode of the Elect, such as we expect from the conventional belief expressed by Homer at *Odyssey* 4.563,[81] but a place of higher purification, to which all souls go after ordinary purgation to spend or complete their full cycle of time.

I have attempted elsewhere[82] to summarise the variety of divergent proposals within this broad outline, and have argued that *pauci* should be taken with both halves of the sentence, which reads more naturally, and the lines be punctuated in parenthesis. Anchises in effect then explains why he is already in Elysium (*Aen.* 5.734f. and 6.669ff.) and is not undergoing prolonged purification. The Elect, among whom he is himself to be counted, do not in fact need purgation, except for a token acquaintance indicated by *exinde*, and are not subject to reincarnation as are other souls. He and the other inhabitants of Elysium are heroes and demigods already. Anchises, like Homer's Menelaus, was also the consort of a deity. From the artistic viewpoint, too, of course, it was necessary for him to be in Elysium. For it is no good if, when

[81] Over-subtle grammarians, it is true, e.g. *E. Gud.* 242.2ff. doubted whether Menelaus would live for ever in Elysium, and took the prophecy to mean that he would eventually die there, though not in Argos. Advocates of this view sometimes connected the derivation of *'Ελύσιον* from the fact that there the *ψυχαὶ λελυμέναι τῶν σωμάτων διάγουσι*. See further E. Rohde, *Psyche*[8], chap. 2 n. 15, who firmly rejects these fancies. Moreover, certain "intermediate" abodes of the righteous in Pindar, Plato, and others came to be described in elysian-like imagery, but this surely does not justify E. Norden, *Aeneis Buch VI*[3], 16ff. talking of a purgatorial Elysium. None of these abodes is called, at any rate, an Elysium. For further discussion of this point see my article (in the following note), esp. 126—128.

[82] In my "The 'Wheel' and Vergil's Eschatology in *Aeneid* 6", *Symbolae Osloenses* 50(1975), 121—141. I should like to take this opportunity of correcting a slip on p. 124, to which Michael D. Reeve has kindly drawn my attention. When rejecting the remedy of the transposition of lines 743—744 after 747 adopted by the Parma editor, I referred to the Ed. Parm. 1475 instead of to the Bodoni Ed. Parm. of 1793 (this text is retained in the 1795 edition). The latter of course is following Brunck's edition of 1785; his other transposition (at *Aen.* 8.654) is an alternative to Brunck's deletion.

Aeneas goes to meet his father, Anchises is still fumigating in the Neutral Regions just beyond the Styx.

The foregoing analysis invites us to reconsider the infernal geography also. For the view, first met in Servius,[83] that all souls pass into Elysium has led to a widespread assumption that the Vergilian Grove of Lethe forms an integral part of Elysium. But the "Unnumbered Tribes" (*innumerae gentes*, 706) bustling around the River of Lethe in the secluded Grove (*seclusum nemus*, 704) are surely separate from, though visible by, the "Few" in the relaxed Elysian Fields. Aeneas and Anchises having taken a path through Elysium can see into this Grove, but we need not suppose that the souls destined to pass back into the upperworld have also traversed Elysium by the same path. There are, after all, as Rohde recognized long ago,[84] three distinct classes of souls in Vergil's Underworld. And these occupy three separate parts. Just as Elysium, the permanent home for the Blessed Elect, might be thought to balance Tartarus, the permanent home for the Incurably Wicked — the two paths that fork at *Aeneid* 6.540 separate these two abodes — so the Grove populated by the "Unnumbered Tribes", who are the vast majority of the departed, seems to balance the Neutral Regions beyond the Styx, and is evidently the continuum of it.

It can hardly be objected that these two parts of the Underworld are mutually unconnected because the Neutral Regions (or "mythological" Hades) present the souls in a fixed, static state whereas the souls in the Grove (the "philosophical" or "theological" Hades) are said to be resigning their personalities in readiness for a new life in different bodies.[85] For it is a popular idea that ghosts retain the physical bearing of the deceased,[86] and static souls are necessary for recog-

[83] Esp. on *Aen.* 6.745. Servius is somewhat self-contradictory in places, see my article (as in previous note), 122—124.

[84] E. Rohde, *Psyche*^{8}, 449 n. 62.

[85] For a review of the numerous attempts by Sabbadini, Dieterich, Norden, Conington, Conway, Norwood, Büchner, MacKay, Perrett, and others to reconcile the alleged conflicts between the "mythological" and "philosophical" parts of the Vergilian Underworld see Brooks Otis, "Three Problems of *Aeneid* 6", *T.A.P.A.* 90(1959), 165ff.

[86] For the notion, with numerous references, see E. R. Dodds, *Plato Gorgias* (Oxford 1959), 379 on 524a—525a.

nition. What, for instance, would a Dido-becoming-Cleopatra look like? Do we, moreover, really expect to see Dido hung up to the winds, or in the wash, or being fumigated? And it is often overlooked that the souls in the Grove of Lethe are static too. Vergil's ingenuity consists in applying the idea of the ghosts proleptically to the heroes as yet unborn. The future Roman leaders are shown in the Grove not as babies, but in characteristic attitudes. The supreme instance is Marcellus, whose noble and sorrowful appearance[87] characterizes his future prominence and early future death. We may conclude, therefore, that Elysium and Lethe's Grove are occupied by separate classes of souls. The close proximity of the regions is an artistic requirement, to facilitate the viewing by Aeneas and Anchises of the future leaders of Rome on earth.

We can now return to the question whether Anchises' explanation of the whole scheme of Creation, involving the doctrines of reincarnation and of the life-force conceived as a spark of elemental fire, serves any purpose for Rome. At first glance it does not seem to suit either the conventional belief that Elysium is the permanent abode of the Blessed Elect or the nationalistic intention of the poem. For, on the one hand, how can the aim of the soul to escape from the cycle of rebirth and from the body which clogs the soul be reconciled with the historical purpose of the poem, which is to glorify Rome on earth? And, on the other, if the soul is said to have its origin in heaven (*caelestis origo,* 730), do we not expect that it will rise upwards after separation from the body and eventually rejoin the elemental mass whence it originated?

Plato and the platonising Pythagoreans were emphatic on this point. And even the Stoics, insofar as they admitted personal survival at all, tended towards this belief. The popular ideas regarding an infernal Hades or Elysium are in fact in contradiction with Stoic psychology, which held that the fiery soul by its very nature was incapable of descent.[88] When Stoics speak of the *inferi* or of "Hades" as the abode of souls, they apparently use the terms figuratively.[89] Why then does

[87] *Aen.* 6.860ff.

[88] See e.g. Sextus Empir. *Adv. Math.* 9.71 (*καὶ γὰϱ οὐδὲ τὰς ψυχὰς ἔνεστιν ὑπονοῆσαι κάτω φεϱομένας*), and cf. Cicero, *Tusc.* I. xviii. 42, xix. 43.

[89] E.g. Zeno in supposing that the wicked suffered *in tenebris locis* (fr. 147, von

Vergil put such an explanation of the nature of souls into the mouth of Anchises?

One reply to this might be that Vergil writes figuratively also. Norden argues strongly that cosmic conceptions attributed by him to Poseidonius underlie the "mythological disguise" of Aeneas' Descent and Underworld Journey. And he attempts to prove from *aeris in campis* at *Aeneid* 6.887 that Vergil placed his "Purgatorio" in the atmosphere.[90] Taking a hint from this R. D. Williams has recently reargued that Vergil's Elysium is not to be regarded as the ultimate home of the Blessed. And by suitably punctuating the two lines 743—744 above so as to make Elysium the place where all souls go to complete their purification, some to return to earth, others after a longer period of waiting to go on to their ultimate paradise in the sky, he supposes that Anchises all but implies a cosmological explanation of the soul's journey from the air above the earth, where it undergoes purification, to Elysium the moon, before finally proceeding to the sun or the pure ether of God.[91]

Arnim I) or Tertullian *de anima* 54 writing that *reliquas animas ad inferos deiciunt* (fr. 146). Thus too Epictetus speaks of a *κάθοδος εἰς ῞Αιδου*, but at 3.13.5 says *οὐδεὶς ῞Αιδης, οὐδ' 'Αχέρων, οὐδὲ Κωκυτός*. Cf. E. Rohde, *Psyche*[8], 516 n. 52 and J. H. Waszink on the Tertullian passage.

[90] E. Norden, *Aeneis Buch VI*[3], 16ff. See for the acceptance of these views Franz Cumont, *After Life in Roman Paganism* (New Haven 1923), 82 and F. Richards, *The Aeneid of Virgil* (London 1928), 3—84; and for the arguments against this interpretation see my article (above note 82), pp. 136f. n. 15. It is worth repeating here the comparison between Aeneas' Descent and the description by Apuleius *Metam.* 11.23 of Lucius' nocturnal initiation into the mysteries of Isis at Corinth. The words *nocte media vidi solem candido coruscantem lumine* in the Apuleius passage have been taken to refer to the sun which shines in the underworld Elysium, as at *Aen.* 6.640f., but John Whittaker *God Time Being* (Oslo 1971), 34 is surely right in supposing from the preceding words *per omnia vectus elementa* that Lucius has experienced a celestial journey to the sun which shines continuously in outer space and is visible even when it is night on earth. For a hint of this kind it is, however, vain to look in Vergil.

[91] R. D. Williams, "The Sixth Book of the *Aeneid*", *G. & R.* 11(1964), esp. 57—59; and his text and commentary *The Aeneid of Virgil* (London 1972), 148 and 504. The interpretation hangs upon punctuating lines 742—744 (see my p. 177 above) as *igni. quisque... tenemus donec* so as to make 745ff. depend closely upon *tenemus*, and *pauci* is construed with *tenemus* only.

This, however, from Anchises' viewpoint, surely expresses the priorities in reverse. For the main thrust of Anchises' speech, despite his teaching concerning the heavenly origin of souls, remains firmly fixed on Rome and the survival of the Roman race on earth. Anchises' philosophical explanation of souls beside the mythological conception of Elysium is, it is necessary to admit, a juxtaposition of two incompatible beliefs of the afterlife. For according to Anchises' philosophical outline of the elemental spark theory of souls, we would expect that they would eventually escape from the cycle of rebirth and return when fully purified to their fiery source in the sky, whereas Anchises and the other Elect are imagined to be the permanent residents of an underworld Elysium. Moreover, Vergil has not chosen to join the philosophical doctrine to the historical purpose, as did Cicero in the *Dream of Scipio*,[92] for instance, by making service to Rome the path to a disembodied, carefree existence among the heavenly stars. Elysium is the highest reward in Vergil's schema. At *Georgics* 4.226 Vergil also sends the souls of the bees to the stars, and at *Georgics* 1.24 he suggests the possibility of Augustus Caesar's apotheosis, here reflecting cult-belief. If Vergil's primary purpose in the Sixth Book was to show the final destiny of the individual soul after death, the incompatibility of these rival beliefs would be vexing in the extreme. But Vergil was far less concerned with the personal salvation of the individual soul than was Plato. He should not be examined therefore through Platonic or platonising spectacles, as he is by those who suppose that Anchises is referring figuratively to a "Himmelsreise der Seele". Nor is he a would-be Christian eschatologist. For although Vergil lends himself readily to Christian doctrine,[93] he is not in our sense an *anima naturaliter Christiana.* Rather the emphasis of Anchises' speech is Stoic, to the extent that true Stoicism placed the realisation of its ideal in this world. Indeed throughout Aeneas' Descent, as we have seen, Vergil is writing strongly in the apocalyptic idiom expressing the fate of the individual soul chiefly as a contemporary judgement of Roman history,

[92] Esp. at *De re pub.* 6. xiii. 13 and 6. xxvi. 28f.

[93] See for Vergil's influence on Christian eschatology, J. Sheehan, "Catholic Ideas of Death as found in Aeneid VI," *C.F.* 16(1962), 87—109. The influence of Classical Mythology generally on Christian ideas of Hell is very curious and, so far as I know, has still not been well studied.

which is viewed in terms of the future glorification of the Roman race and of the future hope for the mission of the Roman State on earth.

This strikes the right key for a Roman and for all who place the claims of society above those of the individual. It is in this context that Vergil has chosen to introduce the philosophic doctrine of reincarnation in relation to the souls awaiting rebirth in the Grove of Lethe, in which Rome's destiny is marked out as part of the divine scheme. It is hard, then, not to accept that the philosophic afterlife in Vergil is a symbolic setting lending great dignity to Roman history — though to the philosophy the historical purpose cannot be entirely reconciled.[94]

[94] See also the able discussion on "the two goals of the soul" by Brooks Otis, *T.A.P.A.* 90(1959), 169—173.

CHAPTER VII

VERGIL'S GOLDEN BOUGH, THE CUMAEAN SIBYL, AND THE ELEUSINIAN CATABASIS OF HERACLES

1. *The Golden Bough*

From the Ghosts met by Aeneas in the Underworld we turn in this chapter to the rich store of tradition on which Vergil drew for the descent mechanism and the person of the Sibyl. It was characteristic of Vergil's mind that he liked to weld together motifs selected from diverse sources to form a new picture or conception; here with subtle innovation he has made Aeneas into a new kind of catabatic hero, taking the hint for Aeneas' new image not only from the tradition that stressed his piety, but from the Eleusinianized Heracles himself.

Our enquiry into this matter takes us back again to the Approach to Avernus and forces us to consider anew that other prerequisite for Aeneas' descent: the Golden Bough. It hangs, like the Golden Fleece,[1] on an oak (*ilex, Aen.* 6.209) in the middle of a wood. This Aeneas must first fetch for the Sibyl, before he is permitted to descend into the "covered-up places of earth". But how will he discover it? How take it from its tree? The Sibyl's cautionary warning that between her Cave on the acropolis and the Shades a pathless forest and the river Cocytus intervene —

> "Tenent media omnia silvae,
> Cocytusque sinu labens circumvenit atro" (*Aen.* 6.131f.)[2]—

is unnerving. And to obtain the Bough, even if found, might yet prove an obstacle. "It will come", says the Sibyl, "of its own will and easily if the Fates are calling you. Otherwise you will not be able to overcome or break it off by any force or blade":

[1] Ap. Rhod. *Argon.* 2.404f., 1266ff., 4.124f. and 162.

[2] See J. Conington, *P. Vergili Maronis Opera*[4], 2.442 on *Aen.* 6. 131, who points out that Vergil here has *Od.* 11. 157—159 in mind.

"ipse volens facilisque sequetur,
si te fata vocant: aliter non viribus ullis
vincere nec duro poteris convellere ferro."
(*Aen.* 6.146—148)

Possibly, as the Sibyl's words imply, Vergil had intended to make the discovery of the Golden Bough within the forest an elaborate ordeal and test in itself, as the finding of the Golden Fleece was the culminating object of Jason's quest. But in the event the forest presents no real difficulty for Aeneas, who is quickly led, in answer to a prayer, to the tree whence "through the boughs shone the contrasting gleam of gold" (*Aen.* 6.204). The Trojan, unlike Jason,[3] approaches the oak fearlessly, and breaks off the Bough, which, however, delays (*refringit/ cunctantem,* 6.210f.) — strange behaviour for the Bough in view of the Sibyl's earlier prediction.[4] Nevertheless the discovery and acquisition of this passport into the "covered-up places of earth", which Aeneas carries to the Sibyl, as she had requested, is a clear sign of divine favour, and an indication that Aeneas' descent is fulfilling destiny.

The Bough plays no part in the mechanism of Aeneas' descent. For no sooner has Aeneas sacrificed to the chthonic powers in the gloom of the forest, at the lakeside of Avernus, where a deep cave lies concealed —

spelunca alta fuit vastoque immanis hiatu,
scrupea, tuta lacu nigro nemorumque tenebris
(*Aen.* 6.237—238) —

than the earth begins to quake, the Sibyl shouts her orders, and they plunge together into the world below:

ecce autem primi sub lumina solis et ortus
sub pedibus mugire solum et iuga coepta moveri

[3] Cf. Ap. Rhod. *Argon.* 4.149ff. The Bough, of course, being protected by the Fates, needed no dragon to guard its tree.

[4] The position of *cunctantem* is very bold if it expresses, as Servius explains, merely the natural resistance of the plant to being picked off. G. Norwood, "Vergiliana" *C.Q.* 12(1918), 148f. interprets *cunctantem* as showing that Aeneas to some extent can "force fate".

silvarum, visaeque canes ululare per umbram
adventante dea. "procul, o procul este, profani,"
conclamat vates, "totoque absistite luco;
tuque invade viam vaginaque eripe ferrum:
nunc animis opus, Aenea, nunc pectore firmo."
tantum effata furens antro se immisit aperto;
ille ducem haud timidis vadentem passibus aequat.
(*Aen.* 6.255—263)

(And, behold, soon before the first gleam of the rising sun, the ground bellowed beneath their feet, the slopes of the forest-clad mountains began to move, and there appeared shapes like Hounds howling and just visible through the shadows; the Goddess was coming and was very near. "Stand clear!" cried the Priestess, "all you who are unhallowed: stand clear! Be gone from all the Grove. But you, Aeneas, whip blade from scabbard and step forth on your way. It is now that you need courage and a stout heart." Saying no more she plunged frantically down into the opened cavern, and strode onwards. With dauntless pace Aeneas followed where she led.)

Despite the realism of this scene, the details remain remarkably obscure. Which do we suppose of two catabatic traditions is suggested by the description of Aeneas' descent through this *antrum apertum,* which may mean either an "open cave", as Tiberius Donatus interprets it *("antrum, quod semper patebat"),* like the cavern at Taenarum through which both Heracles and Orpheus gained access to the world below, or a "cave which opened", like the Venusberg, which gave way for Tannhäuser?[5]

Since the *antrum* at line 262 must be the above mentioned *spelunca* at the lakeside, whose mouth is said at 237 to gape wide open (*vasto immanis hiatu*), Donatus' supposition that Aeneas' descent was through an ever open cave may seem to be fully justified. No such cave, however, is to be found at Avernus. Vergil's description of the

[5] Stith Thomspon, *Motif-Index of Folk-Literature*[2] (Bloomington 1955—1958) fails to distinguish adequately between these two motifs in the section dealing with Descents, see e.g. F92. For the Venusberg motif see F131.1.

Avernian *spelunca* seems rather to have been taken, at least partially, from Lucretius' Gate of Death, *leti ianua,* which *"patet immani et vasto respectat hiatu",* at *De Rerum Natura* 5.375. Vergil's cave owes something, too, as Conington observes, to the *σπέος 'Αίδαο* in Apollonius Rhodius at *Argonautica* 2.735ff. Now, Lucretius is speaking figuratively when he asserts that the Gate of Death lies ever open — passing through the Gates of Hades is a common euphemism for dying from Homer onwards. And when the Sibyl warns that "Easy is the Descent to Avernus. Throughout every night and every day the door of black Dis stands wide open" (see p. 149 above), she too refers figuratively or euphemistically to the ever ready path to the World of Shades. The same thought lies behind the caustic reply of Heracles, "Go hang yourself" (*κρεμάσαντι σαυτόν κ.τ.λ.*), to Dionysus, when at Aristophanes *Frogs* 121ff. the former was asked to advise on the quickest route to Hades.

In view of these passages, the Sibyl's celebrated warning can scarcely refer to the physical cave through which Aeneas will make his actual descent and return. Aeneas' plea to the Sibyl "to explain the way and fling wide the holy gates" (*"doceas iter et sacra ostia pandas"*, 6.237) suggests, *e contra,* that the hallowed Entrance Gate of the Infernal King needs opening. The event itself at the lakeside indicates that in fact the whole ground moved, and the earthquake-action suggests the earth may have parted.[6] During all this while Hecate approaches (*adventante dea,* 6.258), whose nearness is suggested by the presence of her infernal Hounds, (*visaeque canes ululare per umbram,* 6.257).[7]

[6] The parting of earth takes place in descents as well as in necromancy. Cf. Lucian *Nek.* 6 (where it is said that the Babylonian Magi were able *ἀνοίγειν τοῦ ῞Αιδου τὰς πύλας καὶ κατάγειν ὃν ἂν βούλωνται ἀσφαλῶς καὶ ὀπίσω αὖθις ἀναπέμπειν*) and 10 (*εὐθὺς οὖν ἅπαντα ἐκεῖνα ἐσαλεύετο καὶ ὑπὸ τῆς ἐπῳδῆς τοὔδαφος ἀνερρήγνυτο… κατελθόντες δὲ διὰ τοῦ χάσματος κτλ.*), Apul. *Met.* 11.12 *(terrae claustra cohibens)*, and numerous other instances (but not the Vergilian) cited by Th. Hopfner, s.v. "Nekromantie", *R.E.* 16. esp. 2220—2225, and W. Headlam, "Ghost-raising, Magic, and the Underworld", *C.R.* 16(1902), 57f. Vergil may have had in mind the scene at Ap. Rhod. *Argon* 3.1207—1220 where Hecate came to a sacrifice complete with *βόθρος* and the meadows trembled at her approach, *πίσεα δ'ἔτρεμε πάντα κατὰ στίβον*. But in the *Aeneid* Vergil adapts the necromantic ritual as a preparation for the catabatic journey and the earthquake-action is part of the catabatic mechanism.

[7] Cf. *Aen.* 4.609 *nocturnisque Hecate triviis ululata per urbes* and further Apol-

It is tempting to think from this description that their very shapes, as they howled through the gloom, could be made out by Aeneas and the Sibyl, rather than that they merely "seemed" to be howling.[8] And there seems to be little point in emphasising Hecate's physical presence unless she was coming perhaps to open the Entrance.[9] At any rate Vergil has certainly combined an Underworld Entrance which needs opening with a Lucretian cave with gaping mouth. We might, from the Sibyl's words, have expected the Bough to be the actual means of enabling Aeneas "to enter the covered-up places of earth" (6.140) — could not the Sibyl then simply have knocked with the Bough for the Cave-Entrance to open? However, the Bough in the *Aeneid* has no such function. The sacrifice itself, setting the whole process in motion, renders it redundant for this event.[10]

lon. Rhod. *Argon.* 3.1216f., *ἀμφὶ δὲ τήν* (Hecate) *γε/ὀξείῃ ὑλακῇ χθόνιοι κύνες ἐφθέγγοντο* and Theocr. 2.35 and 12f., *τᾷ χθονίᾳ θ' Ἑκάτᾳ, τὰν καὶ σκύλακες τρομέοντι/ἐρχομέναν νεκύων ἀνά τ' ἠρίᾳ καὶ μέλαν αἷμα*, with G. J. de Vries, "Theocritea", *Mnemosyne* 20(1967), 435. For these Hound of Hell see also Aristoph. *Frogs*, 472. Hecate's connection with dogs is interestingly discussed by S. Karouzou, "An Underworld Scene on a Black-Figured Lekythos", *J.H.S.* 92(1972), 64—73 (plate 18) alleging a scene within Hades on a pre-450 B.C. black-figured lekythos (Nat. Mus. Athens 19765) depicting a chthonic Hecate attached to the form of two dogs, who seem to be drinking the blood of a human figure apparently condemned to undergo punishment. The goddess is sometimes pictured with the head of a dog (Dieterich, *Nekyia*², 51 n. 2).

8 E. Norden, *Aeneis Buch VI*³, 205 notes that *videri* is the standard term used with prodigies, and he quotes Obsequens 17, *arma in caelo volare visa* and 14, *tuba in caelo cantare visa.* Sound and visible movement are indeed sometimes considered as a single phenomenon, see A. S. Pease, *Vergili Aeneidos Liber Quartus,* 406, and with our passage cf. Hor. *Sat.* 1.8.33—35, *Hecaten vocat altera... videres infernas errare canes.*

9 For Hecate's role as "Schützerin vor Tür und Tor" see T. Kraus, *Hekate* (Heidelberg 1960), 106. S. Eitrem, "La Sibylle de Cumes et Virgile", *Symbolae Osloenses* 24(1945), 95—97 and 103f. wonders whether Hecate here holds the function of *ῥηξιπύλη* (*P.G.M.* 4. 2751) or *προθυραία* (Procl. *Hymni* 6. 2. 14 cf. *P.G.M.* 4. 2719 *κλῦθι διαξεύξασα πύλας ἀλύτου ἀδάμαντος*), to which the Sibyl perhaps corresponds as *κλειδοφόρος* (see also following note).

10 For the suggestion, on the analogy of the divining-rod of mistletoe used in modern Europe for the discovery of underground secrets, that this was the original function of the Bough see A. B. Cook, "The Golden Bough and the Rex Nemorensis", *C.R.* 16(1902), 275f. Similarly P. Corssen, "Die Sibylle im sechsten Buch

The first real bar to Aeneas' Underworld Visit is the passage over the Waters of Death, which the possession of the Bough enables him to overcome. At first Charon is thoroughly alarmed at the sight of Aeneas sword in hand, and refuses to admit him in his barque. Aeneas' presence reminds Charon of the trickery and violence of the old heroes Heracles, Theseus and Peirithous, whereupon he complains of his unfortunate experience with these earlier living visitors to Hades:

> "quisquis es, armatus qui nostra ad flumina tendis,
> fare age quid venias iam istinc, et comprime gressum....
> nec vero Alciden me sum laetatus euntem
> accepisse lacu, nec Thesea Pirithoumque,
> dis quamquam geniti atque invicti viribus essent.
> Tartareum ille manu custodem in vincla petivit...
> hi dominam Ditis thalamo deducere adorti."
>
> (*Aen.* 6.388—397)

der Aeneis", *Sokrates* N. F. 1(1913), 8 held that the Bough ought to have denoted the entrance of the cave and that "Wer den Mistelzweig hat, braucht sich die Unterwelt nicht durch das Blut von Opfertieren zu erschliessen." Corssen *op. cit.* 13f. describes the sacrifice as a "blosses Ornament" (since there are no ghosts to drink the blood), which nevertheless "das Motiv des Mistelzweiges unterdrückt". We have, however, no evidence as to these alleged properties of mistletoe in ancient Italy or Greece. Nor is the conjecture convincing that the Golden Bough might have originated from an early descent of Heracles, in which a bough with golden apples was fetched, which then served as an open sesame *to Olympus;* see G. Martin in *Studies presented to D. M. Robinson* ed. G. E. Mylonas and D. Raymond (Washington 1953), 2.1193—1195. On the other hand the motif of knocking on the underworld door, which can be traced back to at least the second millennium B. C. in the Sumerian myth of Inanna's Descent (S. N. Kramer, *J.C.S.*5[1951], 1ff.) and is parodied by Dionysus' banging on the underworld door in Aristophanes, *Frogs* 460f., 503ff., may have been known to Vergil, who may also have known a tradition involving other magical plants having the effect of making rocks move apart; for the tradition in later times see S. Baring-Gould, *Curious Myths of the Middle Ages* (London 1894), 402ff. But in the event Vergil adapts the necromantic ritual for the *catabasis* — see on this esp. Eitrem, *art. cit.* in previous n., pp. 99f. and J. van Ooteghem, *Coll. Latom.* 44(1960), 768f. "nous avons donc ici une multiplication un peu inutile des moyens, une juxtaposition de conceptions différentes: évocation des morts et catabase". Hecate is doubtless attracted by the blood (see n. 7 and cf. Hecate *αἱμόποτις* in the Orph. hymn 294.53 Abel) and this presumably is why the Bough is not needed to open the cave.

("Whoever you are who stride in arms towards my river, come, say why you approach. Check your pace; speak now, from where you are. ... I indeed regretted that I ever admitted Hercules to the lake when he came here, and Theseus too and Peirithous, though they were Sons of Gods and of unvanquished might. The one came to steal by force Hell's own watchdog and enchain him. ... The others undertook to abduct Pluto's [Dis'] mistress from her own wedding chamber.")

The welling up of the boatman's fears at the approach of Aeneas is not allayed by the Sibyl's assurance that this hero has come rather to visit his own father. But when the Sibyl produces the Bough from her garment, saying —

"si te nulla movet tantae pietatis imago,
at ramum hunc...
agnoscas" (*Aen.* 6.405—407)

("But if the sight of Aeneas' fidelity so strong has no power to move you, yet you must recognize this branch") —

Charon is completely won over. He "looking in awe at the holy offering, the Wand of Destiny, which it was long since he had seen" —

ille admirans venerabile donum
fatalis virgae longo post tempore visum
(*Aen.* 6.408—409) —

now punts the boat to shore and ferries the living passengers across the infernal waters.

Charon's recognition of the Bough in this manner has given rise to considerable speculation as to the Bough's literary ancestry. It was argued by Vergil's learned editor Christian Gottlob Heyne in the eighteenth century that the Bough must have been shown to Charon in an earlier *catabasis*, perhaps Heracles' or Theseus' when they made their descents to the world below. For how else, Heyne argued, would Charon have seen it before?[11]

[11] C. G. Heyne, *P. Virgili Maronis Opera*[4] cur. G. P. E. Wagner (London 1830—1832), 2 (Excursus VI), 1015.

Yet plausible as this solution at first seems, it hardly convinces.[12] For the two lines 408—409 describing Charon's recognition of the Bough last seen long ago would be oddly used of Charon's meeting with either Heracles or Theseus, who were not much more than one generation back. And Vergil cannot be said to have represented either of these as having come with the Bough, since Charon seems to say, on the contrary, that they came with unworthy motives, forcing their entry with violence. Nor is the suggestion of J. Six[13] any more convincing, that Vergil derived the Bough from a *catabasis* of Orpheus, since Orpheus neither needed a Bough nor had one while charming his way through the Underworld by the music of his lyre.[14]

If, then, the Bough had not been carried by any descending hero before Aeneas, could it be that Charon had not seen the Bough since its creation or since his appointment, but expected that one day someone would carry it, as Polyphemus in the *Odyssey* had heard (at 9.507ff.) that one day someone called Odysseus would visit him? Kroll's explanation that Charon's recognition of the Bough was virtually forced upon him by the expectation of the Sibyl at 406—407 that the sight of it would affect him favourably, is now widely adopted.[15] But it leaves unanswered the counter-argument as to why Vergil attributes this expectation to the Sibyl in the first place.[16] This may now be accounted for, if the Sibyl knows of the Bough that Charon expects one day to see it, as Proserpine expects that one day it will be brought to her (see p. 197 below).

There exists, too, though this is not of direct importance for the ancestry of the Bough itself, some evidence for suspecting that part of Charon's speech may have been drawn from an earlier descent. For when at lines 392f. Charon says "*nec vero Alciden me sum laetatus*

[12] A. Forbiger, *P. Virgili Maronis Opera* (Lipsiae 1839), 3.119 on *Aen.* 6.409 was nevertheless convinced *("igitur Hercules et Theseus cum ramo aureo venerant")* as was E. Norden, too, in the first edition of *Aeneis Buch VI*, p. 242.

[13] J. Six, "Die Eriphyle des Polygnot", *M.D.A.I.(A.)*, 19(1894), 338f.

[14] The comparison by Six *(loc. cit.)* of the Bough to the willow-tree which Orpheus in Polygnotus' *Nekyia* touches (*ap.* Paus. 10.30.6) is inadmissible since Orpheus appears here in the Underworld after death, see p. 111 above.

[15] It is adopted in the place of Heyne's conjecture (at n. 11 above) by E. Norden in his second and third editions (cf. n. 12 above).

[16] See R. A. Brooks, "Discolor Aura", *A.J.P.* 74(1953), 272 n.9.

euntem/accepisse lacu, nec Thesea Pirithoumque" (translated above), he means not simply that he had been unwilling[17] to allow Heracles into his boat, but that having admitted him he did not escape with impunity. Servius in his Commentary on the passage says as much, adding that in an Orphic work Charon is depicted as having been frightened into admitting Heracles, for which he was then put in bonds for a whole year: "*lectum est et in Orpheo quod, quando Hercules ad inferos descendit, Charon territus eum statim suscepit, ob quam rem anno integro in compedibus fuit.*" From this brief passage we may suppose that behind these two verses in the *Aeneid* lies an Orphic descent.

If Servius is to be believed that behind Charon's complaint lurks an Orphic *catabasis*, its influence can be further traced down to Statius, who ingeniously works into his Theban epic a *catabasis* of Amphiaraos. According to Statius, Dis, the god of the infernal regions, is himself angered by the sudden appearance in the lower world of Amphiaraos, who was swallowed up alive in a cleft of the ground as he fled from Thebes; and the god, like Charon, regrets that he ever allowed Peirithous, Theseus, and Heracles into his realm alive or that he yielded to Orpheus' charms.[18] Amphiaraos, it is true, carries no Golden Bough as such. But his denial to Dis that he has come below with the motives of Heracles is reminiscent of the protestations of Aeneas' innocence to Charon. And it is surely due to Vergilian influence that Amphiaraos, as he delivers his speech, holds up in his hand a bough of dying olive, with which he had fallen below, and asks Dis to "believe these credentials" — "*crede his insignibus*" (*Thebaid* 8.96).

Of the Orphic *catabasis* itself nothing more is known for certain. We may be sure, at least, that Servius did not merely read back into

[17] That Charon expresses himself "unwilling" to ferry Heracles might tempt us to read ἀέκων ("unwilling") in the obelized passage in Hermesianax' Orphic *catabasis* referred to in chapter 4 n. 45 above. However, there appears no reason why Charon there should have been unwilling to do his ordinary job, as distinct from ferrying living passengers.

[18] Stat. *Theb.* 8.52—60. For Statius' further interest in the "descent" theme see also *Theb.* 4.406—645 which, however, like the imitations of the Vergilian descent in Lucan and Silius Italicus (see p. 159 above), reverts rather to the necromantic nucleus of Homer's *Nekyia.*

Vergil what may have been gleaned from the *Thebaid.* For on the one hand Statius makes no reference at all to Charon's punishment, while on the other he makes over to Dis Charon's tale of regret. If, however, we are willing to accept Norden's imaginative supposition of a word play on Charon, *Χάρων*, in the original episode with some such words as *οὐδὲ μὲν Ἡρακλῆα χαρεὶς δεχόμην κατιόντα* meaning that Charon "did not escape with impunity when he admitted Heracles on his descent", there will be quite strong evidence for the Orphic descent having been originally a Greek work.[19] And a Greek work rules out M. Haupt's conjecture that the episode belonged orignally to Lucan's lost *Orpheus* (for which see chap. 4 n. 85 above).[20] It is surely a remarkable fact, and one which should be remembered when considering the ultimate source for the Greek poem, that the theme of the punishment of the boatman for ferrying a living person across the Waters of Death is as old as the *Epic of Gilgamesh.* There (see on p. 26 and cf. also p. 73 above) Urshanabi was banned by Utnapishtim from ever making the crossing again.

The Bough, then, is important in distinguishing Aeneas from the earlier mortal visitors to Hades, and it shows the old heroic code to be inadequate.[21] Whereas the descending heroes of the past were sacrilegious and prevailed through physical strength, Aeneas undertakes the descent in preparation for a civilising mission both with divine approval and in obedience to his father's command. Both his personal qualities (*pietatis imago*, 6.405) and the Bough, the symbol of his divine mission (*fatalis virga*, 6.409), reveal his superiority over his predecessors.

That Vergil represents him as a new type of hero is shown, too, by the poet's artful contrasting of Aeneas to these older catabatic figures.

[19] E. Norden, *Aeneis Buch VI³*, 237, followed by A. Dieterich, *Nekyia²*, 134 n.1. It will be noticed that Norden also assumes that Orpheus must have been the *καταβαίνων* to whom Charon complained about Heracles, as in the *Aeneid* he complains about Heracles to Aeneas. If Heracles were the mortal visitor to Hades, as C. A. Lobeck, *Aglaophamus* 813 note b argues, it is difficult to understand how in an Orphic descent the tale of regret would be fitted in.

[20] M. Haupt, *Opusc.* 2.19. For other discussions see O. Kern, *Orphicorum Fragmenta*, fr. 296.

[21] For similar indications elsewhere in the *Aeneid* see K. Quinn, *Virgil's Aeneid: A Critical Description* (London 1968), 1—22.

Theseus is at the outset represented as liberator on the Cumaean Gates (see pp. 148—150 above), but reveals progressively less attractive qualities from that scene onwards culminating in the description of his punishment in Tartarus at *Aeneid* 6.617f. (p. 128 above).[22] At 119—123 Aeneas links him with Orpheus, Pollux, and Hercules, among those descending heroes whose example he hopes to follow. In this list, the divine birth of the descending heroes is stressed, but not their motives. Not until Charon refers at *Aeneid* 6.391ff. to Hercules, Theseus, and Peirithous, are the motives of these mortal visitors to Hades mentioned, and the thought of them rouses Charon to anger. This is perhaps the reason why Orpheus, though mentioned by Aeneas, is not named by Charon, Orpheus being consistently cast in a favourable light by Vergil, who also makes him a prominent figure in Elysium after his death, and why Theseus is coupled in Charon's list, as he is not in Aeneas', with the sacrilegious Peirithous. Heracles, who was both Eleusinian initiate[23] and blusterer[24], could appear in both lists without contradiction.

So far nothing has been found to upset the claim of the learned literary critic Cornutus of the first century A.D. that the Golden Bough is a poetic figment;[25] and indeed there is much to be said in favour of this view, which takes into account Vergil's ordinary manner of composing poetry. Modern scholarship has attempted, however, to uncover a source of another kind underlying the symbolism of the Golden Bough, based on Vergil's comparison of the Bough to mistletoe. It is to this that we should now address ourselves in the hope of discovering to what extent, if any, Cornutus' verdict needs to be modified.

[22] Cf. J. W. Zarker, "Aeneas and Theseus in *Aeneid* 6", *C.J.* 62(1967), 220—226.

[23] It does not seem sufficiently to have been noticed that the Sibyl's reply to Aeneas that "Some few, whom gracious Jupiter has loved,... have prevailed" ("*Pauci, quos aequus amavit/Iuppiter.../...potuere*", 129—131) reflects Eleusinian language (cf. Hom. *Hymn to Demeter*, 487f., *μέγ' ὄλβιος ὅν τιν' ἐκεῖναι/προφρονέως φίλωνται*), which applies most aptly out of the four *καταβαίνοντες* in Aeneas' list to Heracles because of his Eleusinian connections (pp. 89—92 above). For Vergil's use of Heracles' Eleusinian descent see presently.

[24] The emphasis on Heracles' *vis* and *insidiae*, "violence" and "treachery", in Charon's speech here puts him, of course, in contrast with Aeneas.

[25] Cornutus *ap.* Macrob. *Saturnalia*, 5.19.2: "*[Vergilius] adsuevit poetico more aliqua fingere, ut de aureo ramo.*"

The simile in question is that which Vergil introduces when Aeneas first catches sight of the gleam of the Golden Bough in the shadowy holm-oak tree on which it grows. Both the leafy gold of the Bough and the tinkling of the metal foil in a gentle breeze are compared to mistletoe, "which, though never seeded from the tree on which it grows, encircles a round trunk with saffron-coloured berries, and is always green with young leaves amid the forest in winter's cold"—

> Quale solet silvis brumali frigore viscum
> fronde virere nova, quod non sua seminat arbos,
> et croceo fetu teretis circumdare truncos,
> talis erat species auri frondentis opaca
> ilice, sic leni crepitabat brattea vento.
>
> (*Aen.* 6.205—209)

In the eighteenth century, Heyne and his immediate successors passed over this simile as being unimportant for the interpretation of the poetry. But Vergilian scholars in the latter part of the nineteenth century had at their disposal vast collections of comparative mistletoe-lore which they felt justified in bringing to bear on the exegesis of the passage. In particular Frazer, who gave to his study the title *The Golden Bough*, regarded Vergil's comparison as a mere "poetic device to cast a mystic glamour over the humble plant," and believing that the Bough was the mistletoe adds that Vergil's "description was based on a popular superstition that at certain times the mistletoe blazed out into a supernatural golden glory."[26] He further associated the Bough and the mistletoe with tree-magic.[27] Norden was similarly impressed by the magical properties of mistletoe in Celtic, Germanic, and European folk-belief.[28] And he inferred, after studying a number of other similes behind which he seemed to detect a variety of mythic, cultic,

[26] J. G. Frazer, *The Golden Bough*, 11.284f. Neither common mistletoe (*Viscum album*), which has white berries, nor *Loranthus europaeus*, which is deciduous, entirely fits Vergil's description. Frazer suggests *op. cit.* 315—320 that Vergil may have confused traits from both, and notes that common mistletoe turns golden when dried.

[27] See further pp. 201f. below.

[28] E. Norden, *Aeneis Buch VI*³, 166—168.

and rationalizing equivalences, that behind this simile too must lie a cultic identification.[29]

This line of enquiry assumes that the Bough is in fact conceived of botanically as the branch of a real tree or plant, rather than poetically as of actual gold. Yet the Sibyl calls it "golden in leaf and stem" ("*aureus et foliis et lento vimine*," 6.137). When the "golden-haired produce" ("*auricomos... fetus*," 6.141) of the tree is plucked, another golden twig will put forth leaves "of like metal" ("*simili... metallo*," 6.144). The Bough, according to the simile, has even the sound of metal foil in a gentle wind. And, as we have seen on p. 185 above, it cannot be wrenched from its tree, if it does not come easily in accordance with the fates, by any force or blade. Shall we not say, then, that the Bough belongs wholly to the region of myth and that the comparison of it to mistletoe has as its purpose to make credible the strange growth of the Golden Bough?

Nothing, surely, in the simile entitles us to infer that Vergil was dependant upon, though he may have been aware of, the folk-beliefs associated with the mistletoe. On the contrary, Vergil has consistently described the Bough as made of real gold, like the Golden Fleece wrested by Jason or the Golden Apples in the Garden of the Hesperides. And this may be significant. For these Golden Apples were originally given as a gift to Olympian Juno.[30] Similarly the Golden Bough is said to be "dedicated as sacred to Juno of the Lower World", which "beautiful Proserpine has ordained to be brought to her as her especial offering."[31] The Olympian Juno who is Aeneas' arch-enemy to the end is clearly a separate deity from the Juno who is identified with Proserpine. But the allusion is sufficient perhaps to suggest that behind the Golden Bough glimmers the myth of the Golden Apples.

[29] For Norden's treatment of similes cf. *ibid.* 163—168. At Hom. *Od.* 4.121, for instance, where Helen is compared with Artemis, Norden says that Helen is in fact a *hypostasis* of Artemis. This example is instructive for understanding why Norden feels that at *Aen.* 6.205—9 he can similarly use mistletoe-lore for the exegesis of the Bough. For a weighing of the evidence concerning the cult which Norden identifies behind the Bough see further pp. 200ff. below.

[30] Cf. n. 21 to chap. 3 above.

[31] *Aen.* 6.138, *Iunoni infernae dictus sacer* and *Aen.* 6.142f., *hoc sibi pulchra suum ferri Proserpina munus/instituit.*

In short, Vergil thinks of gold as something too emotive to omit. And not only the Golden Apples upon the tree of the Hesperides and the Golden Fleece upon the oak (see pp. 185f. above), but also the Golden Flowers which gleam from radiant trees in Pindar's Islands of the Blest[32] and the Golden Fruits in Pindar's underworld Elysium[33] may have contributed towards Vergil's Golden Bough. In a list of authors and the flowers to which each might be likened, Meleager of Gadara in his *Garland* sang of "the Golden Bough of the ever divine Plato that gleams everywhere in goodness."[34] This passage, if known to Vergil, must surely have clinched the precise form of the symbol to which all other considerations had led.

Finally, let us consider the light thrown by modern scholarship upon a third line of enquiry into the Golden Bough's ancestry, opened up by Vergil's commentator Servius. In a manner typical of ancient scholiasts, Servius on *Aeneid* 6.136 has contaminated his note from older commentaries thus:

> "Licet de hoc ramo hi qui de sacris Proserpinae scripsisse dicuntur, *quiddam* esse *mysticum* adfirment, *publica* tamen *opinio* hoc habet. Orestes post occisum regem Thoantem in regione Taurica cum sorore Iphigenia, ut supra ⟨2.116⟩ diximus, fugit et Dianae simulacrum inde sublatum haud longe ab Aricia collocavit. In huius templo post mutatum ritum sacrificiorum fuit arbor quaedam, de qua infringi ramum non licebat. Dabatur autem fugitivis potestas, ut si quis exinde ramum potuisset auferre, monomachia cum fugitivo templi sacerdote dimicaret: nam fugitivus illic erat sacerdos ad priscae imaginem fugae. Dimicandi autem dabatur facultas quasi ad pristini sacrificii reparationem."

[32] *Ol.* 2.72.

[33] Fr. 114 ed. Bowra, on which see Sir J. E. Sandys' note in *The Odes of Pindar* (Loeb), 588f.

[34] *Anth. Pal.* iv. 1.47f.:

Ναὶ μὴν καὶ χρύσειον ἀεὶ θείοιο Πλάτωνος
κλῶνα, τὸν ἐξ ἀρετῆς πάντοθι λαμπόμενον.

For the suggestion that Vergil may have known this passage see A. K. Michels, "The Golden Bough of Plato", *A.J.P.* 66(1945), 59—63. It does not however follow *pace* Michels that Vergil was turning to Plato and in particular to his Myth of Er for the conception of Aeneas' "dream"; see further at the end of this chapter.

("Although concerning this Bough those who are said to have written about the rites of Proserpine affirm that it is *something mystic*, the *popular view* is as follows. Orestes, having killed Thoas king of Taurica, fled with his sister Iphigeneia, as we have mentioned already ⟨2.116⟩, and carrying off from that region the image of Diana located it not far from Aricia. Here in her sacred grove, the manner of her sacrifices having changed, there was a certain tree from which it was not lawful that any branch might be broken. Only to runaway slaves was the right granted, that anyone able to break off one of its branches might engage in single combat with the priest of the sacred grove, who was himself also a runaway slave. The priest in the grove was a fugitive to commemorate the ancient flight [of Orestes]. And the opportunity to engage in combat in a sense made up for Diana's ancient sacrifice.")[35]

So runs the account of the "popular view", and in two further sentences Servius returns to the explanation of the writers holding that the Bough is "something mystic": *et ad sacra Proserpinae accedere nisi sublato ramo non poterat. Inferos autem subire hoc dicit, sacra celebrare Proserpinae.* Aeneas, they explain, was about to enter the Underworld "and could not approach the sacred rites of Proserpine except by taking a bough. Indeed to go down into the Lower World is tantamount to celebrating the rites of Proserpine."

In an extension of this note, Servius goes on to set forth an allegorical interpretation of the Golden Bough on the basis of the letter Y which Pythagoras took as an object lesson in ethics, the forks indicat-

[35] Students of Roman religion have advanced two contrasting views of the origin of Diana. Franz Altheim attacks the Frazerian position in *Griechische Götter im alten Rom* (*Religionsg. Vers. u. Vorarb.* 22/1, 1930), 93—172 by taking Servius' account rather literally and inferring that Diana is of foreign origin. The traditional view that Diana was originally a genuine Italic goddess is rightly restored by A. E. Gordon, "On the Origin of Diana", *T.A.P.A.* 63(1932), 177—192 and see further Gordon, *The Cults of Aricia* (Berkeley 1934). 1—20. A. Alföldi, "Diana Nemorensis", *A.J.A.* 64(1960), 137—144 and *Early Rome and the Latins* (Michigan 1965), 85ff. suggests the Hellenization of an Italic goddess in the late sixth century. And if the Diana in Servius Tullius' temple on the Aventine came from Massilia and Ephesus as a federal deity, as is there argued, Diana at Nemi may have come from Cumae when Cumae and Aricia were allied, as Colin Hardie kindly suggests to me.

ing respectively virtue and vice. Vergil's Bough hidden in the wood is now taken to be a similar parable of human life, where virtue is obscured in the confusion of error. The comment prompted A.B. Cook's explanation of the Bough as a divining rod, as mentioned already in n. 10 above. Servius ends his note by drawing upon the view of others, who say that the Bough with which the Underworld is sought is golden because mortals meet their death through riches, and for this he cites the poet Tiberianus (cf. *P.L.M.* 3.265).

Now Vergilian scholars show a curious ambiguity towards Servius. Some defer to his views as though he preserves a veritable mine of reliable information, assuming, no doubt, that, because he is much closer to Vergil than we are, he inherited traditions going back to the first century. Others feel with equal conviction that since he came some four hundred years after Vergil, he resorted to no more than unreliable guesses.

The ambiguity is aptly illustrated by the trust which Norden and Frazer respectively put in the different interpretations recorded by Servius. The former is convinced that the "mystical" interpretation is correct confirming that the Golden Bough played a role in some kind of *μυστήρια Κόρης*, which Vergil knew either directly or from some written document unknown to us.[36] What we know of branch-bearing in the Mysteries of Persephone-Kore, is concisely summarized in F. Lenormant's remarks on the Eleusinian initiates thus: "Les mystes s'y présentaient couronnés de myrte et tenant à la main un bâton de forme particulière, sorte de thyrse très court... Ce pouvait être aussi un simple rameau, et c'est ainsi que sur le célèbre vase à reliefs de Cumes (fig. 2639) Céléus ou Eubouleus porte, en guise de *bacchos,* un rameau d'arbre."[37] This explains in part the link between the Bough and Proserpine in the *Aeneid;* and the dedication of the Bough

[36] E. Norden, *Aeneis Buch VI*^{3}, 171—173 on *Aen.* 6.138 and 142f. (above n. 31).

[37] In Daremberg and Saglio, *Dictionnaire des antiquités grecques et romaines,* s.v. "Eleusinia", 2.570. See for further instances of *mystae* holding staffs F.J.M. de Waele, *The Magic Staff or Rod in Graeco-Italian Antiquity* (Gent 1927), 79—84. On the supposition that the mysteries of Persephone and Hecate might have been confused S. Eitrem, *Symbolae Osloenses* 24(1945), 103f. wondered whether the Bough was originally the attribute of Hecate *προθυραία* (see at n. 9 above). But for this there is scarcely any evidence.

to Juno of the Lower World establishes its essentially chthonian character. But we have no reason to believe that the branches in these Mysteries were actually golden, or that they were taken from the oak, or that they had any other of the associations of the Vergilian Bough. Frazer therefore seized upon Servius' "popular view", and imputed to Norden an error of judgement for passing over it. "I confess", he says, "that I have more respect for the general opinion of antiquity than to dismiss it thus cavalierly without a hearing.[38] Norden replies to this that he will not even allow himself to refute this "Nichtigkeit eines Scholiasten". Servius' pseudo-exegesis, he says, bears the stamp of despair.[39]

What value, then, for the exegesis of Vergil's Golden Bough is to be attached to this scholiast's explanation? By taking with it Vergil's text and a hint from Suetonius and others saying that the priest who reigned in the Arician grove was known as the King of the Wood *(Rex Nemorensis)*,[40] Frazer attempted to account for the ritual of Diana Nemorensis. Through a vast, cumulative argument drawing upon both folkore and comparative anthropology he formulated the remarkable hypothesis that the priest was in truth an oak spirit whose life, or death, was in the Mistletoe, the Golden Bough itself.[41] Moreover, the tree on which it grew was thought not merely to be guarded by Virbius, the first King of the Wood and predecessor of all priest-kings; it was the very embodiment of Diana whose consort he was.[42]

No summary can do justice to the eloquence with which Frazer develops this argument. Under his spell Vergil's readers have long grown accustomed to associate the Golden Bough with primitive tree-worship. But just how conjectural the hypothesis is for the exegesis of Vergil may be judged from the fact that Servius only implies (he

[38] J. G. Frazer, *The Golden Bough*³, 11.284 n. 3.

[39] E. Norden, *Aeneis Buch VI*³, 164 n.1. Similarly C. G. Heyne, *P. Virgili Maronis Opera*⁴, 2 (Excursus VI), 1015: "*Nec tamen id quicquam commune cum Avernalibus locis et ramo aureo Proserpinae habere videtur*".

[40] Suetonius, *Caligula*, 35; cf. Statius, *Silv.* 3.1.55f.; Ovid, *Fasti*, 3.271f., *Ars Am.* 1.259; Valerius Flaccus, *Argon.* 2.404f., and see Seneca, *Phaedr.* 414 for the title *regina nemorum* of Diana herself.

[41] *The Golden Bough*³, 11.284ff.

[42] *Ibid.* 1 40f.; 2. 379ff. Hippolytus when restored to life by Asclepios became identified with Virbius at Nemi; for the main classical references see *ib.* 1.20.

does not directly state it) that the "popular view" identified the Golden Bough with the branch which the candidate for the priesthood of Diana had to pluck from the tree in the Arician grove. And Servius calls neither this branch mistletoe nor its tree an oak. These assertions are made by Frazer, who does not prove them. The evidence for calling the tree at Nemi an oak rests only upon the identification of its branch with Vergil's Golden Bough which grew upon an oak; there is just the possibility that the leaves are oak on a leafy double-headed marble bust found at Nemi in 1885, which may, if F. Granger is right, represent a portrait of the King of the Wood and his successor.[43] And since it is uncertain that the branch at Nemi was Vergil's Golden Bough, or that Vergil's Golden Bough was the mistletoe, it is doubly uncertain that the branch at Nemi was mistletoe: indeed Servius' words *arbor quaedam, de qua infringi ramum non licebat* would naturally be taken to refer to *any* bough of the tree, as though all its boughs were of equal worth.[44] Enhancing, then, as Frazer's anthropological considerations have been for the awe surrounding the Golden Bough, they have not succeeded in providing the premises for his particular Arician hypothesis concerning the priesthood.[45] And what matters for us more, they lead away from, rather than towards, an understanding of Vergil's poem.

Nevertheless the emotional associations between the rites at Nemi and the rites at Avernus should not be overlooked. For if we strip away the Frazerian hypothesis that has been superimposed, the similarities that remain lead us to suspect that Vergil may well have had the cult of Diana Nemorensis in mind. Aeneas, since he has lost all status and the position he once enjoyed, is as close as can be to a fugitive or runaway slave, which is the first prerequisite the contestant for the priesthood at Nemi must possess. And as the breaking of the Arician bough from the special tree in Diana's sacred precinct is

[43] F. Granger, "A Portrait of the Rex Nemorensis", *C.R.* 21 (1907), 194—197, whose view is adopted by Frazer in his third edition pp. 41f. Earlier writers explained the heads as water-gods, e.g. A. B. Cook, *C.R.* 16 (1902), 373. Note that on Frazer's explanation the priest is here regarded as the embodiment of the tree which he guarded.

[44] A. B. Cook, *C.R.* 16 (1902), 371 and 374.

[45] For a spirited estimation of the wider foundation of Frazer's hypothesis also see Cook, *ib.* 365—380.

represented as a difficult task (whether on account of the difficulty of discovering the tree or simply due to its being heavily guarded[46] we are not told), so the Golden Bough is hard to find and impossible to obtain unless the fates permit. Furthermore by breaking the bough the fugitive-contender at Nemi won the right to a duel with the reigning priest-king: Aeneas by breaking the Golden Bough is ultimately designated as the future king of the Latins. And his fighting in the next Six Books culminates in the duel between himself and his predecessor Turnus.[47] These close parallels might still be no more than coincidences if we were not certain of Vergil's knowledge of the Arician cult, but this is proved by Vergil's reference to Virbius in connection with Diana there.[48] Possibly, then, it is also with Arician Diana in mind that Vergil speaks of the Sibyl's Cumaean cave as being in Trivia's Grove *(Triviae lucos)* at *Aeneid* 6.13. The Lago di Nemi is *Triviae lacus* for Vergil, who calls Diana, as well as Hecate, the *Trivia*[49]; and the Cumaean Sibyl herself at *Aeneid* 6.35 is the priestess not only of Apollo but also of Hecate-Diana (*Phoebi Triviaeque sacerdos*, cf. *Aen.* 6.69f.).

In short, although it is perfectly true that in tradition the branch at Nemi has nothing to do with the Sibyl at Cumae, nor the Cumaean Sibyl with Diana, Vergil is far more likely to have transferred the emotional associations of the branch by poetic licence from Diana's cult at Nemi, which is only a few miles from Rome, to the similar crater of Avernus, than to have drawn upon Celtic traditions about the mistletoe. The Arician cult was still flourishing in Vergil's day, and was going strong even in the reign of Caligula and when Pausanias travelled through Italy in the time of the Antonines.[50]

[46] See Strabo 5.3.12, p. 239 who says of the priest, *ξιφήρης οὖν ἐστιν ἀεί, περισκοπῶν τὰς ἐπιθέσεις, ἕτοιμος ἀμύνεσθαι.*

[47] For more details see R. Merkelbach, "Aeneas in Cumae", *Mus. Helv.* 18(1961) 86—90. I may perhaps be permitted to satisfy curiosity by drawing attention here to A. Lang's "Breaking the Bough in the Grove of Diana", *F.L.* 18(1907), 89—91 which cites no less than three parallels in English folklore to the breaking of a bough by a fugitive slave who thereby secures freedom and challenges the being who dwells in the wood.

[48] *Aen.* 7.761—782 (cf. n. 42 above).

[49] *Triviae lacus*, *Aen.* 7.515; cf. *Aen.* 4.511; 6.35 and 69;7.774; 10.537; 11.566 and 836; and for other references showing how deeply rooted was the threefold unity of Diana, A. Alföldi, *A.J.A.* 64(1960), 140f.

[50] Suetonius, *Calig.* 35.3 and Paus. 2.27.4.

2. *The Cumaean Sibyl*

Let us turn now from the associations of the Golden Bough, of which there is more to say presently, in order to consider the roles performed by the Cumaean Sibyl herself. When Norden published the first edition of his great commentary, it was still assumed that the Cumaean Sibyl was part of the established pre-Vergilian Aeneas-legend, and that her role as the priestess of Hecate was part of her traditional function. Both of these assumptions have subsequently been questioned, and it is unlikely, as we shall now see, that either can be rightly maintained today.

In tradition there were two oracular sites in the Avernus-Cumae area: one was the Oracle of the Dead, or *Nekyomanteion*, situated on the shore of Lake Avernus, where Hecate-Trivia had her domain (*Aen.* 6.118, 237ff., and 564); the other belonged to Apollo on the Cumaean acropolis, where the Sibyl experienced her prophetic frenzy (*Aen.* 6.9ff.). And inasmuch as the Sibyl's Cumaean cave is described as being in "Trivia's grove" (*Aen.* 6.13), Vergil seems to have transferred, or rather extended, the grove of Trivia from the lakeside of Avernus to the Cumaean acropolis. This blending of the topography, a poetic device, as I think, to help unify the separate roles in the single figure of the Sibyl, is largely responsible for the confusion, both in local tradition and in the minds of some of Vergil's readers, between the two caves which Vergil actually associates separately with these two sites. Servius, then, does well to distinguish the catabatic cave at Avernus *(qua ad inferos descendebatur)* from the prophetic cave *(ubi fuerat Sibylla vaticinata)* at Cumae.[51] And we do well also to say that these oracular sites exist "in tradition", to take account of the argument outlined above (pp. 68—70) that the Oracle of the Dead existed in tradition only, as distinct from in actual cult practice, the real Oracle of the Dead being at Ephyra in Thesprotia (pp. 58—64 above). The Oracle of the Dead beside the

[51] The confusion is responsible for the transference to Cumae of a popular local legend of Christ's Exit from Hell which properly belonged to the Hades-Entrance at the lakeside of Avernus. See my "Christ's Resurrection at Avernus: a Vergilian Influence", *C. & M.* 30(1969), 300—307 (with which cf. E. Norden on *Aen.* 6.42). Cf. also n.1 to chap. 6 above.

Lake Avernus near Cumae was introduced, as we have seen, when Odysseus' *Nekyia* was localised in the West, probably in the sixth century B.C., and this localisation was upheld by mythographers and poets who made this the scene of Aeneas' consultation.

Now just as in tradition there were two oracular sites, so in tradition, as we learn from Varro's report of Naevius[52], there were two sibyls, the Cumaean and the Cimmerian — to avoid possible confusion with Vergil's Sibyl I refer to these "sibyls of tradition" with a small s. And just as the oracular sites have been conflated in tradition, so the two sibyls have long been identified in modern scholarship as one.[53] The theory is that Varro, not admitting that the sibyl whom Naevius had made a contemporary of Aeneas was really the sibyl of Cumae, sought another name for Naevius' sibyl and called her *Cimmeria*, the distinction being then Varro's, not Naevius'.[54] But the argument does not convince. For it is more likely that Naevius himself, in developing the prophetic element in Homer's *Nekyia,* substituted a Cimmerian sibyl for Teiresias because of the traditional association of Homer's Cimmerians with Avernus; and Naevius knew perhaps that there was no Cumae until 754 B.C. and no sibyl there until *c.* 500 B.C.

The fact that they are distinguished, at any rate, in the pre-Vergilian tradition of the Cumae-Avernus area was first regarded as significant for the *Aeneid* by Peter Corssen, who showed how the conflation of these two sibyls helps us to understand why Vergil's Cumaean Sibyl seems to have occupied the two abodes at Cumae and at the lakeside of Avernus, and why she is made the priestess of the cult of Hecate as well as being Apollo's prophetic instrument on the acro-

[52] Varro *ap.* Lactantius, *div. instit.* 1.6.9: "*quartam* (i.e. *Sibyllam*) *Cimmeriam in Italia quam Naevius in libris Belli Punici Piso in annalibus nominat*" (fr. 12 ed. W. Strzelecki). Varro goes on to name the Cumaean as the seventh sibyl and thus distinguishes the Cimmerian from the Cumaean. The distinction is upheld in other Sibylline lists, e.g. Lydus, *de mensibus* p. 103 (ed. R. Wvensch); schol. on Plato, *Phaedrus* 244B; and cf. further J. G. Frazer's note on Paus. 10.12.1.

[53] Succinctly put by C. Alexandre, *Oracula Sibyllina* (Paris 1856), 2.54: "*Certissimum igitur est, Cimmeriam Naevii et Pisonis, a Varrone memoratam, non aliam esse quam Cumanam Vergilii.*"

[54] Most recently argued by J. Perret, *Les Origines de la Légende troyenne de Rome* (Paris 1942), 103: "La Sibylle qui intervient dans ses vers [*sc.* chez Naevius] est donc selon nous la Sibylle de Cumes."

polis.[55] That Vergil conflated these two sibyls is likely even if the distinction between them were a scholar's distinction made by Varro rather than Naevius'. For it is never safe to assume that there was anything Vergil had not read, which means in this case that Vergil is as likely to have come across the tradition in Varro as in Naevius and to have used it to suit his poetry. However, if we can believe Varro that Naevius mentioned the Cimmerian sibyl in his *Bellum Punicum*, where in the first two books of the epic Naevius narrates the history of Aeneas also, it is highly probable, as Corssen suggests further, that Naevius, in the lost portion of the epic, narrated Aeneas' visit to this sibyl, and that this visit led to an *evocatio* by Aeneas of his father on the shore of Avernus. Eduard Norden, who in the first edition of his commentary believed that the Cumaean Sibyl's role as Hecate's priestess was one of her traditional functions, later accepted Corssen's conclusions and in the second and subsequent editions regarded the Sibyl's claim to be Hecate's priestess at *Aeneid* 6.564f. as an invention of Vergil; he attributed also the association of the cults of Apollo and Hecate to "die dichterische Phantasie Vergils."[56] Consequently Norden held that Vergil took the prophecy of the Cumaean Sibyl from the early legend of Aeneas, and allowed the possibility of her connection with the spirits of the dead from Naevius.[57]

Still more recently Waszink has doubted whether even a prophecy to Aeneas by the Cumaean Sibyl was current in pre-Vergilian legend, and he supposed that Vergil transferred the prophecy to the Sibyl of Cumae from Cassandra, who in the *Suda* s.v. *Σίβυλλα* is reported actually to have been called a sibyl, or from the sibyl who in earlier legend prophesied the *fata Aeneae* at Troy.[58] I am personally

[55] P. Corssen, "Die Sibylle im sechsten Buch der Aeneis", *Sokrates*, N.F. 1(1913), 1—16 esp. p. 12. Cf. also A. Rzach, R. *E.* IIA, II. 2095 s.v. "Sibyllen".

[56] E. Norden, *Aeneis Buch VI*³, 118.

[57] *Ibid.* 198 and 350.

[58] J. H. Waszink, "Vergil and the Sibyl of Cumae", *Mnemosyne* 1(1948), 43—58. The important passages considered by Waszink are Lycophr. 1226—1282, Tibull. 2.5.39—64, Dion. Hal. 1.55, *Orac. Sib.* 11.144ff., and Diod. 4.66. Cf. further H. E. Butler's commentary on *Aen.* 6.890 where the double-prophecy of both the Sibyl and Anchises in the same book and where the inconsistency between the prophecy of the Sibyl and that of Helenus at *Aen.* 3.456ff. are also discussed.

inclined to accept Waszink's conclusion, all the more readily because it agrees with the probability, which I have argued elsewhere, that Vergil has innovated the Aeneas-legend even by bringing Aeneas to Cumae.[59] But whether or not the alleged innovation concerning the prophecy is true, Vergil clearly did not accept tradition as it stood. He has evidently turned the *νεκυομαντεία* narrated by his forerunner Naevius into a *κατάβασις* and modifed the function of the Cimmerian sibyl, or sibyls. Not a single reference definitely states that the Cimmerian sibyl presided over the Avernian *Nekyomanteion*, but the references when taken together add up to this, and, despite the area of doubt, our observation that Vergil by adapting the *nekyomanteia* at Avernus was the first to introduce the *catabasis* into the legend of Aeneas and hence the first to make the Sibyl a guide through the Underworld may stand.

In sum then, it it not unlikely that the Cimmerian sibyl is actually a poetic figment whose name was taken from Homer's Cimmerians. The same might be said of the Oracle of the Dead itself, and the nearby town of Cimmerium is another figment.[60] Vergil made his Sibyl the priestess of the cult of Hecate by the lake of Avernus, but it is unlikely that Vergil found even this last detail in the tradition about Avernus.[61] This, too, seems to have been Vergil's invention, helped perhaps by the existence of Diana's cult at Nemi, and designed to make plausible the two functions of his Sibyl by attributing the cult of Avernus to Apollo's sister in her chthonic form. It

[59] As I argue in my article cited in chap. 6 n. 15 above. That Vergil has innovated tradition concerning Aeneas' (and Misenus') landfall is supported by the probability also that Vergil was the first to make Daedalus visit Cumae (for which see at chap. 6 n. 13).

[60] As the "Cimmerian" sibyl doubtless owed her existence to the traditional association of Homer's Cimmerians with Avernus, so the association is surely responsible for the unfounded assertion that there also existed nearby a town called "Cimmerium". Cf. Pliny, *N.H.* 3.61. *lacus Lucrinus et Avernus iuxta quem Cimmerium oppidum quondam*, and Aur. Vict. *Origo gentis Romanae* 10 (ed. Pichlmayr and Gruendel), where the sibyl prophesies *in oppido, quod vocatur Cimbarionis*, on which Heyne, *P. Virgili Maronis Opera*[4], 2 (Excursus IV), 1012 says, "*Cumarum* non male emendat Arnzenius; an latet *Cimmerion?* Ita apud Tibull. IV, 1,64 multi: *Cimmerion etiam obscuras accessit ad arces*". Sepp likewise proposed *Κιμμέριον*.

[61] As C. G. Hardie, *P.B.S.R.* 37(1969), 32 points out.

may yet turn out, as we have admitted, that the names of the two sibyls are attributable only to Varro, who read them back into Naevius, but if a sibyl presided over the Avernian *Nekyomanteion*, which seems to be the case, the tradition as such would have been known to Vergil and he would assuredly have derived thence the hint to turn his Cumaean Sibyl into an Underworld Guide; which he does so adroitly. And the fact remains: there is no evidence that Aeneas in pre-Vergilian legend ever had a catabatic journey.

In the argument so far, we have not considered on what other prototypes Vergil may have modelled his Sibyl. In this connection we should adduce the newly discovered papyrus attributed to Pindar which associates Heracles' descent with his initiation at Eleusis.[62] One personage to whom the Sibyl should be compared above all in this descent is described by Lloyd-Jones succinctly as follows:

> "Heracles before descending was first purified of the guilt of murder and then given a special claim on the friendship of the queen of the world below by the favour of an august personage, Eumolpus; ... No doubt the favourable reception which Persephone gave to the descending hero was in large measure due to the impeccable credentials he had received from the head of an institution so dear to her and to her mother."[63]

Like Eumolpus here, the Cumaean Sibyl in the *Aeneid* has a hierophantic role. She is, as well as being prophetess and underworld guide, the hierophant who prescribes the proper ritual for Aeneas to perform. And she makes sure that he possesses the right credentials for a favourable reception from the deities of the Underworld. In other words, she controls the approaches to Avernus and the Underworld. Homer's Circe performed a similar role and she was preceded in turn by Siduri in the *Epic of Gilgamesh.* These two females both gave advice to the catabatic hero on the crossing over the Waters of Death;[64] both were hedonistic; and Siduri, since she is called the ale-wife, may be presum-

[62] Pp. 89ff. above.

[63] H. Lloyd-Jones, *Maia* 19(1967), 225.

[64] See above p. 25 (for Siduri) and pp. 38ff. and 78 (for Circe). R. Campbell Thompson, *The Epic of Gilgamish*, 8, asks: "Why should an ale-wife live in remote parts of the sea?" He calls this a "suspicious detail in the story", but clearly Siduri,

ed to have mixed strong drink, as did Circe. Mireaux has even compared the drink prepared by Circe to the *cyceon* drunk by the initiates at Eleusis.[65]

Vergil's Sibyl seems also to have performed the same role as Hermes, who met Odysseus on his way through the sacred glade to visit Circe. Hermes tells Odysseus that his companions have been shut up in Circe's palace like pigs, and he gives him a magical plant which has a black root and a milk-white flower and is difficult for mortals to dig up.[66] This will serve as a protection for Odysseus against Circe's powerful drugs (*Od.* 10.287ff.), after which he is to draw his sword and rush upon her as though to kill her (*Od.* 10.293—301). The resemblance between this plant and the Golden Bough has not, so far as I am aware, received any attention from commentators hitherto. But its curious properties deserve special notice. For as the Golden Bough is impossible to pluck unless the fates are willing, so is this plant of Hermes difficult for mortals to pull. It is called by the gods "Moly" (we are not told what mortals call it) and it doubtless had some secret mystical significance. Possession of the plant may have been a show of divine approval towards a favoured person undergoing some ordeal.

What plant is the Moly? Contradictory opinions were entertained in antiquity; and the inadequacy of Homer's description for the purpose of modern taxonomy of course makes it impossible for us to know. The best suggestion, for what it is worth, is that it is *Allium nigrum*, a kind of garlic which has a white flower and dark root.[67] Reference

like Circe, virtually controlled the approaches to the Waters of Death. Vergil's Sibyl, as has been said, controls the approaches to Avernus and the Underworld. Compare also the banging on the door in Aristophanes, *Frogs* 460f., which is answered by Persephone's maid at 503f. If this parodies the same motif, the sequence has been displaced since it takes place on the far side of Acheron.

[65] See p. 77 above.

[66] *ῥίζῃ μὲν μέλαν ἔσκε, γάλακτι δὲ εἴκελον ἄνθος·*
μῶλυ δέ μιν καλέουσι θεοί· χαλεπὸν δέ τ' ὀρύσσειν
ἀνδράσι γε θνητοῖσι, θεοὶ δέ τε πάντα δύνανται.

(*Od.* 10.304—306)

[67] See e.g. Dioscurides 3.47 ed. C. G. Kühn, *Medicorum Graecorum Opera*, 25.295f. and Theophrastus, *Hist. Plant.* 9.15.7, where it is said that *τὸ δὲ μῶλυ* [*sc. γίνεται*] *περὶ Φενεὸν καὶ ἐν τῇ Κυλλήνῃ*. Of course, in matters of identification the discrepancy between ancient and modern names for the same plant compounds the difficulty.

to the use of garlic or onions appears in Aristophanes' comic portrayal of Dionysus' Eleusinian descent,[68] which may be taken to parody actual rites. But other identifications abound.[69] The literary or folklorist — as distinct from the ritual — ancestry of the Moly plant is perhaps to be found in the "plant of Prometheus" procured by Medea in Argonautic legend, which grew near the foot of the Caucasus mountains.[70] This magical plant, like the mandrake of later legend,[71] was also exceedingly difficult and dangerous to pull; it was uprooted by Medea to be a prophylactic for Jason against the ordeals of Aeetes' flame-breathing bulls and the men born from dragon's teeth. Horace is reminded of this very plant by some garlic *(allium)*, which Maecenas once set for dinner.[72] Rendel Harris went so far as to suspect that the dragon which swallowed and disgorged Jason did not like the taste of it, as the bulls did not like its smell.[73]

Here, however, the resemblance ends. The Moly was to act as a prophylactic or antidote against the drink and drugged food prepared for Odysseus by Circe. The Golden Bough was to be Aeneas' passport to the Underworld. Yet curiously enough, the Bough was never so used. It calms Charon's anger, and ensures for Aeneas a crossing over the underworld waters, as the one hundred and twenty poles ensured

[68] *Frogs*, 554, 621f., and 654.

[69] These are assembled in Steier's article "Moly" in *R.E.* 16.29—33. Observe that insofar as Pliny, *Nat. Hist.* 25.26 says that the flowers of Moly were often represented as golden *("Graeci auctores florem eius luteum pinxere, cum Homerus candidum scripserit")*, the colour of Moly matches that of the Golden Bough. Hence Moly is said in Boisacq's *Dictionnaire étymologique de la langue grecque*[4] (Paris 1950), s.v. *μῶλυ* p. 654 to be a plant with yellow flowers.

[70] Ap. Rhod. *Argon.* 3.843ff. and 1013ff.

[71] The two plants are connected in a number of ways. I have enumerated the points of contact in "A Note on Medea's Plant and the Mandrake", *F.L.* 79(1968), 227—231.

[72] Hor. *Epod.* 3.9—14.

[73] J. Rendel Harris, *Boanerges* (Cambridge 1913), 370—372; and for the swallowing and disgorging of Jason see p. 35 above. The bulls in Argonautic saga are in a sense a doublet of the dragon, being introduced, like the men born from dragon-seed, merely as an additional ordeal for Jason to overcome. If they were taken originally from another legend, as the dragon's teeth were taken from Theban legend, Jason may originally have been protected by the plant from the dragon itself and Harris' view would then have some validity.

Gilgamesh's crossing in Urshanabi's boat. And it is equally curious that we are not told how the Moly was used; it seems to have been forgotten, even when Odysseus drained the dish of drugs and presumably had need of its powers.[74] Perhaps in an earlier story the plant was waved like a bough. In any event the acquisition of the Moly was a prerequisite for Odysseus' favourable meeting with Circe, who in turn is to advise Odysseus on his Journey to Hades. Behind the Golden Bough, then, the ghost of the Moly peers through.

To sum up so far, I believe that for his Cumaean Sibyl Vergil has conflated the traditions of the Cimmerian and Cumaean sibyls and possibly the Trojan sibyl also. The grove of *Trivia* would seem to allude to Diana and her Bough at Nemi. Circe and Siduri in their hierophantic roles and Hermes, too, when he tells Odysseus to carry the Moly plant, seem also to lie behind Vergil's Sibyl. And behind her Bough lie the Golden Apples, the Golden Fleece and other Golden Plants. Mistletoe provides an analogy for its growth on a tree not its own, while for the emotional associations both the Arician bough and the Moly remain convincing parallels. As a passport over the Waters of Death it resembles other poles and oars.[75] Finally, as pointed out by Lloyd-Jones, it is now known that between the Homeric Circe and the Vergilian Sibyl there stood the august figure of the Eleusinian hierophant Eumolpus himself.

3. *The Eleusinian catabasis of Heracles and the Aeneid.*

The Heracles *catabasis*, whose hierophant Eumolpus explains part of the Sibyl's role in the *Aeneid*, seems generally to elucidate several other parts of Aeneas' Underworld Journey also. These influences we will consider presently. But first we should ask ourselves how a knowledge of this Descent of Heracles is likely to have come down to Vergil. Whether or no Norden was right to postulate an archetypal *Ἡρακλέους κατάβασις* (see pages 88—91 above) from which all the extant versions by Bacchylides, Aristophanes, Vergil, Apollodorus

[74] Cf. D. L. Page, *Folktales in Homer's Odyssey*, 55.

[75] See p. 153 above.

and, as we can now add, Pindar derived their common features must of necessity remain conjectural, but certain definite resemblances between the extant versions point undeniably to a well defined tradition which was certainly known to Vergil. We have already mentioned on pages 154—156 above some details concerning Vergil's use of the Heracles tradition for the comparison of ghosts to migrating birds and falling leaves. The question of how Vergil could have derived knowledge of this Heraclean tradition is an interesting one. Norden believed that it is likely to have come from a mythological handbook.[76] Lloyd-Jones, however, inclined to the view that Vergil was unlikely to have relied exclusively on such a source, for the reason that handbooks, even if fuller than Apollodorus, are unlikely to contain such details as the similes borrowed by Vergil at *Aeneid* 6.309—312. He suggested that if Vergil did not know the original Heracles poem itself, then he may have used the version of Pindar.[77] I have argued elsewhere[78] in the matter of the similes that the Pindaric fragment, which has been reconstructed largely from Bacchylides, lacks one detail common to both Bacchylides and Vergil, namely the location of the comparison of the souls on the banks of the underworld river, where it remains located in the later literature of Dante and Milton. And since it is unknown whether in the lost part of the poem Pindar alludes to the similes within the context of the infernal river Cocytus, we must leave open the possibility that Vergil may have known the detail of the location through an author other than, or perhaps in addition to, Pindar, perhaps Bacchylides himself.[79] Subsequent to my writing the above, Lloyd-Jones has kindly drawn my attention to a suggestion of Fraenkel, that Vergil might have read the *Aithiopis* directly.[80] And

[76] *Aeneis Buch VI*³, 239 on *Aen.* 6.395f.

[77] *Maia* 19(1967), 228—229.

[78] *Phoenix* 24(1970), 250ff.

[79] To the slender evidence I had adduced in my article *ib.* 252f. for a knowledge of Bacchylides still in the Augustan age — and E. Paratore, "Bacchilide e Virgilio", *W.S.* 69(1956), 289—296 proves little — add E. Fraenkel's notice in *Horace* (Oxford 1957), 66 n. 6 on *Epode* 13 that Horace, too, may have read Bacchylides' poems; and cf. Porphyrion on Hor. *Carm.* 1.15.

[80] See E. Fraenkel, "Vergil und die Aithiopis", *Philologus* 87(1932), 242—248 = *Kleine Beiträge zur klassischen Philologie* (Roma 1964), 2.173—179, esp. the concluding words: "Mir ist es keineswegs sicher dass bei dem unermüdlichen Fleiss

if this is true, we certainly cannot rule out the probability that Vergil also read the early poem of the Heracles *catabasis* directly, from which the extant versions are apparently derived. We have only to consider how many early epics are cited even by Pausanias, who cannot have known them all from summaries or citations.

The supposition that this tradition of Heracles' descent was drawn upon by Vergil enabled Norden to find solutions to two ancient puzzles concerning alleged inconsistencies in Aeneas' Descent. The first concerns the location of Cerberus in the Underworld. When complaining to Aeneas of how Heracles came to steal by force Hell's own watchdog, Charon remarks:

> "Tartareum ille manu custodem in vincla petivit
> *ipsius a solio regis* traxitque trementem." (*Aen.* 6.395f.).

Line 396, which we omitted in the speech quoted on page 190 above, contains the puzzle. As Servius understands it, Heracles came to steal and drag the dog off "from under the King's very throne". But then Servius goes on rightly to observe that this is inconsistent with Cerberus' appearance immediately across the Styx:

> Cerberus haec ingens latratu regna trifauci
> personat adverso recubans immanis in antro.
> (*Aen.* 6. 417f.).[81]

Heracles is said, however, by Apollodorus to have asked Pluto for permission to capture Cerberus and to have found the dog "at the gates of Acheron";[82] and this seems to offer the solution to the ancient *ζήτημα*. As Norden infers, Heracles in the *Ἡρακλέους*

und dem Aufwande von Gelehrsamkeit, den Vergil an die Vorbereitung seines grossen Gedichts gesetzt hat, es ihm nicht doch noch möglich gewesen sein sollte sich ein Exemplar der damals gewiss nicht mehr sehr verbreiteten Aithiopis zu verschaffen."

[81] Servius *ad Aen.* 6.396 *ipsius a solio regis:* atqui Cerberus statim post flumina est, ut (417)...: nam illic quasi est aditus inferorum, solium autem Plutonis interius est. ergo aut ad naturam canum referendum est qui territi ad dominos confugiunt: aut solium pro imperio accipiendum est.

[82] Apollod. *Bibl.* 2.5.12: *αἰτοῦντος δὲ αὐτοῦ Πλούτωνα τὸν Κέρβερον, ἐπέταξεν ὁ Πλούτων ἄγειν χωρὶς ὧν εἶχεν ὅπλων κρατοῦντα. ὁ δὲ εὑρὼν αὐτὸν ἐπὶ ταῖς πύλαις τοῦ Ἀχέροντος, κτλ.*

κατάβασις must have walked to Pluto's palace in order to obtain his permission and then walked back to the gates of Acheron to collect Cerberus. Editors who suppose, as Servius, that in Vergil's *Aeneid* the Hell-dog was taken by Hercules from Pluto's throne have wrongly taken *ipsius a solio regis* with *traxitque* instead of with *petivit*, and have largely failed to see that the sequence of events as described by Apollodorus fits Charon's description of what happened too. Charon, in fact, says nothing of the whereabouts of Cerberus. The Latin words mean simply that Hercules "asked for the dog from the throne of the King himself," and presumably Heracles "took him trembling" from his place at the start of the Underworld, where Aeneas also meets him.[83] The explicit denial by the Sibyl that Aeneas has come like Hercules to seize the "monstrous guardian at the gate" (*ingens ianitor*, *Aen.* 6. 400; cf. *ianitor Orci*, 8. 296) practically confirms the interpretation.

The supposition that Vergil drew on the Ἡρακλέους κατάβασις also explains the apparent inconsistency when Aeneas was told by the Sibyl to draw his sword as he enters the Underworld —

"tuque invade viam vaginaque eripe ferrum"
(*Aen.* 6. 260) —

only to be told in a subsequent command from the Sibyl not to use it against the Gorgons and other bodiless shapes in the vestibule:

corripit hic subita trepidus formidine ferrum
Aeneas strictamque aciem venientibus offert,
et ni docta comes tenuis sine corpore vitas
admoneat volitare cave sub imagine formae,
inruat et frustra ferro diverberet umbras.
(*Aen.* 6. 290—4)

[83] E. Norden, *Aeneis Buch VI*³, 238. R. G. Austin, "*Aeneid VI*, 384—476", *P.V.S.* 8(1968—9), 53 objects that *petivit a solio regis* is impossible for *petivit a rege* and wonders whether Cerberus rushed boldly to protect his king's person only to regret his show of bravery. However, it is not supposed by Norden that the Latin phrase in question is a mere circumlocution for *petivit a rege*. Rather it is a highly compressed phrase, as is Vergil's wont, which combines the two ideas of Heracles' visit to the King's throne and his subsequent request. Cf. Servius' remark at *Aen.* 1.639 on Vergil's style: "*et est sermo in compendium coactus*".

For as Norden again points out, Apollodorus records how Heracles having descended to Hades drew his sword, but was told by Hermes not to use it against the ghost of the Gorgon Medusa: *ὁπηνίκα δὲ εἶδον αὐτὸν αἱ ψυχαί, χωρὶς Μελεάγρου καὶ Μεδούσης τῆς Γοργόνος ἔφυγον. ἐπὶ δὲ τὴν Γοργόνα τὸ ξίφος ὡς ζῶσαν ἕλκει, καὶ παρὰ Ἑρμοῦ μανθάνει ὅτι κενὸν εἴδωλόν ἐστι* (*Bibl.* 2.5.21).[84] And this motif is to be found also, as we shall now see, in Bacchylides, Aristophanes, and with somewhat greater variation in Homer too. For although no ghostly monsters as such are encountered by Heracles in Bacchylides' fifth *Epinician*, Meleager in lines 71—84 warns Heracles, who had put an arrow to the string, not to shoot at him since he is now only a shade. This seems to be an apt compression of the original roles as preserved by Apollodorus, since the command that Heracles should not shoot comes from Meleager, who is both guide and ghost. Moreover Dionysus' Underworld Journey in Aristophanes' *Frogs* is also modelled on Heracles' Descent, and Lloyd-Jones has compared the monsters whom Aeneas meets *vestibulum ante ipsum primisque in faucibus Orci* (*Aen.* 6.273ff.) to the snakes and beasts whom Dionysus and Xanthias in the *Frogs* expect to meet after crossing Lake Acheron (lines 278ff., cf. 143ff.); when these visitors to the world below have crossed the Lake and knocked on Pluto's door, they are, in fact, threatened by the doorkeeper with the appearance of a host of terrifying monsters, Gorgons among them (465ff.).[85] The two female keepers of the kitchen, who shortly afterwards, at *Frogs* 565ff., appear before Dionysus, and tell how Heracles on a previous visit had drawn his sword and terrified them, are a further parody of the theme, and should, I believe, be regarded as comic doublets of these monsters; they then correspond to Meleager's ghost in Bacchylides' version, to the ghost of the Gorgon Medusa in Apollodorus, and to the horde of monsters including Gorgons in Vergil. Aristophanes thus ridicules the sword-motif and adds a further comic effect concerning these otherworldly kitchen maids since, as Bickley Rogers observes, Heracles was seeking "not them but theirs".[86] We should observe further that the encounter

[84] E. Norden, *op. cit.* 206—207.

[85] H. Lloyd-Jones, *Maia* 19(1967), 219 and 221; cf. E. Rohde, *Psyche*[8], 244 n. 6.

[86] One may compare the amusing scene in F. Anstey's *Vice Versa* (50th imp.

with Meleager took place immediately after Heracles had presumably crossed and seen the leaf-like ghosts on the far bank of the Cocytus river, and that the threatened appearance of the monsters in Aristophanes' *Frogs* is likewise met with after the crossing of Acheron. Lloyd-Jones has supposed that the comparison of the countless ghosts to leaves in the versions by Bacchylides and Pindar came right at the start of the journey through Hades, whereas Vergil "held the simile back" in order to apply it to the countless spirits waiting on the infernal shore to be ferried to the other side.[87] In fact, as has been shown already, Vergil has kept the location precisely where it was in Bacchylides, or has moved it, if anything, to an earlier part of the journey, since Aeneas sees the souls on the near side before crossing the underworld river. The impression that Vergil "held the simile back" actually arises from the displacement of the monsters forward to the vestibule of the Underworld, and Vergil's river was, therefore, pushed deeper into the Underworld. In Homer's *Nekyia*, too, Odysseus being in the end fearful that Persephone might send up a terrible monster with a Gorgon's head (*Γοργείην κεφαλὴν δεινοῖο πελώρου*, 634) contemplated drawing his sword against it. He did not actually use it in this instance for the simple reason that the monster with the Gorgonian head did not appear. Furthermore von der Mühll thinks that Heracles' drawing of the sword on the Gorgon in the Heracles *catabasis* suggested to the author of the *Odyssey* the idea of drawing his sword upon the ghosts at the trench, to stop them from drinking the blood out of turn.[88] If indeed Homer had come across this motif in any early version of the Heracles *catabasis*, one may wonder whether the sword motif was not also transferred to the episode in which Hermes tells Odysseus how to use the sword against Circe.[89]

Now since it is clear as well from Homer and Apollodorus as from art that Heracles was accompanied through the Underworld by Hermes,[90] and since several passages including the Oxyrhynchus frag-

London 1962), 243—5 and 284 where a housekeeper similarly mistakes cupboard love on the part of the master of the house for his true love for her.

[87] H. Lloyd-Jones, *Maia* 19(1967), 222.

[88] P. von der Mühll, *Philologus* 93(1938), 9f.

[89] See for the episode p. 209 above.

[90] Cf. Hom. *Od.* 11.620f., Apollod. *Bibl.* 2.5.12 (quoted on p. 213 n. 82 above);

ment of Pindar give Heracles' descent a definite connection with Eleusis (pp. 89—92 above) where Hermes escorted Persephone from the Underworld,[91] Lloyd-Jones thinks that the suggestion of Norden, who in turn followed a suggestion made to him by Wilamowitz,[92] that the notion of a guide had been derived from the concept of the *μυσταγωγός* or underworld guide in mystery religions is in a sense confirmed.[93] And since Hermes' role in the *Ἡρακλέους κατάβασις* has evidently been assigned by Vergil to the Sibyl who forbids Aeneas to strike at the shades,[94] the Cumaean Sibyl in the Descent of Aeneas has the role of underworld mystagogos as well as of hierophant. And if the Sibyl's role in the *Aeneid* is modelled on Hermes, what is more natural than that she, like Hermes, should carry a golden wand?

And so the argument, which has gone full circle, is brought back to the Golden Bough. The possibility that the Bough might be, among other things, the counterpart of Hermes' golden wand was considered by Heyne, but without the advantage of the arguments we have just outlined. Heyne was content to suggest that "since Vergil was unable to introduce Hermes as the guide of this descent, he assigned *to Aeneas* his golden wand" (my italics).[95] But the new arguments compel us rather to focus attention on the connection between the Sibyl and the Bough, and we are immediately struck by a widespread misconception,

for an artistic representation one may refer to the scene on the Middle Corinthian kotyle described on p. 82 above.

[91] First mentioned in the Homeric *Hymn to Demeter*, 334ff.

[92] See E. Norden, *Aeneis Buch VI*³, 154.

[93] H. Lloyd-Jones, *Maia* 19(1967), 225f. Note that although Odysseus had no guide through Hades, he was accompanied by Hermes on the Isle of Aeaea (pp. 77 and 209 above), where the events are said by Mireaux to resemble an initiation ceremony like that at Eleusis (pp. 77f. above).

[94] Milton in turn has imitated the use of the sword in the Underworld in *Paradise Lost*, 6. 329—331. However, the sword here is actually used in the wounding of Satan: "The griding sword with discontinuous wound Pass'd through him; but th' ethereal substance closed Not long divisible". Cf. the order to Scipio to "hew in pieces" the ghosts in Sil. Ital. *Pun.* 13.441—444.

[95] C. G. Heyne, *P. Virgili Maronis Opera*⁴, 2 (Excursus VI), 1015: "*cum Mercurium adhibere huius descensus ducem non posset* [sc. *Vergilius*], *auream virgam Aeneae assignare maluit*".

found in Heyne above[96] and in Frazer[97] and others,[98] that the Bough was carried through the Underworld by Aeneas. The Sibyl herself, of course, carries it and shows it to Charon (p. 191 above). And inasmuch as the Sibyl has been assigned Hermes' role and could not take Aeneas into the Underworld without first receiving the Bough, the Bough is virtually in its chthonic aspect a double of Hermes' golden wand. This explains, I hope, why the role of the Bough differs widely from that of the sword. There is no need, therefore, to accept a conjecture of Norden that the Bough and the sword are doublets due to a contamination of sources.[99]

Finally let us leave the Sibyl for a moment and look at certain awkwardnesses in the several versions of the *Ἡρακλέους κατάβασις* in the hope that we may glean more of the nature of the Underworld into which Heracles and Aeneas make their respective descents. I refer to a certain incongruity, which so far as I am aware has received no attention from commentators, but which can be readily illustrated from Bacchylides' description of Heracles' descent in the fifth *Epinician.* The opening description begins in a way suggestive of happiness:

ὄλβιος ᾧτινι θεὸς
μοῖράν τε καλῶν ἔπορεν
σύν τ' ἐπιζήλῳ τύχᾳ
ἀφνεὸν βιοτὰν διάγειν·

(lines 50—53.)

(Happy the man to whom God hath given a share in honours, and together with that enviable fortune enjoyment of a rich life too.)

[96] See previous note. Heyne, *op. cit.* 2.909 on *Aen.* 6.405, asserts also that the Bough was shown to Charon by Aeneas: "*cum his Sibyllae verbis ramum aureum Aeneas sub veste tectum nudat*".

[97] J. G. Frazer, *The Golden Bough*³, 11. 294: "Hence when Aeneas, emerging from the forest, comes to the banks of Styx, ... and the surly ferryman refuses him passage in his boat, he has but to draw the Golden Bough from his bosom and hold it up, and straightway the blusterer quails at the sight and meekly receives the hero into his crazy bark."

[98] E.g. Brooks Otis, *Virgil: a Study in Civilized Poetry*, 293, writes that the Sibyl quells Charon's anger by pointing out that "Aeneas is no Hercules... but a *pietatis imago* who carries the *fatalis virga.*"

[99] E. Norden, *Aeneis Buch VI*³, 170f.

The verses contain practically a stereotyped formula for introducing Eleusinian bliss.[100] But when Heracles actually descends into the house of Persephone he sees only the "spirits of unhappy mortals" (*δυστάνων βροτῶν ψυχὰς*, line 63). These are the leaf-like souls, to which we have already several times alluded. Meleager, too, is a sad ghost in this Underworld of unhappy spirits, as the whole encounter between Heracles and Meleager bears witness, especially at lines 160—162, where Meleager laments that it were best for mortals never to be born. Lloyd-Jones who comments upon the Eleusinian descent of Heracles in the Pindaric fragment *P. Oxy.* 2622 does not offer his opinion as to whether or not this Underworld was filled with blessed spirits (as it ought to have been). Yet the probable restoration of two similes in connection with the spirits of the dead in this descent (see p. 155 above) suggests that Pindar, like Bacchylides and Vergil, is portraying the ordinary dead at this point. The restored name of Meleager in the same context further suggests that in the papyrus, as in Bacchylides, a tale of woe was told — unless Pindar suppressed it. It is omitted by Apollodorus. In short, we should beware of assuming, even though Lloyd-Jones has proved a connection between the versions of the *Ἡρακλέους κατάβασις* and Heracles' initiation at Eleusis, that this poem ever told of Heracles' descent into a happy Underworld.

This conclusion invites a further question. If Heracles was initiated at Eleusis, why did he not descend into an Elysium of happy spirits? Apollodorus surely gives the clue: *μέλλων οὖν ἐπὶ τοῦτον ἀπιέναι ἦλθε πρὸς Εὔμολπον εἰς Ἐλευσῖνα, βουλόμενος μυηθῆναι... καὶ παραγενόμενος ἐπὶ Ταίναρον τῆς Λακωνικῆς, οὗ τῆς Ἅιδου καταβάσεως τὸ στόμιόν ἐστι, διὰ τούτου κατήει* (*Bibl.* 2.5.12).

> (Now when Heracles was about to leave to fetch Cerberus, he went to Eumolpus at Eleusis, wishing to be initiated. ... And having come to Taenarum in Laconia, where is the mouth of the way down to Hades, he descended through it.)

Heracles was thus initiated at Eleusis but made the descent, as he often does in the canonical versions, at Taenarum.[101] This awkward

[100] See p. 94 with n. 51 above.
[101] See ch. 3 n. 37 above.

join is a clue which gives away the game. Heracles evidently had no time to waste in an Elysium. He had to be off to Taenarum to get the dog. But Eleusis presumably had the monopoly of the Underworld and its approaches already in the sixth century B.C., and interest in Eleusis was too strong a force to be neglected when the story was being treated.

If this supposition is correct it enables us to survey more surely the development of Heracles' descent, and to throw some light on the date and nature of Norden's conjectured archetype. It appears that not only Vergil but also Homer had a well-defined and articulated tradition about Heracles' descent. Earlier poems on the subject had no doubt been recited, but they were not written down and preserved if indeed Homer's own poems were the first to be worth the immense trouble of writing. The complex theme then was continued orally until in the sixth century B.C. a poet akin to the writer of the Homeric *Hymn to Demeter*, but with an evident Athenian connection, introduced an episode at Eleusis but left unchanged the ghosts like leaves in a sad Underworld. Lloyd-Jones had suggested that this version perhaps circulated about 550 B.C. — it can scarcely be earlier than the beginning of the sixth century — under the name of Musaios, a kind of Attic Orpheus linking Orphism and the Eleusinian cult,[102] whom Vergil introduced as a second guide contrary to tradition. And Boardman now, in an argument we have followed already on pp. 82f. above, associates the new role of Heracles as an Athenian-sponsored initiate with the new-style Cerberus scenes introduced on the vases of Athens about 530 B.C., which coincides with the Peisistratan period of active Athenian intervention in the sacred affairs of Eleusis and presumably with the foundation of the Lesser Mysteries at Athens, with which, as we have seen on p. 90 above, Heracles was also closely connected. This poem, then, must have been contemporary with that movement of otherworldly and underworldly (in a moralized underworld, not merely, as in Homer, a faint phantom of the upper world) religion, which manifests itself not only in Peisistratus' enlargement of the hall at Eleusis, but also in the many Pythagorean and Orphic cults in South Italy.[103] The result was an imperfectly integrated

[102] *Maia* 19(1967), 223f., 226f., and 228.

[103] Cf. on the Italian movement C. G. Hardie's article cited in ch. 2 n. 90 above.

poem, which was used in different ways by Pindar, Bacchylides, Aristophanes, and Vergil. It is also preserved in outline by Apollodorus, who preserves enough to suggest that in the version which he follows initiation secured for Heracles Pluto's permission to take Cerberus, though with a fight. Euripides, too, may have known the poem, for the verses 611—613 of his play *Hercules Furens* show that Heracles' violence was still needed, but against Cerberus, not against Hades himself as in Homer, *Iliad* 5. Hades' permission is likewise implied by Vergil at *Aeneid* 6. 395 (see pp. 213f. above), though Heracles' *vis* is still predominant; while Diodorus 4.26 has the further stage in which Persephone hands over Cerberus already shackled.[104]

The fact that the *catabasis* is an amalgamation helps, too, to explain why, in all versions except the Aristophanic, Persephone appears in an Underworld of ordinary and unhappy spirits. There is good reason to believe that Aristophanes goes beyond his model in describing the joys of the Eleusinian afterlife. For he has replaced the Hell-dog Cerberus by a tragedian, whether Euripides or Aeschylus, and the proper place for deceased poets is among the Blessed Dead. Therefore Aristophanes was able to dispose of the unhappy afterlife of the Taenarum-type which he found in his model, and this innovation also increased the structural unity of his own play. That he had a Descent of Heracles clearly in mind is proved not only by the context of the direct reference to Cerberus at *Frogs* 111, but from the fact that the whole of the ἀγών is modelled upon it with rescued poet substituted for rescued dog. And just as in the Apollodoran version Pluto kindly allowed Heracles to return to earth with Cerberus, so too the god of the dead in the Aristophanic version allowed Dionysus to return with the tragedian of his choice.

Now Vergil's Sibyl is made the guide of Aeneas through the Neutral Regions only. If the Golden Bough, as Norden thought, were the

[104] For these versions see pp. 91f. above. The myth in Diodorus 4.26.1 and Plutarch, *Thes.* 35, which tells how Heracles respectively frees both Theseus and Peirithous and Theseus alone by negotiating with Persephone, can scarcely be dissociated from the version of the myth in which Heracles obtains Cerberus through the intercession of Persephone. This, then, is the source of the version which was later rationalized and followed by Plutarch and others, see p. 63 above.

mystic bough of initiates, we would now have to admit the anomalous situation whereby it was carried not through Elysium, the abode of the Blessed, but through the several regions of the ordinary dead. We have said, it is true, that the link between the Bough and Persephone in a sense confirms Norden's view, but the fact that the initiate's bough was borne through the Neutral Regions is perhaps a compelling reason why Vergil virtually disguised it out of recognition.

Aeneas is, in fact, conducted through the Underworld by two guides. The Sibyl led Aeneas, as Hermes led Heracles in the Apollodoran version, as far as Pluto's palace, where Aeneas then plants the Golden Bough as a gift for Proserpine.[105] The two then cross the threshold into Elysium, which in Vergil's design adjoins the traditional Underworld. Here Aeneas and the Sibyl are met by Musaios, who appears in this part of Vergil's Underworld perhaps by virtue of his close connection with Eleusis or simply by his well attested Orphic associations or both.[106] And as the Sibyl's performance of the role of Circe will not later prevent Circe herself from appearing on the Italian coast (at *Aeneid.* 7.10ff. etc.), so the fact that the Sibyl has just performed some of the duties of the Eleusinian hierophant and mystagogos does not now prevent Musaios from turning up *in persona* to lead Aeneas and the Sibyl through Elysium to Anchises.

The slight inconsistency between the Sibyl at Cumae, who knows the future, and the Sibyl in Elysium, who knows nothing, is of course a price Vergil had to pay for giving her different roles. One must, however, admire Vergil for the skilful manner in which he makes the Cumaean Sibyl fade so completely away in Elysium thus leaving the scene to Anchises. The transition is helped by the change of guide. Musaios was a wise choice, and he serves very aptly, too, as the guide who virtually hands on the torch of Greek culture to the future Roman civilisation, just as Vergil himself was to serve for Dante as the link between the Pagan and the Christian worlds.

Norden attempted to attribute the two guides of Vergil's Underworld to an "überliefertes Motif" stemming from Poseidonius. On the ground that Poseidonius influenced not only Vergil, but also Ci-

[105] *Aen.* 6.635f. and see at n. 31 above.

[106] For the traditions attached to Musaios see *art. cit.* n. 102 above.

cero, Plutarch, and the author of the Hermetic writings, he assumed that Cicero's *Somnium Scipionis*, Plutarch's myth of Timarchus in the *De genio Socratis* (589F—592E), and various Hermetic writings showing Poseidonius' influence could all three be used to explain Aeneas' journey.[107]

However, the case for connecting Vergilian eschatology at all with Poseidonius is far from certain,[108] and the basis for establishing that Poseidonius is the originator of the motif in question is slenderer still. The two figures who appear in Cicero's Dream of Scipio do not even belong to different spheres, as do the two guides in the *Aeneid* and in the apocalyptic myth of Plutarch. The only reasonable assumption then, is that the two figures in Scipio's Dream happened to be two in number for domestic reasons, to enable Scipio to meet both his adoptive father Africanus and his real father Paulus. Plutarch needed two guides to cover different spheres, as did Vergil before him, whose own expanded underworld geography called for the introduction of a second guide. Later Dante was to take the motif of a double-guide from Vergil. Even if we grant Poseidonius' influence on the three works mentioned, still these have for their model the Vision of Er in Plato's *Republic* (614ff.).[109] And against confusing Vergil's Descent of Aeneas with celestial journeys of this sort we have already issued a warning on pages 33 and 181f. above.

It is sometimes suggested that the true parallels to Aeneas' underworld journey are to be found, even so, in Cicero's *Dream of Scipio*,

[107] E. Norden, *Aeneis Buch VI*[3], 43—45 and cf. 33 referring for the Hermetic writings to the Poimandres ed. by G. Parthey, 114ff. (R. Reitzenstein, 339), and Stobaeus *Phys.* 41.68f.; now translated into English with a new commentary by G. R. S. Mead, *Thrice-Greatest Hermes*[3] (London 1964), 2.139ff. and 3.118ff. respectively.

[108] See my article in *Symbolae Osloenses* 50(1975), 136f.

[109] While it is true in the case of Plutarch's myth that Timarchus "descends" into the underground Trophonion at Lebadeia, once he is there he has a soul-wandering experience like Plato's Er (Plutarch's own tale of Thespesios of Soli at *De vindicta* 563B is another such instance) — only for the battlefield of Er the oracular chasm of Trophonios has been substituted. For Plutarch's purpose in selecting the Trophonion as the framework of his myth, the "descent" being strictly superfluous as a mechanism for the phenomenon of soul-wandering, see my article at ch. 1 n. 49 above.

and in such other Roman works as Fabius Pictor's *Dream of Aeneas (Somnium Aeneae),* to which Cicero refers in the *De divinatione* at 1.21.43, on the ground that Vergil conceived of Aeneas' Journey to the Underworld as a Dream.[110] But while recognizing that Vergil's "Gates of Sleep" through which Aeneas and the Sibyl are dismissed from the infernal world at *Aeneid* 6.893—898 are a special problem,[111] I do not believe that they imply that Aeneas' whole experience in the lower world has been a dream. In Vergil's day dreams of famous people had become, in fact, almost cliché,[112] and this is perhaps one reason why Vergil represents Aeneas' underworld journey as being poetically actual. In representing it so, Vergil has chosen to be in direct poetical competition with Homer; and in the course of this task, as we have seen, by skilful poetic conflations which reveal at the same time Vergil's working method and his faith in inherited culture, he embraces the whole of the catabatic tradition. Nor has he neglected the eminently Roman work of Naevius that introduces the illustrious Italian tradition of a sibyl into a necromantic consultation of Aeneas on the shores of Avernus. But by introducing the *catabasis* into this legend of Aeneas, Vergil has attempted something entirely new in Latin literature.

[110] For this notion see e.g. J. Perret, *Virgile: Connaissance des Lettres*, 115f., Brooks Otis, *T.A.P.A.* 90(1959), 171, and cf. n. 34 above.

[111] Whether Vergil's adaptation from *Odyssey* 19.562—567 of Homer's Twin Gates of Sleep and Vergil's choice of the Gate through which Aeneas and the Sibyl make their exit from the Underworld were intended to hold any implication for Aeneas' journey other than of indicating purely and simply (with an aura of mystery) the means of his and the Sibyl's dismissal has never been satisfactorily explained. Since Aeneas and his guide were not *umbrae verae* but living persons, Vergil could scarcely have them leave by the Gate of Horn. He therefore sends them out through the only other exit. It is important to grasp that in their new context, as adapted by Vergil, the two Gates of Sleep are the "Gates of the Underworld", as Valerius Flaccus at *Argon.* 1.832 perhaps recognized, leaving no choice, therefore, for the living visitants but to pass out through either the one or the other of them.

[112] On Homer's appearance in Ennius' dream and many other pre-Vergilian dreams see W. R. Hardie, "The Dream of Ennius", *C.Q.* 7(1913), 188—195, and H. R. Steiner, *Der Traum in der Aeneis* (Stuttgart 1952), 9—22.

SELECT BIBLIOGRAPHY

(In particular, editions of classical authors and articles in standard works of reference are here omitted.)

ALFÖLDI, A. *Early Rome and the Latins* (Michigan 1965).

ANDERSON, W. S. "Calypso and Elysium", *C. J.* 54(1958), 2—11.

ARIAS, P.—M. HIRMER—B. SHEFTON. *A History of Greek Vase Painting* (London 1962).

ASTOUR, M. C. *Hellenosemitica*[2] (Leiden 1967).

AUSTIN, R. G. "*Aeneid* VI, 384—476", *P.V.S.* 8(1968—1969).

BACON, J. R. *The Voyage of the Argonauts* (London 1925).

BALDRY, H. C. "Who invented the Golden Age?" *C.Q.* 2(1952), 83—92.

BARING-GOULD, S. *Curious Myths of the Middle Ages* (London 1894).

BARRETT, A. A. "The authorship of the Culex", *Latomus* 29(1970), 348—362.

BARRON, J. P. "New Light on Old Walls: the Murals of the Theseion", *J.H.S.* 92(1972), 21—45 and plates I—VII.

BÉRARD, C. *Anodoi : Essai sur L'Imagerie des Passages Chthoniens* (Suisse 1974).

BÉRARD, J. *La Colonisation Grecque de L'Italie Meridionale et de la Sicile dans L'Antiquité*[2] (Paris 1957).

BÉRARD, V. *Les Phéniciens et L'Odyssée*, 2 vols., (Paris 1927).

—— *La Résurrection d'Homère* (Paris 1930).

BOARDMAN, J. "Herakles, Peisistratos and Eleusis", *J.H.S.* 75(1975), 1—12.

BOLTON, J. D. P. *Aristeas of Proconnesus* (Oxford 1962).

BOWRA, C. M. "Orpheus and Eurydice", *C.Q.* 2(1952), 113—126.

—— *Greek Lyric Poetry*[2] (Oxford 1961).

BRADFORD, E. *Ulysses Found* (repr. London 1971).

BROMMER, F. *Herakles. Die zwölf Taten des Helden in antiker Kunst und Literatur* (Köln 1953).

—— *Vasenlisten zur griechischen Heldensagen*[3] (Marburg 1973).

BROOKS, R. A. "*Discolor aura.* Reflections on the golden bough", *A.J.P.* 74(1953), 260—280.

BROWN, Theo. "St. Joseph of Arimathea at Glastonbury", *F.L.* 57(1946), 75—79.

BURROWS, E. See in HOOKE, S. H.

BURY, J. B. "The Homeric and the historic Kimmerians", *Klio* 7(1906), 177—188.

BUTLER, H. E. *The Sixth Book of the Aeneid* (Oxford 1920).

CARPENTER, Rhys. *Folk Tale, Fiction and Saga in the Homeric Epics* (Berkeley 1946).

CASKEY, L. D. "Odysseus and Elpenor on a Pelike in Boston", *A.J.A.* 88(1934), 399—400 with plates.

CLARK, R. J. "A Note on Medea's Plant and the Mandrake", *F.L.* 79(1968), 277—231.

—— "Trophonios: The Manner of his Revelation", *T.A.P.A.* 99(1968), 63—75.

—— "Christ's Resurrection at Avernus: A Vergilian Influence", *C. & M.* 30(1969), 300—307.

—— "Two Virgilian Similes and the *ʽΗΡΑΚΛΕΟΥΣ ΚΑΤΑΒΑΣΙΣ*", *Phoenix* 24(1970), 244—255.

—— "The 'Wheel' and Vergil's Eschatology in *Aeneid* 6", *Symbolae Osloenses* 50(1975), 121—141.

—— "Vergil, *Aeneid*, 6,40ff. and the Cumaean Sibyl's Cave" *Latomus* 36(1977), 482—495.

—— "Misenus and the Cumaean Landfall: Originality in Vergil's Use of Topography and Tradition", *T.A.P.A.* 107(1977), 63—71.

COCKLE, W. E. H. "P.OXY. xvii. 2078", *C.R.* 20(1970), 136—137.

COLDSTREAM, J. N. "Hero-cults in the age of Homer", *J.H.S.* 96(1976), 8—17.

CONINGTON, J. NETTLESHIP, H. and HAVERFIELD, F. *P. Vergili Maronis Opera* 3 vols. (3rd. and 4th. eds. London 1883—1898).

CONWAY, R. S. *New Studies of a Great Inheritance* (London 1921).

COOK, A. B. "The Golden Bough and the Rex Nemorensis", *C.R.* 16(1902), 365—380.

—— *Zeus: A Study in Ancient Religion*, 3 vols. in 5, (Cambridge 1914—1940).

COOK, J. M. "The Agamemnoneion", *B.S.A.* 48(1953), 30—68 with plates.

CORSSEN, P. "Die Sibylle im sechsten Buch der Aeneas", *Sokrates* N.F. 1(1913), 1—16.

CROON, J. H. *The Herdsman of the Dead* (Utrecht 1952).

CUMONT, Franz, *After Life in Roman Paganism* (New Haven 1923).

DAGRON, G. "La Vie Ancienne de Saint Marcel L'Acémète", *Analecta Bollandiana* 86(1968), 271—321.

DAKARIS, S. "The Dark Palace of Hades", *Archaeology* 15(1962), 85—93.

—— "Das Totenorakel bei Ephyra", *Antike Kunst* Beiheft 1(1963), 35—55.

DALE, A. M. *Euripides: Alcestis* (Oxford 1961).

DAVIDSON, H. R. E. (ed.). *The Journey to the Other World* (London 1975).

DIETERICH, A. *Nekyia: Beiträge zur erklärung der Neuentdeckten Petrusapokalypse*² (Leipzig 1913).

DISANDRO, C. A. "Una nueva fuente para el libro VI dela Eneida", *Humanitas* 3(1957), 117—125.

DOBSEN, J. F. "The Posidonius Myth", *C.Q.* 12(1918), 179—195.

DOREY, T. A. "Homer and Virgil: the World of the Dead", *Orpheus* 3(1956), 119—122.

DREW, D. L. "Horace, Odes I. xii. and the Forum Augustum", *C.Q.* 19(1925), 159—164.

DRONKE, P. "The Return of Eurydice", *C. & M.* 23(1962), 198—215.
DUNBABIN, T. J. *The Greeks and their Eastern Neighbours* (London 1957).

EDMONDS, J. M. *The Fragments of Attic Comedy*, 3 vols., (Leiden 1957).
EICHHOLZ, D. E. "Symbol and Contrast in the *Aeneid*", *G. & R.* 15(1968), 105—112.
EITREM, S. "La Sibylle de Cumes et Virgile", *Symbolae Osloenses* 24(1945), 88—120.
ENK, P. J. "De Labyrinthi Imagina in Foribus Templi Cumani Insculpta", *Mnemosyne* 11(1958), 322—330.

FALKENSTEIN, A. "Zu Inannas Gang zur Unterwelt", *Archiv für Orientforschung* 14(1942), 113—138.
—— review of C. J. Gadd and S. N. Kramer *Ur Excavations Texts VI* (London 1963) in *Bibliotheca Orientalis* 22(1965), 279—283.
—— "Die Sumerische und der Akkadische Mythos von Inannas Gang zur Unterwelt" in *Festschrift Werner Caskel* ed. E. Gräf (Leiden 1968), 87—110.
FARNELL, L. R. *The Cults of the Greek States*, 5 vols., (Oxford 1896—1909).
FLETCHER, Sir Frank, *Virgil, Aeneid VI* (Oxford 1941).
FÖRSTER, R. *Der Raub und die Rückker der Persephone* (Stuttgart 1874).
FRAENKEL E. "Vergil und die Aithiopis", *Philologus* 87(1932), 242—248 = *Kleine Beiträge zur klassischen Philologie* (Roma 1964), 2. 173—179.
—— "The Culex", *J.R.S.* 42(1952), 1—9.
FRANKFORT, H. *Kingship and the Gods* (Chicago 1948).
FRAZER, Sir James G. *Pausanias' Description of Greece*, 6 vols., (London 1898).
—— *The Golden Bough: A Study in Magic and Religion*³, 12 vols., (London 1907—1915).
—— *Apollodorus*, 2 vols., (Camb. Mass. 1921).
—— *Folk-lore in the Old Testament*, 3 vols., (London 1918).
FRIEDMAN, J. B. *Orpheus in the Middle Ages* (Camb. Mass. 1970).
FURTWÄNGLER, A. and REICHHOLD, C. *Griechische Vasenmalerie* (Munich 1904).

GAGÉ, J. "Romulus-Augustus", *M.E.F.R.* 47(1930), 138—181.
GALINSKI, G. K. *Aeneas, Sicily and Rome* (Princeton 1969).
—— *The Herakles Theme* (Oxford 1972).
GANSCHINIETZ, "Katabasis", *R.E.* 10.2359—2449.
GASTER, TH. H. *Thespis, Ritual, Myth, and Drama in the Ancient Near East*² (New York 1966).
—— "A Hittite Seasonal Myth", *F.L.* 84(1973), 339—343.
GORDON, Cyrus H. *Ugaritic Literature* (Roma 1949).
—— *Before the Bible* (London 1962).
GRAVES, R. *The Greek Myths*, 2 vols., (Harmondsworth 1960).
GRESSMANN, H. and UNGNAD, A. *Das Gilgamesch-Epos* (Göttingen 1911).
GRIFFITH, J. G. "Again the Shield of Aeneas (*Aeneid* VIII. 625—731)", *P.V.S.* 7(1967—1968), 54—64.

GRIFFITHS, J. G. *Plutarch: Isis et Osiris* (Cardiff 1970).

GUÉNON, R. "La Caverne et le Labyrinthe", *Études Traditionnelles* 214(1937), 349—354 and 215(1937), 385—390.

GUTHRIE, W. K. C. *Orpheus and Greek Religion* (London 1935).

HALL, H. R. "The Two Labyrinths", *J.H.S.* 25(1905), 320—337.

HAMMOND, N. G. L. *Epirus* (Oxford 1967).

HARDIE, COLIN G. "The Great Antrum at Baiae", *P.B.S.R.* 37(1969), 14—33.

HARDIE, W. R. "The Dream of Ennius", *C.Q.* 7(1913), 188—195.

HARRIS J. RENDEL. *The Homeric Centones and the Acts of Pilate* (London 1898).

HARRISON, E. B. "Hesperides and Heroes: A Note on the Three-figure Reliefs", *Hesperia* 33(1964), 76—82 with plates 11—14.

HARRISON, Jane E. *Myths of the Odyssey in Art and Literature* (London 1882).

—— *Prolegomena to the Study of Greek Religion* (Cambridge 1903).

—— *Themis* (Cambridge 1927).

HEADLAM, W. "Ghost-raising, Magic, and the Underworld", *C.R.* 16(1902), 52—61.

HEIDEL, A. *The Gilgamesh Epic and Old Testament Parallels* (Chicago 1946).

HELLER, J. L. "A Labyrinth from Pylos?" *A.J.A.* 65(1961), 57—63 and plate 33.

HEURGON, J. "Orphée et Eurydice avant Virgile", *M.E.F.R.* 49(1932) 6—60.

HEYNE, C. G. *P. Virgili Maronis Opera*[4] cur. G. P. E. WAGNER, 4 vols., (London 1830—1832).

HIGHET, G. *The Classical Tradition* (Oxford 1949).

HOOKE, S. H. (ed.). *The Labyrinth* (London 1935).

HUBAUX, J. "Misène", *A.C.* 2(1933), 135—166.

HUGHES, R. *Heaven and Hell in Western Art* (London 1968).

HUNT, A. S. *The Oxyrhynchus Papyri*, 17(London 1927).

HUXLEY, G. L. "Odysseus and the Thesprotian Oracle of the Dead", *P.P.* 13(1958), 245—248.

—— *Greek Epic Poetry* (London 1969).

JACOBSEN, T. and KRAMER, S. N. "The Myth of Inanna and Bilulu", *J.N.E.S.* 12(1953), 160—188.

JACOBSTHAL, P. *Theseus auf dem Meeresgrunde* (Leipzig 1911).

JAMES, M. R. *Apocrypha Anecdota* in *Texts and Studies: contributions to Biblical and Patristic Literature* ed. J. A. ROBINSON, 10 vols., (Cambridge 1891—1952), vol. 2, 1893.

—— *The Apocryphal New Testament* (corr. ed. Oxford 1953).

JENSEN, P. *Das Gilgamesch-Epos in der Weltliteratur* 2 vols. (Strassburg and Marburg 1906—1929).

JONES, D. M. "Euripides' *Alcestis*", *C.R.* 62(1948), 50—55.

KAROUZOU, S. An Underworld Scene on a Black-Figured Lekythos", *J.H.S.* 92 (1972), 64—73 and plate 18.

KERÉNYI, K. *Labyrinth-Studien* (Zürich 1950).

KERN, O. *Orpheus* (Berlin 1920).
—— *Orphicorum Fragmenta* (Berolini 1922).
KHAN, H. A. "Horace's Ode to Vergil on the Death of Quintilius: I,24", *Latomus* 26(1967), 107—117.
KILPATRICK, R. S. "Archytas at the Styx (Horace *Carm.* 1.28)", *C.P.* 63(1968), 201—206.
—— "Two Notes on Horace *Carm.* 1.28.21—23", *C.P.* 64(1969), 237.
KINKEL, G. *Epicorum Graecorum Fragmenta* (I. Leipzig 1877).
KIRK, G. S. *The Songs of Homer* (Cambridge 1962).
—— *Myth: its Meaning and Functions in Ancient and other Cultures* (Cambridge 1970).
—— "Greek Mythology: Some New Perspectives", *J.H.S.* 92(1972), 74—85.
KNIGHT, G. WILSON. *The Shakespearian Tempest* (Oxford 1932).
—— *Shakespearian Production* (London 1964).
KNIGHT, W. F. JACKSON. "A Prehistoric Ritual Pattern in the Sixth *Aeneid*", *T.A.P.A.* 66(1935), 256—273.
—— *Roman Vergil* (revd. ed. Harmondsworth 1966).
—— *Vergil: Epic and Anthropology*, ed. J. D. CHRISTIE (London 1967), comprising *Vergil's Troy* (pp. 1—134; 1932), *Cumaean Gates: A Reference of the Sixth Aeneid to the Initiation Pattern* (pp. 135—287; 1936), and *The Holy City of the East* (pp. 290—303; 1939).
—— *Elysion: Ancient Greek and Roman beliefs concerning Life After Death* (London 1970).
KRAMER, S. N. "The Epic of Gilgameš and its Sumerian Sources: a Study in Literary Evolution", *J.A.O.S.* 64(1944), 7—23 and 83.
—— "*Inanna's Descent to the Nether World* Continued and Revised", *J.C.S.* 5(1951), 1—17.
—— (ed). *Mythologies of the Ancient World* (New York 1961).
—— "Cuneiform Studies and the History of Literature: The Sumerian Sacred Marriage Texts", *P.A.P.S.* 107(1963), 485—527.
—— *The Sumerians*[2] (Chicago 1964).
—— "Dumuzi's Annual Resurrection: an Important Correction to 'Inanna's Descent", *B.A.S.O.R.* 183(1966), 31.
KRAUS, E. *Die Trojaburgen Nordeuropas* (Glogau 1893).
KRAUS, T. *Hekate* (Heidelberg 1960).
KROLL, J. *Gott und Hölle: Der Mythos vom Descensuskampfe* (Leipzig und Berlin 1932).
KUNZE, E. *Archaische Schildbänder* (*Olympische Forschungen* II. Berlin 1950).

LAMBERT, W. G. and WALCOT, P. "A New Babylonian Theogony and Hesiod", *Kadmos* 4(1965), 64—72.
LAMBRECHTS, P. "La 'résurrection' d'Adonis" in *Mélanges Isidore Levy* (Bruxelles 1955), 207—240.
—— *Attis: van Herdersknaap tot God* (Brussel 1962).

LANG, A. "Breaking the Bough in the Grove of Diana", *F.L.* 18(1907), 89—91.
LANGDON, S. *Babylonian Menologies in the Semitic Calendars* (London 1935).
LAWLER, L. B. *The Dance in Ancient Greece* (London 1964).
LAYARD, J. "The Journey of the Dead", in *Essays Presented to C. G. Seligman* (London 1934), 113—142.
—— "Maze-Dances and the Ritual of the Labyrinth in Malekula", *F.L.* 47(1936), 123—170.
LEE, M. OWEN. "Orpheus and Eurydice: Myth, Legend, Folklore", *C. & M.* 26(1965), 402—412.
LESKY, A. "Alcestis, der Mythus und das Drama", *Sitz. der Akad. der Wissensch. in Wien* 203. 2(1925), 1—86.
—— "Griechischer Mythos und Vorderer Orient", *Saeculum* 5(1955), 35—52.
LINDSAY, J. *The Clashing Rocks* (London 1965).
LINFORTH, I. M. *The Arts of Orpheus* (Berkeley 1941).
LLOYD—JONES, HUGH. "Heracles at Eleusis: P. Oxy. 2622 and P.S.I. 1391", *Maia* 19(1967), 206—229.
LOBECK, C. A. *Aglaophamus* (Königsberg 1829).
LOBEL, E. *Oxyrhynchus Papyri*, 32 (London 1967).

MCKAY, A. G. "The Greeks at Cumae", *Verg. Dig.* 3(1957), 7—10.
—— "Aeneas' Landfalls in Hesperia", *G. & R.* 14(1967), 3—11 with plates.
—— *Ancient Campania*, 2 vols., (Hamilton 1972).
MATTHEWS, W. H. *Mazes and Labyrinths* (London 1922).
MAVROGORDATO, J. "Modern Greek Folk-Songs of the Dead", *J.H.S.* 75(1955), 42—53.
MERKELBACH, R. "Eine orphische Unterweltsbeschreibung auf Papyrus", *Mus. Helv.* 8(1951), 1—11.
—— *Untersuchungen zur Odyssee* (Munich 1951).
—— "Aeneas in Cumae", *Mus. Helv.* 18(1961), 86—90.
MEULI, K. *Odyssee und Argonautika* (Berlin 1921).
MEW, J. *Traditional Aspects of Hell* (London 1903).
MICHELS, A. K. "The Golden Bough of Plato", *A.J.P.* 66(1945), 59—63.
MIREAUX, E. *Les Poèmes Homériques*, 2 vols., (Paris 1948).
MÜHL, P. Von der. "Zur Erfindung in der Nekyia der Odyssee", *Philologus* 93(1938), 1—11.
MÜLLER, K. O. *Orchomenos und die Minyer*[2] (Breslae 1884).
MURRAY, Gilbert. *The Rise of the Greek Epic*[3] (Oxford 1924).
MYLONAS, G. E. *Eleusis and the Eleusinian Mysteries* (Princeton 1961).

NICOLSON, M. "Milton's Hell and the Phlegraean Fields", *Univ. Toronto Quart.* 7(1938), 500—513.
NILSSON, M. P. *The Mycenaean Origin of Greek Mythology* (Cambridge 1932).
—— *Homer and Mycenae* (London 1933).
—— *Greek Popular Religion* (New York 1940).

—— *The Minoan-Mycenaean Religion and its survival in Greek Religion*² (Lund 1950).
—— *Geschichte der griechischen Religion* (I³ and II² Munich 1967 and 1961).
NORDEN, E. *P. Vergilius Maro: Aeneis Buch VI* (lst. and 3rd. eds. Leipzig—Berlin 1903 and 1926).
—— "Orpheus und Eurydice", *Sitz. Berl. Akad. der Wissensch. Phil.-histor. Kl.* (1934), 626—683 = *Kleine Schriften zum klassischen Altertum* (Berlin 1966), 468—532.
NORWOOD, G. "Vergiliana", *C.Q.* 12(1918), 141—150.

OPPENHEIM, A. L. "Mesopotamian Mythology II", *Orientalia* 17(1948), 17—58.
—— "Mesopotamian Mythology III", *Orientalia* 19(1950), 129—158.
OTIS, B. "Three Problems of *Aeneid* 6", *T.A.P.A.* 90(1959), 165—179.
—— *Virgil, A Study in Civilised Poetry* (Oxford 1964).
OWEN, D. D. R. *The Vision of Hell: Infernal Journeys in Medieval French Literature* (Edinburgh 1970).

PAGE, D. L. *Greek Literary Papyri* (London 1950).
—— *The Homeric Odyssey* (Oxford 1955).
—— *History and the Homeric Iliad* (Berkeley 1959).
—— *Folktales in Homer's Odyssey* (Camb. Mass. 1973).
PAGET, R. F. "The 'Great Antrum' at Baiae: a Preliminary Report", *P.B.S.R.* 35(1967), 102—112.
—— *In the Footsteps of Orpheus* (London 1967),
PATCH, H. R. *The Other World According to Descriptions in Medieval Literature* (Camb. Mass. 1950).
PERRET, J. *Les Origines de la Légende troyenne de Rome* (Paris 1942).
PFEIFFER, R. "Hesiodisches und Homerisches, Zu neuen und alten Papyri", *Philologus* 92(1937), 1—18.
PFISTER, F. "Herakles und Christus", *A.R.W.* 34(1937), 42—60.
PHILLIPS, E. D. "Odysseus in Italy", *J.H.S.* 73(1953), 53—67.
POCOCK, L. G. *Odyssean Essays* (Oxford 1965).

RICHARDSON, N. J. *The Homeric Hymn to Demeter* (Oxford 1974).
ROBERT, C. *Die Nekyia des Polygnot* (Halle a. S. 1892).
—— *Die Griechische Heldensage* (Berlin 1920—1926).
ROBERT, F. *Homère* (Paris 1950).
ROHDE, E. *Psyche*⁸, trans. W. B. Hillis (London 1925).
ROSE, H. J. "Herakles and the Gospels" *H.T.R.* 31(1938), 113—141.
—— *A Handbook of Greek Mythology*⁶ (London 1958).
ROUX, R. *Le Problème des Argonautes* (Paris 1949).
RUEGG, A. *Die Jenseitsvorstellungen vor Dante*, 2 vols., (Einsiedeln 1945).

SANDARS, N. K. *The Epic of Gilgamesh* (revd. ed. Harmondsworth 1964).
SÄVE-SÖDERBERGH, T. *Pharoahs and Mortals* (Indianapolis 1961).

SCAZZOSO, P. "Riflessi misterici nelle 'Georgiche' di Virgilio", *Paideia* 11(1956), 5—28.

SCHLUNK, R. R. *The Homeric Scholia and the Aeneid: A Study of Influence of Ancient Homeric Literary Criticism on Vergil* (Michigan 1974).

SEGAL, C. P. "The Character and Cults of Dionysus and the Unity of the *Frogs*", *H.S.C.P.* 65(1961), 207—242.

SEVERYNS, A. *Le Cycle Épique Dans L'École D'Aristarque* (Paris 1928).

SHAFFER, A. *Sumerian Sources of Tablet XII of the Epic of Gilgamesh* (Pennsylvania Ph. D., 1963).

SHEEHAN, J. "Catholic Ideas of Death as found in *Aeneid VI*", *C.F.* 16(1962), 87—109.

SILVERSTEIN, T. *Visio Sancti Pauli, the History of the Apocalypse in Latin, together with Nine Texts* (London 1935).

—— "Did Dante know the Vision of Saint Paul?" *Harvard Studies and Notes in Philology and Literature* 19(1937), 231—247.

SIMPSON, W. *The Jonah Legend* (London 1899).

SIX, J. "Die Eriphyle des Polygnot", *M.D.A.I.(A.)* 19(1894), 335—339.

—— "Mikon's fourth picture in the Theseion", *J.H.S.* 39(1919), 130—143.

SNELL, B. *Scenes from Greek Drama* (Berkeley 1967).

SOLMSEN, F. "Greek Ideas of the Hereafter in Virgil's Roman Epic", *Americ. Philos. Soc.* 112(1968), 8—14.

SPEISER, A. E., see in *A.N.E.T.*

STEINER, H. R. *Der Traum in der Aeneas* (Stuttgart 1952).

STOKES, M. C. "Hesiodic and Milesian Cosmogonies", *Phronesis* 7(1962), 1—37.

STRAUSS, W. A. *Descent and Return: The Orphic Theme in Modern Literature* (Camb. Mass. 1971).

STUBBS, H. W. "Satan, Loki, and Prometheus", *Orpheus* 3(1956), 152—156.

—— "Troy, Asgard, and Armageddon", *F.L.* 70(1959), 440—459.

—— "Virgil and H. G. Wells: Prophets of a New Age", *P.V.S.* 9(1970), 34—53.

—— "Underworld Themes in Modern Fiction" in DAVIDSON, *q.v.*, 130—149.

THANIEL, G. "Vergil's Leaf- and Bird-Similes of Ghosts", *Phoenix* 25(1971), 237—245.

THOMPSON, R. Campbell. *The Epic of Gilgamish* (Oxford 1930).

THOMSON, G. "Mystical allusions in the *Oresteia*", *J.H.S.* 55(1935), 20—34.

—— "The Greek Calendar", *J.H.S.* 63(1943), 52—65.

THOMSON, J. A. K. "Dolon the Wolf", *C.R.* 15(1911), 238f.

—— *Studies in the Odyssey* (Oxford 1914).

TISCHENDORF, C. de. *Evangelia Apocrypha*[2] (Lipsiae 1876).

TREU, M. "Die neue 'orphische' Unterweltsbeschreibung und Vergil", *Hermes* 82 (1954), 24—51.

TURCAN, R. "La catabase orphique du papyrus de Bologne", *R.H.R.* 150(1956), 136—172.

URE, A. D. "Demeter and Dionysus on Acrocorinth", *J.H.S.* 89(1969), 120f.

VALK, M. van der. *Beiträge zur Nekyia* (Kok, Kampen 1935).
—— *Textual Criticism of the Odyssey* (Leiden 1949).
VERMASEREN, M. J. *The Legend of Attis in Greek and Roman Art* (Leiden 1966).
VERRALL, M. de G. "Two instances of symbolism in the Sixth *Aeneid*", *C.R.* 24 (1910), 43—46.
VÜRTHEIM, J. *Stesichorus' Fragmente und Biographie* (Leiden 1919).

WAELE, F. J. M. de. *The Magic Staff or Rod in Graeco-Italian Antiquity* (Gent 1927).
WAGENVOORT, H. "The Journey of the Souls of the Dead to the Isles of the Blessed", *Mnemosyne* 24(1971), 113—161.
WALCOT, P. *Hesiod and the Near East* (Cardiff 1966).
WALCOT, P. *see also* LAMBERT
WASZINK, J. H. "Vergil and the Sibyl of Cumae", *Mnemosyne* 1(1948), 43—58.
WEBSTER, T. B. L. "Homer and Eastern Poetry", *Minos* 4(1956), 104—116.
—— *From Mycenae to Homer*² (London 1964).
WELCKER, F. G. *Der epische Cyclus*, 2 vols., (Bonn 1835 and 1849).
WEST, M. L. *Hesiod: Theogony* (Oxford 1966).
WHITMAN, C. H. *Homer and the Homeric Tradition* (Camb. Mass. 1958).
WHITTAKER, J. *God Being Time* (Oslo 1971).
WILAMOWITZ-MOELLENDORFF, U. von. *Homerische Untersuchungen* (Berlin 1884).
—— *Isyllos von Epidauros* (Berlin 1886).
—— *Euripides Herakles* (Berlin 1889, 2nd. ed. 1909).
—— *Die Ilias und Homer*² (Berlin 1920).
—— *Pindaros* (Berlin 1922).
WILKINSON, L. P. *The Georgics of Virgil* (Cambridge 1969).
WILLIAMS, R. D. "The Sixth Book of the Aeneid", *G. & R.* 11(1964), 48—63.
—— *The Aeneid of Virgil* I. (London 1972).
WITZEL, P. MAURUS. "Zur sumerischen Rezension der Höllenfahrt Ischtars", *Orientalia* 14(1945), 24—69.
—— "Ischtar gegen Tammuz?" *Orientalia* 21(1952), 435—455.
WOODHOUSE, W. J. *The Composition of Homer's Odyssey* (Oxford 1930).

YAMAUCHI, E. M. "Tammuz and the Bible", *J.B.L.* 84(1965), 283—290.
—— "Additional Notes on Tammuz", *J.S.S.* 11(1966), 10—15.

ZARKER, J. W. "Aeneas and Theseus in *Aeneid* 6", *C.J.* 62(1967), 220—226.
ZUNTZ, G. *Persephone* (Oxford 1971).

A. INDEX OF ANCIENT AUTHORS OR WORKS NAMED

Large and small arabic numerals refer to pages and footnotes respectively, Roman numerals to chapters. References are not usually given separately to notes appearing on pages cited.

B. GENERAL INDEX

Large and small arabic numerals refer to pages and footnotes respectively, Roman numerals to chapters. Usually references are not given separately to notes appearing on pages cited.